T0148614

A Journey
from the Depression
to Space Age

A JOURNEY
FROM THE DEPRESSION
TO SPACE AGE

MARY BECHTOLD

authorHOUSE®

AuthorHouse™
1663 Liberty Drive
Bloomington, IN 47403
www.authorhouse.com
Phone: 1-800-839-8640

© 2011 Mary Bechtold. All rights reserved.

No part of this book may be reproduced, stored in a retrieval system, or transmitted by any means without the written permission of the author.

First published by AuthorHouse   12/12/2011

ISBN: 978-1-4670-6176-6 (sc)
ISBN: 978-1-4670-6154-4 (ebk)

Library of Congress Control Number: 2011918429

Printed in the United States of America

Any people depicted in stock imagery provided by Thinkstock are models, and such images are being used for illustrative purposes only.
Certain stock imagery © Thinkstock.

This book is printed on acid-free paper.

Because of the dynamic nature of the Internet, any web addresses or links contained in this book may have changed since publication and may no longer be valid. The views expressed in this work are solely those of the author and do not necessarily reflect the views of the publisher, and the publisher hereby disclaims any responsibility for them.

CONTENTS

Chapter 1:   Relatives 1

Chapter 2:   Marys Childhhood 25

Chapter 3:   High school 79

Chapter 4:   College 93

Chapter 5:   Marriage 103

Chapter 6:   Teaching 121

Chapter 7:   Counseling 135

Chapter 8:   Children 149

Chapter 9:   Eugenc 172

Chapter 10: Kennel 200

Chapter 11: Prison 218

Chapter 12: Stories of Animals 230

Chapter 13: Interesting life stories 248

CHAPTER 1

RELATIVES

Castile Creek was the site of many baptisms

When my mother was a small child, her family attended the Mt. Zion church located outside of Gower, Mo. Her family went to church in a buggy drawn by horses from their farm.

Mt. Zion was built during the time of slavery. Slaves are buried at the graveyard. The congregation itself is of southern Baptist origin. Church services are still held there.

My mother was baptized in Castile Creek. The preacher held her in his arms and she was completely submerged in the water. It is impossible to be baptized that way today since our creeks are so polluted and filled with rubbish.

Primitive conditions

The church itself is located in rural country. On one side it is surrounded by fields of grain and grazing cattle. The grounds consist of two primitive outhouses, and a cemetery where anyone can be buried. Cemetery plots are free. My father has already been laid to rest there. My grandparents are also buried there, as is my mother's older sister who died of diphtheria at and early age. Her cousin's parents are also buried there.

It is a beautiful cemetery with old trees and surroundings. I always enjoyed going on Memorial Day to pay my respects to my ancestors. We would take our lunch and flowers to spend a peaceful day in the country.

Much of the social life in the early 1900's centered on the church. The congregation had basket dinners, put on plays, held a contest on who could finish reading the Bible first. The prize that they would win would be a King James Bible. In the summer they had Bible school for the children. The young people would rent a truck, all pile into the back of it and go to Fairyland Park in Kansas City.

Quilting club

The women at the church lived around Star field and had a club where they quilted, made garments for the needy and enjoyed each other's fellowship at their luncheons monthly. Many of the women moved from the area, but they still come back for the club meeting.

Bertha and Clyde Dale

American farmers paid the price

In the 1930's it seemed as though the American farmer in the Midwest was paying the price of laying the soil wide open and thinking the fertility of the soil would go on for ever without putting any nutrients into the soil, rotating the crops or giving the soil a rest.

Dust storms arose in the dry season in the plains area, where surface cover of vegetation had been stripped away. A combination of drought and dust storms destroyed the top soil and the economy of large areas of Texas, Oklahoma, Colorado and New Mexico.

Day into night

My relatives tell tales of these dust storms blowing in from Oklahoma and Kansas. The dust particles would cover the sun, and it looked like it had a black ring around it. Day turned into night and people would go into their houses and close the doors and windows tightly. In spite of that, dust particles would come in and cover everything with a fine layer of gray soil. People would wear handkerchiefs over their nose to protect their lungs from the dust particles.

As if life wasn't difficult enough for my parents and other relatives, a plague of locust or large grasshoppers came to devastate what crops and gardens they had managed to raise.

When numbers of grasshoppers increase, they become more gregarious, active and conspicuous. They form groups of hoppers and migrate by day, mating and reproducing as they travel. These hoppers develop longer wings, shorter legs, and other identifiable characteristics. Once started a locust plague may last several years until they die out from lack of food.

I remember my relatives bringing in the rakes used to cut hay so the grasshoppers couldn't eat on the handles. Cloths left on the lines were eaten up promptly after they landed. You could hear the whirring of their wings as they lighted in your area. There were so many of them, it looked like they were covering the sun. They banged against your windows and spit out the black juices that stained your windows. These swarms of invading insects left no green stuff standing.

As if dust storms and giant grasshopper's invasions were not enough, tornados or cyclones occurred in the Mississippi Valley.

One of the largest and strongest tornadoes on record is the Tri-States tornado of March 18, 1925. This twister traveled 219 miles mostly in Missouri and parts of Kansas and Illinois—and killed 689 people.

Shared the space

A story told by one of my relatives is that a tornado touched down in their farmyard. The wind pulled all the feathers out of their chicken's skins and left them unharmed, buck naked and cold in their yard. All of my relatives headed for the root cellars for shelter and shared the space with the vegetables and meats.

Another tale I remember is the wind taking all the shingles off the house and driving them into the side of the house. The rain poured in but the house and furniture remained intact.

These hardy farmers of the 1930 have lived through locusts, tornadoes, and dust bowls, but raised their families and then went to fight Hirohito and Adolph Hitler in their lifetime. Quite an accomplishment.

Children learn many good life lessons

I think of the many things my mother has been to me and has done for me. I would not be the person I am today were it not for her. I like to watch Dr. Phil and he lists the ways that good parents influence and guide their children's lives. My mother lived during the depression and raised us during hard times. Her philosophy of child rearing came many years before Dr. Phil wrote his books on parenting but, he would have approved of her methods.

Mothers do so many things for their children. One of the greatest gifts my mother gave me was the belief in a higher power. I began to say my prayers at night before I went to sleep when I could barely talk. I still receive comfort from saying the Lord's Prayer. Mother saw to it we went to Sunday school. I got grounded in the Christian faith in Sunday school.

From her I learned compassion for all people. I was taught respect for older people, handicapped people and people of other races and religion. We were taught respect for our parents and elders. If you got in trouble in school, you got in trouble when you got home. My mother did not blame the teachers. She figured we had a hand in getting into trouble.

When we were small my mother read us stories. We developed a love of reading and an appreciation of books. She took us to the public Library and we checked out books. My mother stayed home and took care of the house and us. We always had nutritious food and three meals a day.

Some of my favorite foods were her pineapple upside down cake and donuts. She taught us how to keep a clean house, cook and minister to children. My one fault, and I still have it is not putting things away after I use them.

The Protestant work ethic was installed in us. Until we were old enough to work part time jobs, we had jobs at home to do. Mother helped my dad, and I went to work after school in the library. I worked five days a week and Saturday. I did this all the way through high school and college. I learned the value of work and money to buy the things I wanted. I was started on the road to independence and taking care of myself

Mother was a teacher and had to pay to go to high school. I was the first grandchild, spoiled and wanted to stay with my grandparents on school days. My mother and dad made me go home and go to school. My brothers and I didn't play sick and if we did, we stayed in bed all day. That was not fun and we went to school the next day.

Curfews were just that. We were to be home at a certain time. One night, I decided to test it. Two hours late, we pulled up and house lights came on. Mother came out with curlers, bare feet and nightgown. Boyfriend peeled out of there like the devil was after him. After that, I met my curfew.

I am lucky my mother is still here to talk to and have her guidance. Thank you, Vivian Dale for a job well done.

Ann and Albert Dale

Families celebrate together

I can remember family gatherings of the Dale family when I could see four generations starting with my great-grandparents and coming down to me. My place in this family was very important to me as a child. These relatives who loved me gave me security and a feeling that I had a place in the scheme of things. I knew how a Dale was expected to act by seeing role models before me.

Probably the most important family gathering we attended was the Christmas dinners. My great-grandparents had eight children who were all married and had children of their own. At Christmas, my great grandfather's farmhouse was filled with 100 or more people wearing their Sunday best. All of us went there after we had attended church.

One Christmas in particular in 1935, we drove to my great-grandfather's house in a Model A Ford with a rumble seat. I always liked riding there even though the air was brisk, and the roads were muddy and covered with fresh snow. The country looked like a winter wonderland. Thank goodness the road was frozen; otherwise we might have been stuck.

As we arrived, I could see a group of relatives, adults and children waving at us. All of the children enjoyed playing in the huge old farm house with its beautiful furniture and old toys. We could smell wonderful smells emanating from the kitchen. The women gathered there, helping put the huge feast on the table. We always has roast goose, quail, rabbits, deer steaks, huge mounds of potatoes and gravy and every kind of salad imaginable and delectable delights for desserts, pies, cakes, sweet rolls, etc. The men and small children were served first. Women and older children ate at the second table. I liked eating with the women. I got caught up on all last year's neighborhood scandals. I hated it when they caught me listening and wouldn't finish their stories and would say "little pitchers have big ears"—this meant me.

Grandma's Christmas tree would be seven feet tall, freshly cut and decorated with popcorn, candy canes, homemade snowmen and pretty bows. Under it was a present for each of us. What fun it was to watch each person open their gift.

Times were hard in the 1930's but family love made up for monetary rewards.

Clyde and Bertha Dale

Mary Bechtold

My Grandmother,
the cement who held two generations together

My grandmother kept her family of four children and the families of these children who came in contact with her and her overwhelming presence which radiated love.

She was born in Paradise in the late l880's. Her family was a religious one who attended church every Sunday. She married Clyde Dale and they had four children. My grandfather was a fun loving hard drinking card playing man. Grandpa inherited a farm from his family. He lost the farm by squandering his money and spending it foolishly. My dad 'Gilbert Dale, their son, went to work in the fields at eight years of age to help put food on the table. After her children were teenagers, one of my grandmother's sisters moved to Kansas City and bought a house. My grandmother liked that idea and she got all of her belongings together and hired a truck to take her to the house she had bought. She told my grandfather he could stay in Paradise or move with her. He lingered in Paradise for several months after she and her children moved into Kansas City. He drove in inebriated and acted like all should be glad to see him.

My grandmother always disciplined her children and grandchildren. My grandfather on the other had spoiled his children and grandchildren. It was like she had another child which was my grandfather. If one of her children and grandchildren had problems they always went to grandmother for advice. One of my aunts came home with a baby and the baby's father. My grandmother took them in and they lived with her for many years. The father of the child flew the coop and was never heard from again, after a few weeks. As the eldest grandchild I stayed with them as often as I could. I got to do as I pleased ate what I wanted and ran wild tearing up my aunt's dolls. My grandfather wanted me to stay there instead of go to school. My mother, dad, and grandmother made me go home so I could go to school. I had an aptitude for learning and did well. When I won a scholarship to go to college, my mother and grandmother cheered me on saying a woman needed a way to support her-self independent of a man. My parents and grandparents were there cheering me on at my college graduation.

I owe a lot to this strong independent woman who was Bertha Dale. She encouraged me to push myself in higher education. I always knew that I had a home with my grandparents if I ever needed it. I would stay nights after I became a teacher with them when it was too snowy to drive home.

I could never understand why my grandmother put up with my grandfather. She said that she had no way to support herself and four children alone. She said she did not know what to do with him or without him so she just kept him. She went on to say this is why every woman should be prepared to take care of herself and her children alone. Thank you Bertha Dale for being there to guide and help me when I needed you.

Incidents led to belief

One is always looking for signs that there is a hereafter and life beyond death. The following incidents made believers out of my mother and me.

My father died suddenly at the age of 56. This left my mother a widow and alone. She got her a job and learned to drive after that. She slowly put her life back together and began to see other men. She liked one man better than all the other men and was considering marrying him. He went to Montana for a month and, after a whirlwind courtship, married another woman.

After that, one night my mother was sitting alone in the dark feeling sorry for herself and crying. She felt that life was not worth living. As she lay in her bed something compelled her to get up and go into the other room. As she started into the hallway, she saw a light in the other room. She was drawn toward the light.

As she got near the light, she began to feel warm, and be at peace with herself. She heard a voice say, "Don't despair, you are not alone. You have me." Calm descended over her, and she immediately felt comforted.

Many years went by, and I was having trouble establishing my growing kennel business. I was eagerly awaiting a pet shop check. The mail man pulled up and put several letters into the box. I was burning trash at the time. I went to the mailbox and picked up the mail. I went to stir up the fire. As I bent over, I dropped the letters down beside the coals into the trash. A feeling of utter devastation came over me. I just knew my check had been burnt up.

I was the only one at home. I heard a voice say, "check the fire. You'll be fine."

I checked the fire and one envelope was singed. I opened it and there was my check. The voice again said, "Believe and all things are possible." My business prospered after that. Many times after that day, I'd remember the voice and know that everything would be fine.

Good old story to tell on Halloween

When I think of old time funeral I recall the funeral carriage was very ornate—black with white satin on the inside. On the white satin the deceased was displayed in his Sunday best with the casket left open. The hearse was drawn by six black steeds with evenly matched gaits. Family members rode behind the horse drawn hearse in surreys.

One of the stories I can remember being told at Halloween has to do with funerals. It seems an older man had lapsed into a coma with a very slight pulse and with no evidence of breathing. He was lying on the embalming table awaiting the embalmers. He sat up and the embalmers ran out shrieking. Had the supposedly dead person done that a few moments later, he might not have been so fortunate. On a dark October night this story had a sobering effect on those of us who wanted to play tricks.

My mother's summer vacation

In the early 1900's, my mother was a child. She lived on a farm near Gower, Missouri. In the summer, she helped her father cultivate and plant his crops. She drove two mules to help plant the fields. One day a summer storm came up and it thundered and crackled with lightning. The mules became spooked and ran away with my mother still attached to the reins. The mules finally stopped before she was harmed. She never knew why they stopped, but suspected it was through the intervention of her guardian angel.

Some of her other chores were to milk the cow every morning and night. She also fed and watered the chickens and gathered the eggs.

For recreation in the summer, her family went to Stewartsville for Fourth of July celebration. A fire cracker called a spit devil flew up under her dress and hit her leg causing it to bleed. They rode the Ferris wheel, the Merry-go-round, and other carnival rides. They ate lots of hot dogs and ice cream.

Summer picnics were held in Agency, Mo. Her family rode on horses to Gower and took the train to Agency, Mo. They played all kinds of games of chance, looked at unusual creatures like mermaids and two headed dogs. There were so many different kinds of food that you didn't want anything else for a week. All the kids stuffed themselves on cotton candy.

There was movie once a week in Gower. All the children walked five miles in Gower to watch the silent movie in front of the General store. My mother liked the Green Hornet stories.

Before school started, the Barnum and Bailey circus came to St. Joe. Her whole family rode the train and stayed overnight there. She remembers being fascinated by the trapeze acts, the vaudeville acts, fortune tellers, and the girls who rode the trained elephants.

Church played a big part in their summer vacations at Gower. They had church picnics, basket dinners, put on plays and had bible study.

Some teenagers hate to go to high school now and quit before they finish. My mother's parents had to pay for her going to school. She worked in the library and helped clean a lady's house to help pay the tuition. When she graduated, she won the key for the best all around student scholastically and gymnastically. Today we don't realize what a privilege a free education is. When I think of the challenges that faced my mother's generation, I think my generation who grew up in mechanical age were spared the hardships of her generation. We are also drifting away from the Protestant work ethic and Ten Commandments that her generation lived by.

Family wakened to flooding

Many are the times I remember my mother saying, "Never live by a river or a low place between two hills. Live on top of a hill." Her strong feelings on this subject came from her early childhood.

Her family lived in the Plattsburg and Gower area of Northwest Missouri at the time. They lived in a house located by a creek. The house was closest to the creek. In 1913, most farmers traveled by horse and buggy. In the early spring of that year, it had rained hard for over a week. My mother's family went to bed and was awakened by the sound of rushing water and debris washing around their house.

They were unable to get out of the back or front door. Her father climbed out the window and swam back to the barn which was located on higher ground. He hitched up the horses and the wagon and swam back to the house where water was already one foot high inside. He carried my mother, her brother and my grand-mother to the waiting wagon.

They stayed with neighbors until the rain subsided, and the waters of the creek and branch went down. They went back to their ruined home and cleaned up their furniture and belongings and moved to a farm located on higher ground. My mother said every thing smelled for years after the flood.

My mother had night-mares for many years about this flood experience, since she lost her pet rat terrier and the chickens in the hen house, when the water covered their roosts.

Bare feet in the summertime

Some of the happiest times of my life were when we would get together as a family with Edith and Orville Livingston on their farm.

My brother, Bob and I were small, school aged children. Their children, my cousins, Orville Lee and Jackie Livingston, and my brother and I would play in open fields of corn taller then we were. Bobbie and Jackie played together while Orville Lee and I found shade trees and would be content to read comics or detective magazines.

Sometimes we would play baseball. I was never a great player. I usually got the outfield when we had more than four players. I was prone to poison ivy. Many were the times I contacted it when I roamed in weeds taller than my head.

On Memorial Day and the Fourth of July, all the Dales would get together for picnics. Oh the mounds of food we had, fried chicken, corn on the cob, potato salad, deviled eggs, tea and all the soda pop you could drink. I had many cousins on the Dale side—seven girls and four boys. We had our baseball and kickball team. The girls liked to play house. The boys would only play house if we agreed to play baseball or kickball with them.

Four of my cousins lived on a farm with a stream running through it. We all liked to play in it and walk around with bare feet. As misfortune would have it, I stepped on a piece of glass and it stuck in my foot. What an operation to get it out. My dad pulled it out while my mother held me still. She disinfected and bandaged it. I howled while the antiseptic was being applied. It really burned. All my cousins called me a chicken.

After my junior year of college, I met and interesting Romeo, Roscoe. He was a friend of Ralph's who dated my friend Vernilda. Roscoe and Ralph liked the outdoors. They liked to fish and hunt and go out in boats on the water. We went swimming and boating on the lakes in the area. The ironic part was that I couldn't swim. I depended on them to rescue me if I fell in. Many were the times after outings with them that I came home badly sunburned.

We also enjoyed going to drive-in movies. The summer went by quickly, Roscoe went to work and I went back to finish my senior year of college. I still remember the summer we four spent as one of the best times of my school years. As I reminisce, I think about how care free we were in our early twenties.

Grandmother deserves acclaim for family role

This month's topic should be people who you remember who have been part of your daily life in Missouri. These are the ordinary people who you come into contact with who make an impact upon your life. It is not a famous person but someone who comes and goes from this life with little fanfare that lives on in the memories of others.

Such a person was my grandmother, Bertha Dale, who was born and lived part of her life in the Paradise/Smithville, Mo., and area. The remaining years of her life were spent in Kansas City.

Now that I am a grandmother, I can appreciate the sacrifices she made to make my life and that of her children better. She lived through the transition from the horse and buggy days to the takeover by the automobile as the mode of transportation.

When her father became ill, she took him into her home and cared for him until he died. I didn't know him, but I remember several pieces of his furniture. I always wanted the bookcase desk that my grandmother had. I didn't inherit that, but I got a hatbox dresser that was his. My daughter wants that dresser as part of her family history.

My grandmother was a loving woman who spoiled her grandchildren but could be stern when the occasion demanded it.

I like banty chickens when I was a child. When we lived in the country, I could keep the banty chickens myself. My parents began traveling with Koss Construction Co, during the war years. I was unable to take my banty chicken. I left it with my grandmother.

When my grandmother came to visit us, she had the chicken in a carrying case. When she found we couldn't keep her, she took her back with her on the train. My chicken and I were reunited in Grandview, Mo. We settled in one place, and my chicken had a happy life until an owl got her.

I thought of my grandmother recently when my grandson called me saying he couldn't keep Boomer, his dog. He asked if I'd let Boomer stay here until they found a place where they could have dogs.

My grandmother may not have been a famous lawyer or politician, but she was a good mother and grandmother. When I think of famous Missourians, I think of Bertha Dale and the women like her who lived through the days of the Great Depression, Prohibition and the times when women were second-class citizens and didn't have the right to vote. I, myself, having lived many years in the 20th century, have seen many changes in the lives of women. My grandmother encouraged me to be the best I would be, and I consider her one of the unsung millions of Missouri's great past.

Grandmother provides stability for her family

My grandmother had a profound influence on my life. She was of Scots-Irish stock and came from a religious family who spent most of their time in church. My grandmother as a result, rebelled against church going after she married.

She met my fun-loving grandfather in the Smithville, Mo., area. He had a large family of brothers and sisters. His parents were farmers; He enjoyed drinking, card-playing and chasing women. My grandmother was the one who offered the stability in the family and held it together. My grandparent liked to dance the night away at the local square dances.

As the first grandchild, I was fussed over by my grandparent, aunts and uncles. I loved to stay with my grandparents because I got most everything I wanted. I can remember drinking so much pop and eating so much candy that I got sick and threw up. My grandmother was the one who applied the swats when I got out of line.

I can remember her millions of guppies. I think I inherited my love of tropical fish from her. My house is filled with reminders of her crocheting and bottle collections. I had a crocheted pineapple tablecloth and doilies for tables and chairs.

When my grandparents were alive, I stayed two nights with them when I taught at Central High School and it was so snowy I couldn't get home. I always knew that I was loved and welcome in their home.

My grandfather was a handsome man who always loved life. He liked to tell jokes. I inherited my love of dancing from him. I think my dislike of card-playing came from the games of cards my relatives played for money.

My grandparents lived through World War I and the Great Depression. They worked hard to feed their families and keep them together. My grandfather did farm labor, factory work or whatever he could find. I grew up knowing that you had to work for what you get in this world. I try to give my grandchildren the love and security that I got from my grandparents. There's nothing like that warm, fuzzy feeling that I got from them. I wish that all children could have felt as wanted as I did during my childhood with my parents and grandparents.

Quilting, crocheting fashion two pastimes

The two handicraft techniques that I have knowledge of are quilting and crocheting. My grandmother was experienced in crocheting, and my mother loves to put together quilts.

Quilting is a process of stitching together two layers of fabric filled with some soft substance (usually cotton) to form a kind of textile sandwich. This quilted fabric is most often used in a bed covering called a quilt, but is also used for clothing upholstery and decoration.

The first quilts in America were brought by Dutch and English colonists and were made by appliqué. It was the patchwork quilt, however, that reached its highest artistic development in the United States. As a result of scarce sewing materials and a need of artistic expression, pioneer women lavished great attention on ingenious geometrical designs. Many quilts were signed and dated. By 1883, handmade quilts were on three quarters of the beds in the country. With the advent of inexpensive machine-made bed coverings, however, quilt making declined in the early years of the 20th century. In the 1960's interest in quilting revived. By the mid 1980's quilting had become the most popular form of needlework.

Little is known of the early history of crocheting. Much modern crochet is executed with soft yarns and is used to make garments and bedcovering. Crocheted continues to be a home handicraft, and contemporary artists employ crochet along with other techniques to create large wall hangings and fiber sculptures.

One of my prized possessions is a tablecloth crocheted by my grandmother, Bertha Dale. She made doilies for tables, backs of chairs and divans. My linen closet had many examples of her handiwork. The tablecloth is made with a pineapple design and is one of my prized possessions. She gave it to me for my college graduation.

When my husband and I were married in 1953, we received a sheet and pillowcases with crocheted flowers on them. I still have these sheets and enjoy looking at them.

My mother makes beautiful quilts. She has made many quilts with Sunbonnet Sue on them. I have two matching quilts for my twin beds with Sunbonnet Sue on them.

In earlier years, she made a quilt with all the state flowers and state birds on it. These designs were embroidered in each block. She is making quilts for her great-grandsons with footballs on them. Making the blocks for the quilts, it brings back fond memories of earlier times spent with these relatives of mine and the time that loving hands spent making these items. I only hope that my children treasure these items as much as I have.

Clyde, Bertha, Kathryn, Francis, Gilbert—Dale

Tragedy changes holiday celebration

My mind travels back to the 1920's my dad, Gilbert Dale was ten years old. He was trying to get his mother and sister's attention. He had found a live dynamite cap that had been left behind by a W.P.A. road crew. He took out a match and lit it. It got his sister's and mother's attention. He had blown out his eye and two fingers on his right hand. They rushed him to the hospital. The doctors could not save his eye or two fingers. All his life he wore a glass eye and was handicapped by the loss of his fingers and eye.

As a result of his experience, we never had fireworks on the Fourth of July. We went to other celebrations where firecrackers were shot off. This was a tradition that we had in my family and my family after I married. I took my children to fireworks celebrations in Cameron and Hamilton, Mo. My business of a busy kennel kept the dogs excited by the unusual sound of fireworks. We sat on our back deck looking at the fireworks going off in the sky. The sound of dogs barking and fireworks created a lot of noise.

I saw on television recently that two teens were trying to put fireworks together to make a larger bang. A teen girl was nearby. She was burned badly and is in a burn unit at a hospital. Another man shot off his hand with a large firecracker and destroyed the inside of his home. What a waste of human energy to cause such tragedies.

Our countries birthday a wonderful celebration, I will sit on the deck and think of the sacrifices our forefathers made. I hope they are watching us and know that the sacrifices that they made are appreciated by their descendents who are free.

Methods for achieving curls become easier as years go by

When I think of hairdos and hair, I remember looking at the wedding pictures of my grandparents.

My great-grandmother wore her long hair in a pompadour in front and a bun in the back. The dresses were elaborate and beautiful, with many buttons and embroidery. The clothes seemed to match the hairdos.

My great-grandfather had side whiskers and a big moustache.

On of my earliest memories as a child was a trip to the beauty shop with Mother and Grandmother. My grandfather gave each of them a dollar to pay for the permanents. Money may have been scarce, but good looks had to prevail.

We walked into the shop, where several operators were working. The machines they used looked like Dr. Frankenstein's contraptions. They were attached to the ceiling, and electricity was used to curl the hair.

The hair was wound around metal rods that were attached to the machines. Can you imagine what these women looked like, Attached to these? There was always the danger of being shocked or having your hair burned. But both my mother and grandmother were happy with their new hairdos.

My mother's next hair changing project took place using a chemical reaction instead of electricity to provide the heat. My mother stepped out of that beauty parlor with waves and curls. She looked like a true flapper and daughter of her generation. There was only one problem you could not wash the solution out of your hair for one week. Even the cats and dogs gave my mother a wide berth as they put their paws over their noses.

I didn't get permanents as an adolescent; I used pin curls, which was the last thing I did before I went to bed. I wore shoulder length hair, and the pin curls worked except when it was damp, when my hair went limp and straight.

When I started to teach school in the 1960's, I wanted a different hairdo. I went to the beauty parlor and had my hair cut short and dyed red. I was no longer a brunette, but a redhead. I continued this for a number of years until I decided that I should use a rinse. Now, I am a brunette with gray overtones. I believe at times that I am more gray than brunette.

Women early in history used color for hair and various devices to curl hair. Cleopatra probably could not have charmed Julius Caesar without her hairdresser and makeup artist. She was one of the greatest female vamps in all history.

Gilbert Dale, Clyde Dale, Bertha Dale

Greatest gifts come without price

The greatest gifts I ever received were not ones that had a price value. They were gifts given with love from my parents to their child.

From the earliest times, I can remember I always felt valued. My grandparents, the Dales, always applauded all the accomplishments I achieved.

My mother, Vivian Dale, always said that you could accomplish whatever you wanted if you worked at it hard enough. Her faith in me helped me to develop the self-esteem to believe and to try for all the things I ever wanted to do.

Another gift that she gave me that cannot be measured monetarily was a deep and abiding faith in God. She always saw that my brothers and I attended church and Sunday school.

These priceless gifts are ones that I tried to pass onto my own children and grandchildren. The Unites States of America is a country in which one can raise him or her-self up out of poverty and go as far as desired if one is willing to work for it.

Women did not receive equal opportunities with men until they received the right to vote and joined the work force during the Second World War. My dad was a product of the old school, that woman's place was in the home. When I won a college scholarship, he was pleased and came to all of my college graduations.

In my work as an elementary counselor, many of the children I work with lack the parental encouragement to develop their full potential. It is a rare child that succeeds when his parents are not cheering him on. This is why it is so important that children have mentors.

I have received many gifts at birthdays, Christmas and on other occasions, but none of them are as important to me as the non-measurable gifts my parents gave to me.

My mother still has encouraging words when she praises me for articles and things that I write, and the volunteer work that I do.

The Ten Commandments set out by Moses for the Hebrews thousand of years ago are just as applicable today as they were then.

James, Vivian, Dave, Edith Buckridge.

Christmas arrives late

The most unusual Christmas celebration I have ever heard about was in the early 1900's when my mother was a child in a rural Clinton County, Mo., community.

Her parents were frugal, had working farmers who planted corn and wheat with their mules and hand pushed plows. Her parents did not believe in celebrating Christmas per se. They had candy, cheese, nuts oranges and apples at Christmas, but they never put up Christmas tree or decorated it and put presents under it.

My mother attended a one room schoolhouse. Every Christmas in Clinton County, Mr. Schaeffer, an older gentleman who loved children, went to all the schoolhouses in Clinton County driving his big truck filled with toys. He unloaded toys and carried them into the schoolhouse. Each child was allowed to pick one toy. My mother's best Christmas present was a 24 inch kewpie doll.

Two years after my mother married, my brother and me, under my mother's supervision, decorated my mother's first real Christmas tree with colored paper chains and homemade popcorn balls. We children received a tricycle and a little red wagon.

Eugene, Mary Bechtold—Robert, Ruby, Vivian, Dale

Scented memories include family, businesses and holidays

My sense of smell has always been highly developed as I think back over my past life. Many memories of good and bad smells slip into my mind.

From my younger days I remember the smell of holly-hocks on their graceful stems. They stood tall and straight as they guarded the outhouse which has the granddaddy of the smells. Bumblebees loved the earthy smells of the outhouse. They also like the hollyhocks.

One outhouse still remains at the old Mt. Zion Cemetery outside Gower. My mother and her cousins attended that church. On Memorial Day, we would visit the graves of deceased relatives. My father, my mother's parents and her cousin and her husband are all buried there. It is difficult to find hollyhocks in gardens now. I do remember them since they are associated in my mind with Memorial Day and outhouses.

Another earthy smell came from a business enterprise when I ran a kennel and brokering business. Since over three hundred dogs lived in my kennel, we had to have a way of disposing of the manure. We put in a sewage lagoon. To me the kennel and the dog's odors smelled like money. I still remember with my nose the awed feeling when I walked into a whelping room and smelled dogs, large and small, fairly early in the morning before they were fed and cleaned. I always went into the kennel where the adult dogs would come running out when I yelled, "Hey dogs!"

My nose twitches when I think of fried chicken mashed potatoes, green bean and other goodies that we had at family gatherings. I enjoyed the smell of my mother frying homemade donuts. I like putting the sugar on the donuts. Pineapple upside down cakes smelled good when they came out of the oven on a cold evening when I got home from school.

My Brother Bob's wife Ruby makes delicious tacos with all the trimmings. When she served these at dinner with a lettuce salad, the smell of anticipation would get my salivary glands going.

My husband's mother had a kitchen always filled with delicious smells. I always enjoyed going to her kitchen because she cooked whatever she knew you enjoyed. Endive salad with potatoes was one of her specialties. Her daughter, Martha follows the family tradition and Christmas and Thanksgiving dinner now.

Last, but not least of my memories, is the smell of incense. Incense is used at Easter and other important times of year in my church. Christmas Mass in the evening is a wonderful time of smells and sights. This is the time of year that you feel closest to your family.

C C C Program brings relief

In October 1929, the stock market crashed, wiping out 40 percent of the paper value of common stocks. The Depression deepened, confidence evaporated and many lost their life savings. By 1933, the value of stock on the New York stock exchange was less than a fifth of what it had been in 1929. Business houses closed their doors. Factories shut down and banks failed. By 1932, approximately, one out of every four Americans was unemployed.

In 1933, President Franklin D. Roosevelt brought an air of confidence and optimism that quickly rallied the people to the banner of his program known as the New Deal. "The only thing we have to fear is fear itself," the president declared in his inaugural address to the nation.

An early step for the unemployed came in the form of the Civilian Conservation Corps, a program enacted by Congress to bring relief to young men between 18 and 25 years of age. The CCC enrolled jobless young men at work camps across the country for about $30.00 per month. They engaged in a variety of projects: planting trees, maintaining national forests and conserving coal, oil, gas, sodium and helium deposits, to mention a few.

Work relief came in the form of the Civil Works Administration. Although criticized as "make work," the jobs funded ranged from ditch digging to highway repairs to teaching. Created in November 1933, it was abandoned in the spring of 1932. Roosevelt and his key officials continued to favor unemployment programs based on work relief rather than welfare.

My parents, Vivian Buckridge and Gilbert Dale, were married in 1930 at the height of the Depression. I was born in November 1931. My father worked at whatever job he could to make money. He worked on whatever government project were set into motion. He would meet the trucks that would take him to the work projects and get home long after dark, so tired that he could hardly eat before falling asleep. The projects that my mother remembers are his working on the river and in a rock quarry.

Other individuals I have talked to in my generation remember the Depression years in different ways. Ben Silvers of Hamilton, Mo., remembers the black clouds resulting from the dust bowl. He lived in

Nebraska at the time. "When you saw those black clouds rolling in," he said, "man and beast alike headed for shelter."

Houses would be filled with fine dust, no sun could be seen, and paint would be taken off buildings and cars.

Bernard said, "The Depression was a period when only the strongest survived. Farmers would raise corn and they had no one to bring it in and they used it for heat in the winter."

The WPA projects put men to work earning enough money to buy flour, salt, sugar and clothing. On payday, one would get money or script to purchases items.

Gene Walker of Hamilton remembers droughts during the 1930's and millions of grasshoppers and locusts eating the crops. He said, "There were 118 days of no rain, day after day." Dust storms came rolling and houses were inundated with black dust. You had to go inside or you couldn't breathe.

The Depression was a great equalizer. Most people were in the same boat. Individuals rode the rails going to a better place like California or the "land of opportunity," they thought. Many stopped at homes asking for a meal. The cry, "Buddy, can you spare a dime?" was widespread.

No sooner had we started to come out of the Depression than along came World War II. We had to mobilize our country to fight an enemy on two fronts, which threatened the freedom of the world.

CHAPTER 2

MARYS CHILDHHOOD

Clyde and Bertha Dale

Living Paradise

I was born in 1931 in Paradise, Mo., in the midst of the great Depression. Smithville was located about 10 miles from paradise. Today, Smithville has Smithville Lake, which is popular with boaters, swimmers and picnickers in the spring, summer and fall.

Paradise itself consisted of about 60 families. There was one grocery store and filling station. This was the Hafferty store. One doctor served the community, Dr. Rupe, who made house calls. Dr. Rupe delivered my brother, Bobbie and me at home.

My grandparents, the Clyde Dales, lived in Paradise, and my great-great-grandparents, the Albert Dales, lived in Smithville. I had six great uncles, who lived on farms around the area. I can remember the family getting together. We must have had over 100 people there: what a feast.

There was a Baptist and Methodist church in Paradise. The two room schoolhouse was close to the Methodist Church. I started school there, and so did my brother. I liked school and especially all the books that were in the library. At recess, they rang an old-fashioned bell, and we played kick ball and tag. One of the stories told about me in first grade was about me walking in a ditch full of water, getting my brand new boots soaked. My brother didn't want to go to school, so he climbed out the window and went home. My mother and a switch brought him back.

On winter evening the men would go to Hafferty's store and sit around the wood stove and gossip and play cards. At Christmas time, my dad would go to the store for candy. We got to go to Grandma's from awhile. When we came home, Santa Claus had left our toys and a treat of chocolate drops, jelly beans and candy corn.

Those years in Paradise passed quickly, and the economy improved. My grandfather and grandmother moved to Kansas City, and we followed them. Sometimes, when I take a trip down memory lane, I fondly remember Paradise as it used to be in the first 10 years of my life. These memories are of the family get-together; you got to see your family more often. Now families are scattered and we do not have good times like we used to.

Vivian and Gilbert Dale with Mary as a Baby

Long winter began on Halloween

The weather was lovely, with temperatures in the fiftiess and sunshine the week before Halloween. On Halloween night, Oct. 31, 1931, the winds blew and the weather changed suddenly—snow and blustery winds made their way to Paradise, Mo.

My mother went into labor on Halloween night and Mary Lee Dale Bechtold was born in a remote farmhouse on a hill outside Paradise. My mother, father and grandparents were there, anxiously awaiting the birth of their first grandchild. I came into this world hollering loudly at being exposed to this cold world. My grandmother, Bertha Dale, gave me watermelon tea to start my kidneys moving. I was born a minute after midnight—too late to be a Halloween baby—and lucky enough to be born on All Saint's Day.

The Dale clan got together to celebrate the first grandchild. My father was hoping for a boy and he got me. My grandfather was ecstatic. Now he had another girl to spoil. My aunt, who was only ten, was replaced and unhappy to have a rival.

Times were hard and my dad worked on WPA jobs and farms doing anything he could do to make money. The long hard winter took its toll on him and he got rheumatic fever. Mother took care of us both. I was kept in bed with him so we would both stay warm. The drafty cottage was heated with a wood stove and my mother had to go outside and bring in wood. Clothes had to be washed in a tub and scrubbed on a washboard. Cooking was on a wood stove and bath water had to be heated on it.

I am telling this story about my birth from stories told to me. That winter was long and harsh with snow piled until March. Times may have been hard but my relatives were sturdy people who were the descendents of pioneers who settled our country. I knew all of my relatives and celebrated holidays with them. I always felt wanted and like I belonged to a group of people

Mary and Bobby Dale

Country classes include 'Three R' along with other subjects

I started to school at Paradise, Mo., in a one-room schoolhouse. I walked about half a mile to get to school. I didn't like my first teacher, but the one who took her place after she got married was a good teacher. My friend, Anna Madelyn Coons, and I flourished under her guidance.

I learned to read in the Dick and Jane readers. My penmanship left something to be desired since I wrote left-handed. Every writing primer was designed for right—handed people.

Our school in the 1930's had one room and was built with a wood frame. All eight grades attended these schools. My mother tells about the schools of her day. They were one-room schoolhouses. Behind the school was a woodshed, large enough to stable horses. There were two outhouses, one for the boys and one for the girls, located at the back of the lot.

Like most school of this time, this school was equipped with a globe and dictionaries. Near the teacher's desk was a wood stove which the teacher filled up with wood in the winter before school started. The walls were covered with blackboards. On the wall you could find framed pictures of George Washington and Abraham Lincoln. The American flag stood in a prominent place.

In front of the teachers desk was a recitation bench on which students sat when it was their turn for instruction or to recite lessons. The rest of the floor space was taken up with rows of student desks. Desks might seat one or two persons.

Subjects taught in rural schools were the "three Rs," reading, 'riting and 'rithmetic. Civil government and geography were typically taught as well. Other topics such as etiquette and human relations were fitted in. Many rural schools used the McGuffey's reading series, which included essays and poems on things a person would need to know, Penmanship was emphasized and many hours were devoted to it.

My mother's family at Gower had to pay for her to go to high school. Her years in the one-room school prepared her for high school. She received the Schuster Key for being the best all around student. My mother went to Warrensburg to prepare for being a teacher after she graduated from college. When she had received her training, she got a teaching job in a country school. She taught for several years until she got married and moved to paradise, Mo. She taught at Camel, a one-room school-house in Clinton County, Mo.

Some of the games that were played at all country schools at noon and recess were Ante-1-over, Red rover and baseball.

Christmas programs were an important event in country schools. Early in the fall recitation would begin and students would begin practicing to recite poems, perform readings or learn a part in a play. On the day of the program, relatives and friends would arrive and the play would begin. At the end of the program, Santa would stop by and every child would receive a small gift. A potluck dinner would follow, where everyone stuffed himself.

The last day of school had the added excitement of report cards. Parents would arrive before noon and try to beat their kids in a ball game. A potluck dinner would follow, and school was out for the summer.

I myself am the product of two years in a country school. I received a good foundation and love for reading and learning. My husband, Eugene, went through eight years at a country school in Boonville, Mo. In his farming area, life revolved around the one-room school-house. Nothing remains of the old schoolhouse. Now there is a housing development where it used to stand.

By the turn of the century, the population began to shift to cities and country school began to lose students and tax support. School district consolidated, pooling their resources to provide better teacher, broader curriculums and opportunity for extracurricular activities. By 1966, the one-room country school had become a thing of the past.

Cousins gathered to play ball

Baseball came to the United States with the English settler who left the mother country for adventure in the New World. Baseball has its origins in two games that are played in England, cricket and rounders. Rounders is a game that is played with a ball and bat and involves hitting all the bases.

The game itself took strides forward when the Knickerbockers Baseball Club was organized in 1845 in New York City. In 1857, the National Association of Baseball players representing various baseball clubs drafted a special code of rules. Also in 1857, Amherst College and Williams College played the first inter-collegiate baseball game and Amherst won.

As a child under ten, I can remember going to the park in Smithville, Mo., to watch my uncles and the other young men of Smithville play against the young men of neighboring towns on Sunday afternoons in the spring and summer. This was also a good time for me to get acquainted with my cousins and the other children who came to watch the games.

We sometimes took balls and bats and organized our own teams. I was never a good baseball player. I was always chosen last and got a good position in the outfield. Balls never seemed to light in my area. If I caught a ball, it was an accident.

Being left handed had disadvantages. I always held the bat in the wrong hand and pitchers had problems with me standing in the wrong direction. A female baseball star I was not!

Catalog makes fantasies to order

As a child, I spent my free hours with the Sears and Roebuck and Montgomery Ward catalogs. My brother Bob and I inherited the old catalogs after the seasons for ordering were over.

We sharpened our scissors and started cutting. The first thing we did was to cut rooms to hold our furniture for rooms like the bedroom, living room, kitchen, etc. We made any kind of rooms and building that our imaginations could conjure up.

We cut our paper dolls from the children's section of the catalog, adults from the adult section, and made wardrobes for them. We gave them names and created lives for them. They were parents, children, schoolteacher, cab drivers and any kind of roles we dreamed up for them to play. We were only limited by imagination in the lives the paper dolls could lead and the places they could go.

If we needed cars, detectives or something the catalogs did not have, we only had to snip a few pictures from my dad's detective stories and my mother's "True Stories."

When we read library books that we were fond of, we re-created the stories with our paper dolls. We especially liked dog and horse stories. My brother Bobbie and I spent hours with our paper dolls and their imaginary lives.

Other things we both enjoyed were stories that we heard on the radio. I've always liked stories like "I Love a Mystery." "The Shadow" and "Amos and Andy."

Our whole family, in the winter, would put together puzzles. We kept a card table set up with the puzzle and its pieces scattered on it. After we had finished our dinner and homework, we always sat down and worked together trying to finish the puzzle by kerosene lamplight and in front of an old wood stove.

Another way I wiled away my time, when we went visiting, was listening to my mother and her cousins talk. They always talked about everything that had occurred since the last get-together. Being the only girl had its advantages. While they were cooking, I'd listen to the latest updates on who had babies, got married and the latest crimes. Her cousins were interesting women, and I could lose myself in listening to them talk. I developed a habit of listening as a child; that helps me in my work today.

The pre-television family was closer because the family members interacted with each other instead of sitting docilely as the family members do today, staring the "boob tube," Families who limit TV time today spend more quality time together and have closer relationships.

Catalogues played a major role in her young life

When I was small, catalogues played a major role in my life. My brother and I would cut out figures of men and women, boys and girls furniture, and appliances from the catalogues and make imaginary lives for them when we played.

The boys and girls would be people we went to school with in the one room school house in Paradise, Mo. We played for hours at a time with these paper figures. By the time the figures were getting frayed, a new book with sparkling figures, new houses and people, were ready to join our group of free paper dolls. We also cut out suits of clothes that would fit them.

After the cutting, we didn't throw away the catalogue; it went to the two-seated outhouse with old magazines. 'Squeezable soft Charmin toilet paper was too expensive. If it were warm in the out house, we spent a lot of time looking at the pictures. If the north wind was whistling around, 'get in and get out' was our motto.

My mother ordered a Shirley Temple doll and a baseball bat for us for Christmas when we lived in Paradise. We came home from school for lunch and the postman delivered the mail at that time. He knew he had Christmas packages for us, so he came back after we had gone back to school so we wouldn't know what we were getting.

After I got married, had children, and moved to a rural area on a farm, the catalogue still played and important role in my life. We got both the Montgomery Wards and Sears and Roebuck catalogues. I was busy running a dog kennel and ordered a lot of gifts from the catalogues. The fashion conscious daughter put her initials beside the pretty clothes and make up pictures in the book. My horse-loving daughter put her initials beside horse statues and Barbie dolls who rode horses. After my orders were delivered, I hid the gifts in the trunk of my car. They hunted with no success. After they caught onto the hiding place, I'd hide them in the feed sacks in the barn and hung them up so that mice couldn't get them.

Gilbert, Vivian, Bobby and Mary Dale

Depression gifts still remind

On the shelf an old, yellow teddy bear, battered and bent, shows his age as he sits in the back closet of my new home. What a story he could tell if he could talk! Across the room, a red wagon, dented with peeling paint, waits for the little boy who has since become a man. These two items represent the most cherished Christmas presents that my brother and I ever received.

It was a cold, snowy Christmas in the early 1930's. Vivian and Gilbert Dale had no idea where the Christmas presents for their two small children were coming from. During the Depression, jobs were hard to come by. Gilbert worked when he could on the WPA projects and the various farms in the Paradise, Mo., and Smithville, Mo., area. The old farmhouse they lived in was heated by a wood stove. Only the living room and the kitchen were warmed. The bedrooms had feather mattresses and iron bed warmer, heated from the wood stove.

Clothes were washed by hand on a washboard. Baths were weekly, and the water was carried from the pump outside and heated on the stove. Just surviving these hard winters represented a monumental accomplishment. There were no televisions; only battery operated radios. Entertainment came at night while working puzzles, reading, playing games, talking and doing homework by lamp-light. We were not passive viewers, but active participants.

Christmas loomed close. What would the young parents do? They put up their tree with homemade decorations of popcorn and colored paper. The children's excitement became more apparent as Christmas Eve approached.

On Christmas Eve, Gilbert was later than usual coming home from work, and Vivian became worried. Finally he came in with a five dollar bill clenched in his fist. Vivian wanted to know where he had gotten the money, and he said, "I gave one pint of blood and was paid for it.

They went to the Hafferty General Stored in Paradise and picked out the teddy bear and red wagon to make two you children happy.

The little boy and girl, are now senior citizens themselves and go shopping for their grandchildren, but they still remember the sacrifice that their father made to give them a happy Christmas . . .

Depression years necessitate much 'making do'

When you are short of money, you learn to use ingredients that you have instead of buying prepared items. My parents were married during the Depression in 1929. Then, you only bought the necessities and made your own items. My mother, Vivien Dale, made her own soap. She made lye soap and used this for washing clothes by hand on a washboard. She had two children that were small at the same time and keeping us and my father clean took a lot of time. The clothes were beaten after they were rubbed with soap, then rinsed by hand and hung out to dry in the fresh air winter and summer.

Produce was grown in our own garden. Some of the vegetables were tomatoes, lettuce, potatoes, sweet corn, peas, green beans, rhubarb and watermelons and muskmelons. After they had ripened, tomatoes and vegetables were canned and preserved in glass jars. We had no freezers. Potatoes, apples and all kinds of fruits were stored in a cellar underground. Iceboxes came along and the iceman delivered blocks of ice every day to keep our food cool. Then, along came electricity and the refrigerators.

Chickens were kept as layers of eggs and as meat for the table. One horrific job was cleaning out the hen house. My husband, Eugene, remembers the smell today, since he cleaned the henhouse in Boonville, where he lived on the farm.

Flour came in large quantities, in printed feed sacks. This cloth feed sacks made nice dresses. Mrs. Bechtold, my mother-in-law, made dish towels, dresser scarves and potholders out of them. My husband watched his mother pick out flour in the feed sack patterns she liked. The women at the local store in Paradise where I lived liked these sacks, too.

I can remember eating dandelion's greens in the spring. My husband's family ate mustard greens. These made great substitutes for lettuce and green stuff that we eat today and buy in the supermarkets.

Families in rural areas made do with one and two room schoolhouses. The teacher taught grades one to eight. She was janitor, fire starter, nurse and psychologist, as well as teacher. School let out early in the spring so the older children could help with the crop planting.

In the spring, everyone went berry picking. You gathered mulberries, blackberries and gooseberries. What delicious pies and cobblers they made. They were also good with cream and sugar.

One thing I can remember using on my hair after soaping and rinsing was vinegar to soften the hair. My hair was curled for special occasions with rags wound around to make curls.

Also, when there were no indoor bathrooms, we made do and took one bath a week, the littlest child first and the parents last. All used the same water with hot water added. In the warm summer, water holes at the creek made good bathing places

We used newspapers and magazines for wiping paper in outhouses. No Mr. Weebles to check our paper for softness like he does in the Charmin ads. Bees in summer like the manure smell in outhouses. We always checked to see what kind of insect was there before we sat down. Who wanted a bee sting on the rear?

There were no air conditioners in 1930. On hot nights, everyone slept on screened in porches or out in the open. Our dogs enjoyed having us and the blankets to snuggle up to. Also, so did many insects and crawly things. I can remember today looking up at the stars as I said my prayers out in the open.

Life was simpler in the 1930's and 1940's. Extended families stuck together and all relatives pulled together to help each other. Everyone was in the same boat, struggling to get ahead and happy to make do with what they had.

Easter Finery opens season in style

Whenever, I think of spring, I always think of Easter Sunday; the parade of ladies and children in all of their finery.

We always ordered our Easter finery from either the Sears Roebuck or the Montgomery Ward's catalog. My clothes ensemble always had white shoes and fancy dresses that were not made for active children. Grass stain on white shoes is a definite parent turnoff. On that particular day, little girls were supposed to sit demurely in their finery watching everyone else have fun.

The ole Easter bunny brought candy eggs and colored eggs, which we loved to hunt for. When I was very young, I always watched for the Easter bunny to come hopping up with my basket of goodies. Like Santa Claus, he was something I always managed to miss.

Another Easter pleasure for us was cute little dyed, live chickens. I loved those chickens until they grew up, sprouted feathers and became he-man roosters with few traces of the lovable chickens brought by the bunny. Our roosters, which always crowed at the crack of dawn wanted to fight with you and were generally lords of the barnyard. They ruled their henhouses with iron feet

My mother used to read the seed catalogs to find the proper seeds for the vegetable she planted. After ordering her seeds and planting them, she'd line my brother and me up as helpers. We got to weed the garden, water it, pick the vegetables, etc. My mother always said my brother made a better gardener than I did. Is it surprising then today that he has a big, beautiful garden and that mine is confined to two pots? In these pots, I grow interesting tomatoes, one plant to each pot. I love fresh vegetables, especially when someone else grows them.

Spring is here again, and I'm buying a mosquito plant to help keep the mosquitoes away as I sit on my porch watching the birds at the bird feeder. Spring is a renewing time for me as I sit in the warm sun watching the birds scratch for worms and cultivate the potted pansies, violas and miniature roses that comprise my gardening effort.

Easter hat prompts old love memories

I attended church services in the late 1930's and in the early 1940's. The song "In your Easter Bonnet" has added significance as I think about it.

Every Easter, I would get new shoes, new dress and a new hat. This new hat was straw usually with a ribbon hanging down.

All of the girls, who attended the Baptist Church in Paradise, Mo., and the one-roomed school house, claimed handsome Phillip as their boyfriend, whether openly or secretly.

He would come to church dressed in his new suit and shoes. All of the young ladies, me included, would almost fall out in the aisle swooning when he walked by.

You would have thought he was Elvis Presley before his time.

He ignored me every Easter until I was nine years old. My mother had made me a white organdy dress with a big pink sash. I had white leather shoes and a white straw hat with a pink ribbon.

This Easter, Phillip sauntered down the aisle at church and sat down behind me. I can still remember my heart fluttering as I wondered why he was sitting there.

I didn't have to wait too long. I felt a swift tug on the ribbon on my hat. Soon this hat was being passed from boy to boy while the minister tried to inspire the congregation with the biblical passages about the resurrection of Christ.

I finally got my hat back, slightly gray now and missing a ribbon.

I felt triumphant because Phillip has chosen me out of all his giggling admires. It was worth the scolding I got for ruining my hat to be Phillip' choice.

Eight—year old decides she'll do things differently as an adult

One New Year's resolution I remember making and keeping was in 1939 when I was eight years old. Over the years, Christmas and New Year's was celebrated at my grandparent's and great-grandparent's houses. I vowed that when I got married, I would always have the men and women eat at the same table. We had a large, extended family with lots of uncles, great-uncles, aunts, etc. I could smell the food from the kitchen—chicken, ham and every other kind of goodie. My grandmother told everyone, "Let's eat."

I lined up, but men were served first. It was an old tradition left over from farming days, when men came in from the fields and had to hurry back. To an eight year-old, it seemed as though those men took forever to eat. They were not hurrying back to the field, but to a card game. I thought the men got the best food, and I got the "running gears."

I've been married for over fifty years, and at my house, men and women eat at he same table. There's equal opportunity for food for the females.

As I was growing up, I watched the effect of "old man alcohol" on people. My grandfather likes to drink; he said it relaxed him. One New Year' night, I stayed with my grandparent in Trimble, Mo. My grandfather came stumbling in about 3 o'clock in the morning. He woke me up and I watched him stumble in the back door, holding onto the wall. On New Year's Day, I made a resolution that I would never get drunk and get out of control. I have kept that resolution to this day.

I was engaged while I was going to college. I made a resolution when I started college to graduate. My fiancé came home from the service in my junior year. He wanted to get married and move to Arizona. I would have had to stop college and move. We celebrated New Year's together and he went to Arizona alone and I went back and finished college. I have never regretted that decision, because after that I met my future husband Eugene

Certain youthful beliefs, fantasies carry over into life as adult

When I was a child, space technology and development were a few light years away. Orville and Wilbur Wright had taken off in their flying machine and Charles Lindbergh was a national flying hero. Our economy was changing from an agrarian to an industrial power, making automobiles and airplanes.

Families stayed together and the women stayed home to raise the children. The father was the head of the house and was the sole breadwinner. Women were subservient to their husbands and his wishes were law in most households. Women had only had the right to vote since 1917. I was born in 1931.

As a child, I remember going to church and Sunday school, and receiving a good foundation in the Bible and Christianity. I try to live by the Ten Commandments. I drifted away from the church in my teens and early 20's, but gradually came back into the fold in my early 30's.

As a child, I always resented women and children eating at the second table in family dinners. After the men had been served, the women and children then ate. I always felt that all of us were equal in the sight of God and should all eat together. We have always done that in my home. My father taught my brothers to drive. He did not think a woman needed to drive. My husband fell heir to the task of teaching me to drive at twenty two. I also got my own car, since we worked in different places and on different shifts.

I taught my daughters how to drive and they got their own cars at sixteen. I also taught them that they needed an education beyond high school so that they could provide a living for themselves and their children if needed. I encouraged them to go for higher education, and told them that they could do anything that they wanted to.

We believed that your gender did not affect what you could do or the aspirations that you would have for yourself. Higher education is something that my father felt was unnecessary for females. My mother supported me so that I could go on to college on a four year scholarship.

As a child, I was taught to respect and listen to older people. This is something that children should learn early. You can learn from hearing about the experiences and lives of those who came before you. Even as an adult and married, I always felt that I was not alone and knew that my grandparents were cheering me on in whatever I did and were there if I needed help and advice.

I felt that guardian angels lived up in the heavens above and would swoop down to protect me if I needed help. This belief has carried over into later life. When I was running a kennel, I went to get the mail and burn the trash at the same time. As I lit the fire, I dropped a large check into the trash that was burning. The fire died down long enough for me to retrieve the check without being burned and with the check intact.

Another time, I was the only one home and locked myself outside of the kennel and the house. I got colder by the minute. I heard a voice say: "Look In the key box on the nightlight . . ." Lo and behold, there was the key to both buildings. There was no one there when I heard the voice, but I know that is was my guardian angels.

Another childhood fantasy that I have never outgrown is the belief in elves, fairies, little people, angels, ghosts and other beings. I read every fairy story ever written. I still like fantasy, science fiction, ghost stories about alien beings. I expect my liking to write came from these very same musing.

I believe that all of us should keep a little of the childhood wonderment in our lives, even if we live to be a thousand years old.

Beliefs about luck, health affect child's outlook

When I was a child, I was influenced by many superstitious beliefs. Many of my relatives carried a rabbit's foot on a keychain for luck. I can remember my grandfather telling me that a buckeye carried with a rabbit's foot brought you twice as much luck.

Living in Kansas City gave me plenty of opportunities as a child to jump over cracks in the sidewalks. The old saying went if we stepped on a crack; we broke our mother's back.

The above practices that I have mentioned are superstitions. Superstitions can be defined as irrational and resulting from ignorance or a fear of a belief of unseen and unknown. The word implies a belief in unseen and unknown forces that can be influenced by object or r rituals. Magic, witchcraft and the occult are referred to as superstitions. Elements of magic associated with religion and its beliefs have been regarded as superstitions also. Amulets are used to ward off evil spirits. Good luck charms like horse shoes, coins, lockets, four-leaf clovers and religious medals and lockets are kept or worn to ward off evil and to bring good fortune.

My brother and I spent many a summer afternoon fighting the honeybees, trying to find a four-leaf clover among the good-smelling purple blooms. I don't remember finding the elusive four-leaf clover, but I did learn a lot about ants, tumble bugs, chiggers and other crawling insects.

Some of the superstitions I remember are cultural instead of religious: a bride always wears something old, something borrowed and something blue. When couples are newly married, the groom carries the bride across the threshold of her new house. This custom is based on the fear that if the bride should trip entering the home, it is a bad omen for the marriage. One of the things I remember as a newlywed was the clattering of the tin cans tied to the car as we left the wedding reception. This custom probably came about as a result that noise makers would frighten away evil spirits. The same principle applies to New Year's Eve noisemaker and firecrackers on the Fourth of July.

Spilling salt is thought to bring bad luck. Salt was once a very valuable commodity and wasting it was a real loss. It was the chief means of preserving a purifying food. A believer in superstition who spills salt on the table will take a pinch of it and throw it over his left shoulder into the face of the devil who sitting there.

I have worked with people who feel that Friday the 13th is a good day to stay at home. Fear of the number 13 has religious roots. At the last supper of Jesus and his disciples, there were 13 persons, one of whom was Judas the traitor. Today, many tall buildings omit the 13th floor, going from twelve to fourteen.

I have a friend who will go around the block if she sees a black cat starting across the road. Avoidance of black cats has religious origins as well. During the middle Ages, it was believed that witches could turn themselves into black cats. Thus, when such a cat was seeing, it was thought the witch was a cat in disguise.

Another practice that I have known about since childhood is that breaking a mirror brings the breaker seven years of bad luck. Since a mirror reflects the self, distortion of the image was a sign of coming trouble. The Romans allotted seven years for the human body to renew itself after a mirror was broken.

Man may be able to land a space probe on Mars that sends pictures through space, and I am a product of the educational technology, but I'm not so far removed from my primitive ancestors that I still shudder at a black cat starting across my path. I also wear a St. Christopher's medal for divine protection. What complex creature we human being are

Let's Play Dress up

My brother Bobbie and I played dress up. I loved my grandmother's winter Coat with the big fur collar. She wore her hair short and waved on one side. I tried wearing it and it dragged behind me. In that coat, I played being a gangster's moll liked a moll for Pretty Boy Floyd. My brother had a suit coat ten sizes too big and it had pin stripes. He also had a cap that he pulled over his eyes. His toy cap pistol made up the rest of the outfit for what we considered a gangster. My dad had a car with a rumble seat. My brother would get in the front seat and I would sit beside him. During the depression, gangster exploits made the headlines of the newspapers and we heard on the radio newscasts.

Another favorite imagination game that we played was being pirates like Bluebeard. We would get in an old washtub and set sail for the Caribbean. I wore a peasant blouse and long skirt. My brother wore a rag around his head and ragged pants with bare feet. We knew that pirates took whatever they wanted. We had our eyes on the neighbor's cherry tree. We climbed it and ate our fill of cherries. We were caught and received a lecture and could not go to the movie shows shown on the screen on Saturday night in front of the grocery store. We hated that because we were missing a segment of the continuing Tom Mix movie.

Life may have been hard in the 1930's but we enjoyed life with make believe games and get together with our cousins and families who lived close.

"Calamity Jane" goes to camp

My most memorable vacation before 1949 was my first experience in leaving Missouri and living in the great outdoors.

I was very excited as my parents drove me to the bus that would take me and 19 more excited kids to Des Moines.

We pulled into the camp in time for our evening meal. This meal was cooked outside, and we had hot dogs and toasted marshmallows cooked in the fire. We sang old church songs before we turned in to our small cabins that had two walls made of screen.

For a city dweller, the sounds of the night were frightening. The deep harrumph of the tree frog and the screeching of the night owl had replaced the rumbled and clatter of the 31st Streetcar.

The next day we had a hiking trip scheduled. Now that sounds like fun! You'd think. Forty of us trudged off with our leader, an energetic 20 year old. We sang "Onward Christian Soldiers," at the top of our lungs. Our guide cautioned us about staying on the path. I saw a beautiful wildflower on the side of the path. As I started to pick up the flower, this big black rope launched itself at me. I screamed, and all the happy campers came running back. My hero, Dave charged up. His only comment, "you only saw a black snake, and he was twice as scared as you." I felt like catching the first bus home.

The campers had to prepare their own food. I drew K.P. detail. My job was to peel the potatoes and cut them into small pieces for boiling. Half way through peeling, I sliced a deep gash in my finger. Immediately, I was rushed to medical and got my finger stitched and bandaged. Bye-Bye K.P!

We used outdoor toilets. One night I had to go, but the toilet was busy. I decided to go into the bushes. Stupid mistake! I must have backed into a growth of poison ivy. By the next morning, I was itching so bad that I could not sit on my rear end. I scratched and the poison ivy spread over my whole body. This was only Wednesday. We had two days left of camp.

The camp director called my parents who drove up to get me.

Gilbert and Tim Dale

My favorite family toys

When I was a child, my favorite toy was a doll with auburn hair and blue eyes. I carried her around and pushed her in a doll buggy. I still have that doll in my home today. She sits in a place of honor. She could use a new wig and a pair of shoes. She reminds me of happy times and has withstood the ravages of time.

One of my other favorite toys was a living banty hen. I liked to watch the baby chickens that she hatched. When we moved to Kansas and Oklahoma, we moved my banty chicken with me.

My husband, Gene, and my brother, Bobby, liked their Red Ryder wagons. It was a privilege when my brother let me haul my dolls in it. They both like their BB Guns. My husband used his BB gun to shoot out all the windows in the barn. Sparrows used to annoy us with their droppings. My brother Bobby liked to shoot at them, my husband got into trouble with the gun and shooting out the barn glass windows.

My nephews liked sacks of toy army men and jeeps, tanks and all the equipment that came in the sacks. They played for hours with them winning many battles.

My daughters in the 1960's liked to play with the Barbie's. Julie had horse figures and sat her Barbie's on them. She would use barns and stables and play for hours. Mari Jean wanted a Barbie head that she could arrange and rearrange the hair on. She also got makeup for the doll and painted her face many times. Barbie equipment, dolls, Kens, trailers, houses, airplanes, horse's dogs and other Barbie material were wrapped under my Christmas tree for many years.

My brother Tim had a bicycle that got him around the neighborhood. He as an adult graduated to a motorcycle. His prized possession was a dog name Daisy. Daisy was a male Shetland sheepdog. He kept running away from his former home and finally became by brother's. When he and my parents went on vacation, Daisy went too. He liked certain people. He did not like my husband or my friend Vernilda. He would sneak up behind them and give them little nips on the leg. Thus concludes the story of "The Dale Family and their pets", both inanimate and alive.

Homemade Toys

My favorite toys were those that were homemade. We used catalogues and magazines for material to make the toys. We cut out paper figures and let our imaginations run rampant. Mother and father paper dolls had all kinds of wardrobes provided by the clothing displayed in the Sears and Roebuck, Montgomery Ward and the Spiegel catalogues. The childr5en we cut out were close to our own age. If we wore out the figures from constant use, we just put our scissors to use cutting our more.

We used cardboard boxes to house the furniture we cut out for the paper dolls. We cut paper animals and pets from magazines and farm catalogues.

Our paper dolls took us too many foreign lands on trips we dreamed up for them. Our paper dolls lived lives of famous radio personalities, movie stars, admired teachers, and neighbors. We let our psyche roam and the seeds of many novels started in the humble play of my brother Bobby and I.

My own children enjoyed playing with paper dolls and housing made from catalogues. My granddaughter likes to cut out paper figure and give them names. This creative play is much better that sitting passively in front of the television set.

Vivian Dale sitting by Christmas tree

Christmas memories past and present

Whenever I think of Christmases gone by, I remember the stories my mother told me about her Christmases as a young child. Her family did not celebrate Christmas in the traditional way. The family of four lived on a farm near Star field, Mo. She went to a one-room schoolhouse and walked or rode a horse.

Her family never had a Christmas tree. The children got and orange or an apple for a present. My mother always said to herself, "When I have my family, I will always have a Christmas tree every year."

At school, they always celebrated Christmas. The children were given presents by a wealthy school board member; He would drive up in a horse-drawn sleigh. Each child got to pick what they wanted. One year my mother picked a cupie doll which my mother kept until she died. She passed it on to me.

My mother lived to be ninety seven years old. My dad died fifty years before she did. She always had Christmas at her house, until she was eighty. She finally let me take over and have the Christmas dinners. The last two years of her life, she lived in a nursing home. She insisted on having a Christmas tree in her room. She also sent out Christmas cards to friends with my help. Her family was farmers. When my mother was born, she was vaccinated with diphtheria vaccine. Her sister died a few days before she was born with the disease. Her family always thought that they got the disease from a mother cat and kittens that had colds and fever and died at the same time that her sister did. The sister was eight.

When I was small, my parents got their Christmas tree from the nearby woods. We made the decorations for the trees. We cut out angels, bells and colored them. We made paper chains for the tree and put them all around the tree. The tree would not have been complete without popcorn strung together on a string which went up with all our other decoration. On Christmas we went with our dad and came home to find out that Santa had been there. We especially like the chocolate treats and peppermint candy canes. On Christmas we went to a family gathering where we played and ate roast turkey and all of the kinds of desserts that you can imagine.

With my mother's death on Feb 7, 2008, one of the most courageous spirits I have ever known left this Earth for a better place. She passed on this belief in Christ and a life after death to her family. She instilled belief in the Ten Commandments in her children. Wherever she is now, there will be a Christmas celebrations. At my house, I will put up a Christmas tree and eat the traditional feast much sadder without my mother. I am sure that her spirit will be watching our get together.

Christmas nostalgia

Each Christmas when I see the Santa's in the store and the faces of the children, I remember one of my own childhood Christmas Eves, while we lived in Paradise, Mo.

My father would take my brother and me to the local grocery store to see the toys and Christmas tree. I always enjoyed these things because the store had all kinds of good smells from candy and evergreen to herbs and spices. Each year my father would buy my brother and me chocolate drops and sweet orange slices. We always stayed about and hour at the store. My mother always stayed at home. When we go home the Christmas tree would be shining with lights and the popcorn balls we had strung and candy canes. Somehow present appeared under our tree and we opened the presents that we had given each other as well as what Santa Claus had left. My parents always told us that Santa stopped early and came by later with specially picked toys.

I never questioned them but continued to believe in Santa Claus until one night in the early 1940's I woke up with start thinking I heard Santa on the roof. I tiptoed out of bed and hid behind the door, thinking to catch the benevolent old gent in the act. I saw none other than my dad placing a beautiful doll for me and a wagon for my brother under the tree. My dad said to mother, "We might as well eat Santa Claus's cookies."

Each Christmas Eve I think of my parents as I have played Santa Claus to my children and grandchildren.

Keeping Christmas a Surprise

Sneaky ways we find out what is in our Christmas presents early. One event I remember from my childhood is admiring a beautiful doll in a store in Oklahoma City. We went in this store to buy groceries and other goods. The twelve inch doll that stood in the window captivated me and I stood transfigured in front of her. While mother was buying groceries, she could find me easily rooted to the spot in front of the doll. The gorgeous doll graced that window until five days before Christmas. Then she disappeared. On Christmas morning I woke up and went to the Christmas tree. There under the tree stood the doll and she has my name on her. I didn't know where mother hid the doll but I did not see her until Christmas Day. That same doll still lies on my bed a little bedraggled but a symbol of my families love. My parents are gone now but I still can remember that Christmas morning so long ago and the happiness I felt with my doll.

My two daughters, Marijean and Julie learned how to wrap and un-wrap the packages so that you could never tell they had been touched. I caught the culprits one day examining the packages and rewrapping them. I decided after that I was going to stop putting the packages under the tree until Christmas Eve. I had developed many hiding places for them in their childhood years. I put them in the trunk of my car and that was safe enough until Marijean was helping me put groceries in the trunk and she spied the presents. I had to change the hiding place. One of my favorite places was in the kennel building in feed sacks. Another place I used was putting up gunny sacks in the barn it took them a long time to discover that hiding place.

Now that they have their own homes and children, I miss trying to hide presents so they can't fine them. I wonder how good their children are at finding their presents.

Sneaky ways we find out what is in our Christmas presents early

One event I remember from my childhood is admiring a beautiful doll in a store in Oklahoma City. We went in this store to buy groceries and other goods. The twelve inch doll that stood in the window captivated me and I stood transfigured in front of her. While mother was buying groceries, she could find me easily rooted to the spot in front of the doll. The gorgeous doll graced that window until five days before Christmas. Then she disappeared. On Christmas morning I woke up and went to the Christmas tree. There under the tree stood the doll and she had my name on her. I didn't know where mother hid the doll but, I did not see her until Christmas Day. The same doll still lies on my bed, a little bedraggled but a symbol of my family's love. My parents are gone now but, I still can remember that Christmas morning so long ago and the happiness I felt with my doll.

My two daughters, Marijean and Julie, learned how to wrap and unwrap the packages so that you could never tell they had been touched. I caught the culprits one day examining the packages and rewrapping them I decided after that I was going to stop putting the packages under the tree until Christmas Eve. I had developed many hiding places for them in their childhood years. I put them in the trunk of my car and that was safe enough until Marijean was helping me put groceries in the trunk and she spied the present. I had to change the hiding place. One of my favorite places was in the kennel building in feed sacks. Another place I used was putting up gunny sacks in the barn it took them a long time to discover that hiding place.

Now that they have their own homes and children, I miss trying to hide presents so they can't find them. I wonder how good their children are at finding their presents.

Clever advertising campaign entertains drivers

The best examples of old time advertising that I still remember and repeat are some of the old Burma Shave ads. We would ride along in the rumble seat of our Model T Ford and check out the Burma Shave signs. This was before television and before we had radios. We didn't watch movies on the road nor do puzzle books, but we enjoyed checking out the signs . . . Like my relative said:" No one could read just one line; you had to read every line till you got to the end.

As one of the rhymes said:" If you don't know/ whose signs these are/ you can't have driven/ very far/ Burma Shave."

Clinton Odell developed the brushless shaving cream he called Burma Shave. At a time when folk's were really starting to travel America by automobile, the brushless cream eliminated the problem of packing a way shaving brush and mug. Odell had an excellent product and all he lacked was a marketing plan.

Allan Odell convinced his father to spend $200.00 for some material to construct high way signs. In 1926, using recycled lumber, Al fabricated the first Burma Shave verses and erected one set of sings along route 35. Within weeks, drug stores began running out of Burma Shave and ordering, more. In the next year more signs were set up and orders poured in; sales for the first year hit $68,000. During World War 11, homesick GIs would erect Burma-Shave look alike signs in Alaska, Germany and even Antarctica.

All good things come to and end. The Odell Family sold their company to Gillette, which in turn became part of American Safety Razor. By 1966, every Burma Shave sign had disappeared from America's highways.

Here are a few jingles that I remember after looking them up in the library;

"Guys whose eyes/are in their backs/get HALOS crossing/ railroad track? Burma Shave"

"A Christmas hug/a birthday kiss/awaits the woman/ who gives this/ Burma Shave."

You can take a trip down memory lane by reviewing these signs. I like most of them better than I liked television ads today. They turn up the volume on these ads and I have to turn them down.

Ears brought all the ads home

The sense I used in the past that was influenced by advertising campaigns was my ears.

The radio with its programs influenced the products that depression families used when they chose liquids to drink, products to clean their bodies and make themselves more beautiful, etc.

Grand Ole Opry

The Grand Ole Opry was a weekly institution in my family. We enjoyed listening to the show broadcast live from Nashville, Tenn. Some of their sponsors were Prince Albert and bull Durham.

My grandfather bought Prince Albert and rolled his own cigarettes.

I always thought that smoking was a nasty habit and had no desire to smoke.

Reading signs in car

Another product I'll never forget was advertised on the public highways.

Burma Shave signs would be posted for miles. You'd read the limerick and there at the end would be the words "Burma Shave".

If I'd shaved at that time, I would have automatically bought Burma Shave.

Many of my hours spent in the back seat of the family care were reading the Burma Shave signs. I still find myself looking for them when I travel.

Other radio shows that sold products were Amos and Andy—Pepsodent toothpaste for the bright smiles; Lum and Abner—Oval tine; My Gal Sunday-Ivory soap.

We still use Ivory soap, 100 percent pure, at our house today.

Wheaties on the radio

Cereals were sold on radio programs, like Jack Armstrong for Wheaties, the breakfast of champions.

The Tom Mix show sold Kellogg products. You always got coupons for prizes in cereal boxes.

Kids gobbled up the cereal so they could get cards, rings, airplanes, cars, magnifying glasses, de-coder rings, dolls, etc.

My husband at age 6 spent some time in the hospital. He enjoyed throwing his cereal airplane out the door into the corridor so the nurses could chase it.

Flour sack fashion

Dresses, curtains, and dish towels were made out of flour sacks.

The kind of flour you bought depended a lot on the current feed sack pattern.

Many families got their eating utensils. Especially dishes, from Mother's Oats.

Grocery stores also offered whole sets of dishes for the purchase of so many groceries.

Jewel Tea offered prizes like dishes and silverware if you bought their products.

I liked to buy and read magazines telling about my favorite movie stars.

I bought lipsticks, soaps, and makeup hoping I'd look like the movie stars that endorsed these particular products.

Student acting

My students at the grade school where I work acted out some of the commercials on television to see if the others could guess the products.

We saw that the advertisers are as successful today as they were in the past when we only heard them on the radio.

Entertainers contribute to musical memories

My musical memories date back to my childhood. I can remember listening to the Grand Ole Opry on the radio at my grandparent's home in Paradise, Mo. Hank Williams Senior, songs and Patsy Cline lyrics were especially popular with my family. All her songs I remember go back into the folklore of American culture. They were about; unrequited love, drinking in honky-tonk cafes and painted doves. Gospel songs by cowboys on their guitars were especially moving, "The Old rugged Cross" and "I come to the Garden Alone," to name a few.

My husband, Eugene, still likes Patsy Cline, Hank Williams Sr. and the more traditional cowboy music better than he does Rockabilly and modern cowboy music.

As I was growing up in the 50's I liked Fats Domino and his rocking piano. I especially liked "Going Home," "Ain't it a Shame," "Blueberry Hill," "I'm Walking," and: A Whole Lot of Shaking Going on."

I am still a Fats Domino fan. Fats outsold every 50's rock and roll pioneer except Elvis Presley. He was inducted into the rock and roll hall of Fame in 1986.

Bill Haley and the Comets was another sound that I liked. Their song in 1952 was "Rock Around the Clock," which became the sound track for "Blackboard Jungle," a talked about movie in 1954. My favorite song of theirs was "Shake, Rattle and Roll."

Even today, I still like rock and roll music. Its fun to execute a few rock and roll dance movements as I dust and vacuum. My husband thinks I'm going to throw something out of joint or gear and have to visit the chiropractor.

At our house, I play my rock and roll records when Eugene does his volunteer work and is gone. Rock and Roll scared the parents of my generation, who thought we were going to the devil when we screamed our heads off at Elvis when he did his pelvic gyrations. The caveman probably shook his head when his teenagers jumped up and down and beat on animal skin drums.

So end this story of my musical trip into my past. I hope you enjoyed it.

Mary Bechtold

Entertaining indoor activities fight off snowy blues

When the snow fell and the winter winds howled in from the north, it was time for varied activities. Indoor fun consisted of various card games—pinochle, bridge, solitaire, pitch and rummy and board games like Monopoly, Life, Carom and Dominoes.

My mother made snow ice cream when the snow first fell. I can still taste it. It was fun to sit around the fire at slumber parties and tell ghost stories and compare notes on manly "hunks" we knew.

Winter was also the time for getting groups of teenagers together in Kansas City for a night of fun at the Plamor. I always enjoyed roller skating more than I did ice skating. I did both, though, since you can meet lots of eligible males in the ice skating rink. It was easy to get acquainted with them by bumping into them accidentally on purpose.

My parents originally came from the Gower and Paradise region. Even though we lived in Kansas City, my whole family went back to Gower where they had square dances.

My second cousin, Orville Lee Livingston, and I enjoyed dancing at these dances. My dad and mother enjoyed all kinds of dances. Many of my cousins still participate by giving demonstration all over the country.

Ginnie B., a friend of mine, grew up in a family of eight. There were always plenty of brothers and sisters to join in the winter fun. They would take the hoods of cars and use them for sleds on the old gravel roads. These metal sleds really moved. They lived near a river where the water had backed up and was not very deep. Even if you fell and the ice broke, you couldn't drown. You would probably feel like you were freezing to death.

Another pastime of her family was ice fishing; cut a hole in the ice, and wait for and unsuspecting fish to grab your bait—fresh fish at temperature below zero.

Skating parties could also bring hot chocolate and wiener roast. When one of her brothers got into the water while they were skating, her sister left her skates on and drove the car in skates to get help.

My husband, Eugene, and his sister Alrita, rode on their sled at ages 4 and 5, pulled by a hound dog wearing a harness that their mother had made.

You won't find me ice skating today but you can still find me working puzzles, playing card games and reading. These are some of the winter things I enjoyed earlier.

Tim Dale in front of house

Family stands vigil after boy drinks coal oil

We lived in a large farmhouse that was heated with a coal stove. My brother and I had gone to school, and my mother and 2 year old brother were at home.

My mother had let the fire go out, and was trying to light it with coal oil, the liquid. She turned her back and when she turned around; my little brother had the coal oil up to his lips.

My mother had no way of knowing how much he had drunk. She went up to the neighboring dairy farm and got pure cream for my brother to drink. My brother never got sick, but we all watched him anxiously for 24 hours.

Mary Bechtold

Folks escape heat under eaves, shade trees

When I think of porches and swings, I think of times gone by where life moved at a slower pace than it does today.

Pre-Civil War plantation had big shaded porches where the inhabitants could sit on a hot summer day and cool themselves.

Victorian homes in the 1890's had porches where the family gathered on summer evenings. If the nights were hot enough, they slept on screened-in porches or out in yard on cots or in tents.

Before air conditioning, people made use of their yards and nature's air conditioning. Leisure summer days and evenings were spent in the shade, swinging on the porch, watching the children chase lightning bugs. The only sounds you could hear were the creaking of the tree frogs, crickets and the porch swing as it moved back and forth rhythmically.

In the 1940's and 1950's my family (the Gilbert Dale family), lived at 2845 Spruce in Kansas City, Mo. We had a screened—in-porch that had lots of uses. We sat on it to cool down when it was hot. Our dog Daisy liked it, too. Lawn chairs were used on this porch in the heat of the summer. This porch could tell a tale of the comings and goings of my brother Robert, and me as teenagers.

I had my wedding reception on this porch and in that house. The house was demolished to make way for highway improvements and where it once stood there are now concrete roads and bridges.

My husband, Eugene, had a porch at Boonville that went all the way around the farmhouse.

When prohibition came, all bars were closed. A huge refrigerator from a bar was kept on this porch, where milk was kept cold: the Bechtolds were dairy farmers. This porch also had a porch swing and chairs. Lizzie Bechtold sat here on hot summer days, preparing her vegetables for canning.

On sultry summer nights, the family gathered on the porch with visitors to watch barefoot children playing tag. Cots were set up under the trees for sleeping.

Many nights the children were surprised by what kinds of nocturnal creatures they would see go by. On one wanted to see the skunk with its potential for disastrous smells. To me, porch swings and porches were our predecessors' way of coping with the heat—nature's own air conditioners.

Games can't hold her interest

"Batter up"! When I hear those words, my thoughts go back to my childhood. We lived in the country near Smithville, Mo. My mother had cousins who lived close; we'd get together and play baseball. All my cousins were boys. We would mark off at ball diamond and "batter up." I was never a good player; my position was always far outfield. When I was up to bat, I missed unless the pitcher actually hit the bat with the ball. Being the only girl, I took a lot of ribbing.

In the country school I attended I got the same position last outfielder. I was the last person picked for the team. I would never have qualified for a baseball scholarship.

In high school, we had to have two years of gym classes. I remember having to shinny up ropes and climb back down. Also, we played baseball outside. Guess where I ended up—last outfielder. I never had a talent for sports. My lack of athletic ability never bothered me. I always had my nose in a book, and I think I developed more muscles in my head than in my arms.

I had boyfriends who played baseball, hiked, swam and fished. I always went along, but never developed any proclivity for those things. Later, when I ran a dog kennel, I wished I had developed more muscles. Carrying dogs; 50 pounds bags of feed, and small children, I could have used more muscle power.

My daughters and their children are much more athletic. They ride horses, train horses, play football and basketball. They did track and basketball in high school. In grade school, they belonged to summer baseball teams. I delivered them to haves and watched them play.

My husband likes car races, football and baseball games. I have my head stuck in a book or watching forensic science programs on television. "Batter up" never captivated me.

Invention of movies brings new medium to entertainment scene

When Thomas Edison and his assistant, William Dickerson, invented and patented the kineograph and kinescope at Menlo Park, N.J., in 1891, motion pictures had their primitive beginning. Soon all over Europe and the United States people were experimenting with making pictures that you could see move by turning a crank and looking into a box.

From the invention came the movie projector. Some of the earliest potable films were newsreels and documentaries. In the 1920's some of the famous silent screen film stars were Rudolph Valentino, Charlie Chaplin, and Mary Pick ford, Clara Bow, Douglas Fairbanks and Greta Garbo.

The average United States citizen in the 20's and 30's was poor and struggling to make ends meet. The Depression was in full swing. The neighborhood grocery store in a small town would show a continued serial on Saturday night. Then the local farmers and townspeople would come into town to buy groceries.

Movie houses sprang up in larger towns. For a dime, you could forget your troubles and watch a Roy Rogers Western, a tale of love and woe or historical movies. In the early 1930's the screen stars talked and you no longer had to read what the people were saying at the bottom of the screen. Cartoons like Betty Boop, Sylvester the Cat and Mickey Mouse kept the audience entertained.

My husband's mother loved movies and went to see every new Shirley Temple with her children in Boonville, Mo. The farm work would wait. Her daughter, Martha Ann wore Shirley Temple curls.

All the cereal that you ate had some sort of mementos of Tom Mix, Roy Rogers, Hoot Gibson and Gene Autry. Even John Wayne got in to movies as a singing cowboy. He couldn't sing so someone else sang for him.

Until I moved to Kansas City in the 1940's I didn't attend many movies, we listened to programs on the radio, such as "The Green Hornet, "Amos and Andy" and "I love a Mystery." My brothers and I with my dad would go to the Troost Theatre to see gangster movies, who-done-its and horror films. My mother never went; she didn't like to be scared.

In my teen years, groups of my friends and I would go to Saturday afternoon matinees and watch two hours of cartoons for twenty five cents. You could enjoy the antics of the cartoon characters. Drive-in movies sprang up and carloads of us would go to the movies and enjoy the companionship of friends and eating popcorn.

When I look back, I remember the movie year's with fondness. I was an Elvis Presley fan. I went to see every movie he made.

Television and VCR's have replaced movie theaters. Individual's rent movies and invite friends over to watch them at home. It is not the same as seeing the lights go off in the theater and the plot unfolds on the screen with hundreds of others sitting there in the audience with you.

Keepsakes recall memories of family

The keepsakes and treasures that I have are related to my relatives and the various decades of my life. My mother's parents used lamps and kerosene to light them. I have a beautiful lamp that is hand carved glass. I very seldom use it, but it comes in handy when the electricity goes off and one cannot see with out these lamps or flashlights.

I still have reading certificates that I received in the late 1940's and 50's. Reading was never a chore for me. I always enjoyed books and could be found with my nose stuck in one. I read all the horse and dog books I could find and then graduated to historical romances. One could visit far away countries when engrossed in an intriguing story.

My other treasured remains of my high school years from 1945 to 1949, are pictures I took of the Central High school campus and friends. I have a bound copy of the Central High Luminary of 1949, the year I was first page editor. I also have copies of my yearbooks. These keepsakes are dusty and the pages turning yellow.

Moving on, one of my favorite keepers is a skull ashtray which is printed with "University of Kansas City," which has grown into University of Missouri and Kansas City.

Pictures of sorority friends are seen in my old albums. College yearbooks picture their graduates as forever young.

Life moves on to marriage years. Some of my favorite keepsakes are the tea set sent to me by my husband when he served in England and the anniversary clock he bought that was made in Germany.

Quilts rank high on my list of favorite things. My mother handmade one, with all the emblems of the 50 states flowers, birds and state mottos. I especially like the Sunbonnet Sue I use in my twin beds.

In the 1960's I had a kennel. My daughter, Julie, bought me small statues of dogs that I have sitting around. My friend, Elsie Moutray, made me ceramic dolls. I have two of these dolls in small doll beds.

One could go on and on about their treasures, but one's keepsakes are a life remembered.

Life before plumbing presents health concerns

In America today, a person would never purchase a home without an indoor toilet and bathtub. In the fast pace of our everyday lives, we fail realize how the plumbers of the past 20 years have helped to eliminate disease, increase life span and provide the conveniences we take for granted each day.

As the cave dwellers were quick to discover, humans could not exist long in close quarters without acquiring a certain air.

The ancient Greeks promoted bodily fitness and cleanliness and their gymnasiums featured hot and cold shower baths.

Of all the ancient civilizations, the Romans were the best plumbers in the world. Their public baths were engineering marvels. In 600 B.C., the Romans introduced hot water boilers with hot and cold delivery systems. Their sewer branches and water supply lines were run with lead pipe. The fall of Rome in 450 A.D. was the fall of plumbing technology as well. Throughout the middle ages, twice as many people were struck down by typhoid, dysentery and cholera than were killed in all the wars. Cleanliness was considered sinful and bathing was rarely permitted. In 1348 the first wave of Black Plague entered England, wiping out on third of the population.

In America, in Colonial times, bathing was frowned upon, illegal in Boston except upon a physician's order. Typhoid, cholera and dysentery were the chief threat to survival in New York in the early 19th century. Finally, in 1946, New England passed the National Plumbing Health Age, mandating a flushing toilet or ash pit in every home. As toilets improved and proper correction eliminated disease, they became more popular, and it was in the latter part of the 19th century that human wasted was linked to disease causing organisms.

In the 1930's I was under 10 years of age, and we lived in many houses where there were no indoor toilets. We trotted out to the outhouse winter and summer. If it was very cold, we were allowed to use chamber pots, which had to be emptied.

Outhouses made great places, when it was warmer, to read old magazines, news paper and comic books, which were used for toilet paper. I think my love of detective and mystery stories began in the outhouse.

When Tim, my brother, was small, we had a chicken house by the outhouse. The old rooster listened for the house door to open and chased him-and anyone headed to the outhouse flogging and spurring.

My husband's parents in Boonville kept a large container of water on the wood stove. This water was hot at all times. At Saturday bath time, a tub was put out behind the wood stove and the ritual began. The youngest took the first bath. Hot water was added each time a person hopped in the bath. You burned in front and froze on the back end when you were trying to put on your clothes after a bath.

Keeping wood chopped and in the wood stove was no easy job. Children got to split the kindling and carry in the wood.

Life during the 20's and the Depression era moved at a slower rate than is does today. Physical work was harder and family connections were closer because they had to work together. My memories of my childhood and all my relatives are pleasant because we were close.

Having running water and indoor toilets has made our lives more sanitary and easier. My family connections were stronger in my earlier years because we had to work as a team and spent more time together playing games and doing the chores to keep our household running.

Lot of squawking getting fowl to table

When I think about the process of getting a live animal ready to eat and serve on the table, I remember the process of getting the live chicken from squawking and flapping his wings to dead bird lying on his back stuffed and baked with dressing and gravy.

When we lived in the country, we bought baby chickens direct from the hatchery and raised them as meat for the table or adult egg layers. I got to help take care of the chickens when they arrived; we used lamps to keep them warm. We always rushed to gather them in if it looked like rain because they had a tendency to pile on top of each other and smother the ones underneath.

When you help with the care of animals, you become attached to them. It didn't seem very long before they grew big enough to become food.

When I was eight years old, my mother decided it was time for me to learn about getting a chicken ready to eat. First on the agenda was killing him. This was accomplished by putting your foot on his neck and wringing off his head. Another way was to chop off his head with an ax. I hated to see my friends killed. Even more horrible than that was the headless chicken flopping about until he died.

Before the chicken was killed, hot water was heated to boiling. The headless chicken was scalded so the feathers could be plucked out, leaving the poor chicken naked. I always feel heir to plucking the chicken. The feathers stunk, and I always got scolded for leaving some pin feathers.

After the feathers were off, the chicken was cut up and refrigerated in an ice box until cooking time. Chicken pieces were fried in grease. After being coated with delicious batter and cooked, the wishbone of the chicken was given to us to eat and pull on. The one who got the longest piece of the wishbone would have his wish come true.

My first set of wheels

I am thinking back in time. My first set of wheels was a doll buggy. It looked like any baby carriage except smaller. My grandmother made me blankets and quilts for my dolls. My brother had a little red wagon and he and I played house for hours with our set of wheels. My brother, Bob hauled his cars and trucks in the wagon. We like to play with live animals and give them rides. Kittens and puppies were our favorite customers and got many free rides. I used to dress up cats in doll dresses with matching caps and bonnets. Neither the kittens nor puppies like their clothing. We made a swing for them. It was funny to see the cats and dogs running around in doll clothes. We got a lot of scratches and bites from disgruntled kittens and puppies. These animals would start yowling and barking.

I also loved banty hens. I dressed them up in clothing and took them for rides in my first wheels.

My family moved to Kansas City when I was eight. My next set of wheels came when I wanted to go roller skating at he Playmour arena. All the girls in my class had a crush on Marvin. He went skating on Saturday. We all decided to go and watch Marvin skate. To get in, you had to pay a fee and rent skates. They had four wheels on them. I put on the skates and bravely went in to see my hero. He could do all kinds of tricks on his skates. I held on to the side of the rink. I started off and proceeded to fall on my behind, much to the amusements of my classmates. Marvin was the one laughing the hardest. He came over and said "I'll help you." He did and I learned to say up on my wheels. My first crush turned out to be my hero and rescued me.

Permanent machine from space

Sitting under the dryer at the beauty shop, I happened to glance in the corner of the room. There, before my eyes, sat and old-fashioned permanent machine with clamps to put on the top of curlers.

Each curl was connected with an individual clap plugged into an electrical outlet. My mind drifted back to a beauty shop in the Smithville vicinity where I had gone with my mother when she was going to get a new permanent wave.

It seemed like it took hours for her to get rolled, wired and hooked up. I can remember thinking to myself; you'll never get me to sit under that heavy mess of hardware just to get a man to look at me. The contraction looked like an outer space device come to earth early to plague mankind. I didn't want to be curled up at that age and wear Shirley Temple hair. I thought I'd rather go with straight hair.

We had kerosene lamps in the houses I lived in as a child. My mother had curling irons that you heated in the kerosene lamp. I got my Shirley Temple curls from the device. I can also remember smelling my hair burning if I turned my head to quickly. Who liked a burnt scalp or burnt ears?

Thank goodness for electricity and the electrical curling irons that we use today. I don't mind having my hair permed today.

Life was good in the 1930's and 1940's but gives me the beauty devices and appliances of today as compared with those used earlier.

Pond experience leaves water mark

One summer vacation from grade school stands out in my mind from all others. It was a hot day in July 1939 when I was eight years old. My family, consisting of my parents and my brother Bobby, went to visit my mothers' cousins in Gower, Mo., on the farm.

I can remember walking along dusty gravel roads where the wild flowers—sunflowers and tiger lilies grew in wild profusion and were taller than I was. I liked playing hide and seek in the corn fields between the rows of tall corn. The fields of corn made wonderful hiding places.

Our fathers and mothers were in the house talking and cooking lunch. My cousins and brother had decided to go swimming in the pond to cool off on this hot, muggy July day. All three of them swam like fishes. They took off their clothes and swam in all together.

I stood watching at the end of the pond. Since there were no girls to play with, I followed my cousins around. Throwing caution to the wind, I took off all my clothes except my underpants and jumped in. I couldn't swim, but I could float a little. I got braver and floated and hopped toward the middle of the pond. I put my foot down to balance myself and stepped into a hole and went down with my head under water. My cousins and brother pulled me out and dragged me to the edge of the pond. I sure was embarrassed, but very much alive. I would have drowned if it had not been for them.

When our parents found out about our swimming in the pond we got lectured. The wonderful smell of fried chicken and the trimmings with homemade ice cream and cake helped make the pond episode fade into the background. I still have no great love for water.

Radio days revisited

The first time I ever saw a radio, I was about 3 years old. My grandfather was listening to a Hank Williams tear-jerker on the "Grand Ole Opry" emanating from Nashville, Tenn. Grandpa had a huge radio in a fancy cabinet that had doors that closed over the radio when you finished listening to it. After the death of my grandmother in 1983, I received the cabinet that had housed that radio. If close my eye I can still see my parents, aunt, uncles and cousins sitting around the cabinet on a Saturday night in Paradise, Mo.

I always have been an extrovert and enjoyed being the center of attention. When I was little I like to dance to the radio and perform so everyone would notice me. I would continue going in circles until I dropped to the floor because I was so dizzy.

"The squawk box" as my dad called the radio, had programs that all of us liked to hear. We quaked at the horror stories of "I love a mystery," "The Shadow knows," and laughed at "Amos and Andy".

In my early teens, I loved it when my parents would visit my grandparents and leave me at home alone to listen to my programs. One I like to hear was Walt Bodine and his late-night talk show in Kansas City.

My grandmother had a chicken house that had hens and roosters in it that made lots of noise at night. She solved the problem by installing a radio that lulled them to dream land until the ole rooster saw the sun coming up. In my kennel business, I kept my dogs quit and night by playing a radio with country western music.

I still enjoy listening to the radio as I write or study. Radio is the greatest invention that has come along in my lifetime and has given me a great deal of pleasure.

Rationing, scrap drives, other projects mark years of conflict

Whenever I think about World War II, I think of the rationing program and the sacrifices. In the spring of 1942, rationing was introduced to avoid anger over shortages-not to allow the wealthy to buy commodities.

People were often required to give up material goods. There was an increase of employment. Joining together to support and maintain supply levels meant making adjustments. Efforts included scrap drives, taking factory jobs, goods donations and other projects. The campaigns appealed to Americans to contribute without complaint. Propaganda posters and pamphlets were highly effective tools.

While some food items were scarce, other did not require rationing. Red Star rationing covered all meats, butter, fat and oils. Ration stamps became currency, with each family being issued a War Ration book. The book guaranteed each family a share of the goods made scarce.

Rationing was determined by a point system. With the coupon book, shoes, clothing, coffee, gasoline and tires were distributed. Rationing of tires depended on the distance to one's job. On the whole, the American people united in their effort and, while rationing regulated the amount of commodities going to each family, the U.S. standard of living actually rose during the war.

Recycling was born, with the government's encouragement. Aluminum cans meant more ammunition. Economizing initiatives seemed endless, as Americans worked to conserve and recycle metal, paper and rubber. War savings stamp books were sold to provide war funds, and Americans were united through volunteerism. Communities held scrap iron-drives; school children pasted savings stamps.

Food manufacturers took advantage of the shortages to flaunt patriotism to their profit. The familiar Kraft macaroni and cheese gained great popularity. Two boxes required only on ration coupon. In 1943, 80 million boxes were sold. Cottage-cheese sales went from 110 million in 1930 to 500 million in 1944.

I was ten years old at the beginning of the war. I remember seeing all the posters saying to conserve food and help our troops. We also used our nickels and dimes to buy war bonds. My dad was handicapped; he worked for a road building Construction Company during the war. My aunt worked in a factory in Kansas City building bombers. Patriotism was high and it made you proud to be and American.

Reader still yearns for Paradise lost.

The Paradise, Mo., of 1998 is nothing like the Paradise, Mo., that I remember in the 1930's and 1940's when I lived there.

The small, one-room schoolhouse since had given way to progress—the consolidated school district and the big yellow buses which transport the children. We walked to school rain or shine the equivalent of one-half mile. I especially enjoyed the rain when I could get in the ditches and test out the overshoes to see if they worked.

I was born in a farmhouse outside the town itself. The house itself was heated with a wood stove. We took baths in tubs behind the old wood stove. We did our homework by kerosene lamps. It was quiet, with no TV blaring. We read, played cards, worked crossword puzzles, played with our toys and listened to the radio for recreation.

Hafferty's store sold groceries and other necessities. Men gossiped there and sat around comparing notes on conditions of the times and farming.

Babies were delivered at home with the help of Dr. Rupe. That's how all three children in my family arrived.

The Dales, my great-grandparents, lived in Smithville. We spent holidays there with cousins, aunts and uncles. I got to know all those who came before me, with all their quirks and good qualities.

The roads were muddy between Paradise and Smithville. Many times, the cars would get stuck, and I'd get out and help push the old Model A. I loved riding in the rumble seat.

Sundays were spent in church and Sunday school classes. We learned about the Old and New Testaments there. I still remember these stories about biblical heroes. The hymns I learned in childhood bring me great comfort today.

When we relocated to Kansas City after the Second World War, I missed seeing my relatives in Paradise and Smithville. I felt lost in the larger schools with 100 or more students in my grade. The air smelled dirtier and houses were closer together. I no longer knew everyone like I did in Paradise. Streetcars clanged and banged in Kansas City; I went downtown in Kansas City to shop on this noisy conveyance.

My parent did return to the area surrounding Paradise to go to square dances at Gower. I got to see old friends when the old-time musicians played a hoedown. Some of my first crushes began there.

The Paradise I remember had 200 inhabitants, two churches, a schoolhouse and a general store and was surrounded by lush farmland. The people who lived there cared about each other and helped each other in times of need. The name chosen by the town's founders truly fit it.

When my mind is wandering now, I still like to return to yesterday and the Paradises of my youth. It brings me great comfort.

School room hub of community

Attendance at the one room eighth grade schoolhouse is nil. It is considered fashionable to buy them and build on to them as family dwellings now. Many are spread over the countryside abandoned and neglected as it is no longer a hubbub of activity.

I began my journey into the world of education in the one-room school house at Paradise, Mo., at the age of five. There were three children in the first grade. No one had thought of kindergarten yet. I walked almost a mile to and from school along muddy country lanes. There were eight grades. My favorite place in the school was the four shelves that comprised the library.

The one thing I remember about first and second grade was being whacked with a ruler because all 'normal" human beings were supposed to be right-handed. I didn't develop a tic or speech defect from the teacher who wanted to retrain my "handedness." I can excuse myself today because I still have preference for left-handedness and write with my left.

I read every book in our library 10 or 12 time by the time I reached third grade. I read all the True Stories and True Detectives, etc., which were used for toilet paper in the outdoor privies. Many a happy moment was spent perusing the wiping paper and reading material.

The school houses were centers for community activities. In the fall we practiced for our crowning achievement of the first semester which was the Christmas play. One of my most embarrassing moments occurred when I was supposed to be and angel guiding the three wise men and I tripped and fell.

The spring semester saw the planning of the closing of school and the basket dinners that parents prepared and brought with fried chicken and all other goodies that they could concoct. I dreaded getting up and reciting poetry and passages that we had to memorize.

After one-room schoolhouses class and the school districts consolidated, the schools were used for square dances. All ages came from adults down to babies. If a child went to sleep, they were put on a coat in the corner. I learned how to do all kinds of folk and square dances to violins and guitars.

In the summer, churches had basket diners and unmarried women made them. The woman spent the evening with the highest bidder for her basket. Many courtships and marriages started here at the country schoolhouse. These one-room school houses played and important role in the community and consolidated the farmers who were unduly dispersed over the countryside. They drove up in their buggies and Model-T Fords to compare notes and watch their offspring show off.

In the summer, the children relaxed and helped their parents at home in the garden, with the crops and the animals but we were always glad when September came and the school bell rang calling us back.

Science fiction enthusiasm begins with "Flash Gordon"

The comic strip I remember most was entitled "Flash Gordon." Flash was on a plane coming home to be with his family because of Earth being threatened with destruction by an oncoming planetoid. Flash Gordon and Dale Arden parachuted to safety from the doomed plane. Dr. Hans Zarkow made Dale and Flash go with him on his rocket ship to the planetoid that was threatening Earth. There they tangled with Ming the Merciless, who was bent on cosmic destruction in the land of Mango. Flash and Ming vied for the love of Dale Arden. Alex Raymond created the galactic hero in 1934. Universal Pictures released a serial, "Flash Gordon" In 1936, "Flash Gordon's Trip to Mars" in 1938 and "Flash Gordon Conquers the Universe" in 1940. All three serials starred Gold Medal swimmer Buster Crabb. In addition to the serials there were a host of toys and premiums for Depression era kids and popular radio show. Flash Gordon became a feature length movie in 1980.

King Features still produces weekly cartoon strips Jim Keefe, the current artist, began writing and drawing Flash Gordon's Sunday strip in January 1996. The animated television series regularly draws viewers to flash's cartoon adventures. Flash Gordon even appears on his own U.S. postage stamp.

On of my favorite quiet times was visiting the outdoor privy and sitting there reading Flash Gordon cartoons as I relaxed? I got acquainted with Flash as I looked through the toilet paper literature. I tried to keep up each week. Listening to his adventures on the radio ranked up there with the other programs I liked such an "I love a Mystery" and the "Shadow." Many years have gone by and I enjoy indoor plumbing. I still view mysteries on television along with science fiction stories. I also watch the Discovery channels to try to keep up with the latest space voyages and developments. My enthusiasm for television science fiction and science fiction novels came about because of my quite times reading the funnies in the out house.

Serials, mysteries among favorites

In the heyday of radio in the 1930's and 1940's families sat around the radio listening to their favorite programs. My husband's family listened to serials-"My Gal Sunday," "Abby's Wild Irish Rose," "Lum and Abner," "Amos and Andy," "Tom Mix" and "Gene Autry." The cereal companies who sponsored these programs gave away goodies in the boxes for kids.

My husband, Eugene Bechtold, developed osteomyelitis as a child of 6. He had surgery to remove the bad tissue and the wound was kept scraped so the good tissue would grow back. He spent some time in the hospital. One of his favorite toys, an airplane, came from a cereal box. He would wind it up and send it flying into the hallway. The poor nurses had to retrieve it. He couldn't get out of bed, so he needed some diversion. I'll bet the nurses were glad to get rid of him.

In my family, the Dales, we liked the "Grand Old Opry" from Nashville, Tenn. My relatives never missed a broadcast.

My dad and I liked the mysteries—"The Shadow," with his creepy laugh, and "The Crypt," where you could hear the vault door slowly squeaking and closing. To this day, I still like television mysteries and crime shows with forensic files. I read mystery novels.

My brothers liked the cowboy shows on the radio. They had toy guns, stick horses, cowboy hats and boots.

My husband, Eugene, and his pals in grade school were intrigued by "Tarzan the Ape man." They had woods outside the country schoolhouse they attended in Boonville. They swung from the trees and pretended to be apes and Tarzan. When they got bored with that, they brought their toy guns, hats and ropes and played "Gene Autry." This occurred at their lengthy recesses. On special occasions, they had to wear short pants and knee socks. These special occasions were church, school functions and school parties. Some times, they had to pull my husband out of the drainage ditches to get him in his short pants and Little Lord Fauntleroy suit, as he called it.

All of us remember President Roosevelt talking in his "Fireside Chat," telling us that the United States was going to war, after Pearl harbor was bombed in 1941.

My grandmother, Bertha Dale, would go to bed listening to talk shows in Kansas City, even after television began to replace the radio. I listened to the talk shows on the radio, like Walt Bodine. After midnight, it seems all the creepy characters would call in and they had insomnia. Our television programs, like "Dr Phil" and "Montel Williams" are a follow-up on these radio shows.

Sounds being transmitted in any form have had a powerful impact on our lives and will continue to do so.

Skunk oil, sassafras tea and hot toddies

Have you ever heard of Ex-Lax? I got acquainted with it when I was constipated. That chocolate tasted so good to a four year old. I kept a watchful eye to see where my mother kept them. I took two out and ate them. I spent my time that day sitting in the old outhouse. No more Ex-Lax for me.

My most favorite old-time remedy was the hot toddy. You got this for congestion and a head cold. The ingredients were piping hot water in a cup, one half a shot of whiskey, and one teaspoon of lemon juice and one teaspoon of honey, mixed well. I liked them because it made you sleepy. You had adventurous dreams and your cold got better.

My mother Uncle Rolly drove a van with remedy labels all over it. You could hear him coming because he had a parrot as old a Methuselah. This parrot had a vocabulary more salty than a sailor. He would sing dirty songs, and if you put your finger in his cage, he promptly bit you. He sold my mother curious beauty concoctions designed to make her more beautiful. He also had skunk oil to cure laryngitis.

One of my fateful encounter with old fashioned remedies was Carter's little liver pill. They looked appetizing to a four year old, so I bit into one. It tasted horrible. I never bit into a pill again.

One other remedy my mother learned from her grandmother dealt with athlete's foot. You walked through a fresh pile of cow manure. Believe it or not, it relieved my athlete's foot.

I still have the flannel patch that my mother used with Vapor Rub to cure my congestion. You also got to put your head over a pan of water with Lysol with water that was boiling hot. That sure opened up your head.

I think my favorite remedy was the hot toddy. I am relatively health and living proof that these old-time remedies work.

South paw' endured on indignity after another

"South Paw." I got tired of hearing those two words that just hearing them made me see red. Every child has a certain hand preference for eating, writing and everyday tasks. Some lucky people I know can use both hands interchangeably. Not me, I eat, write and do everything with my left hand. The left side of my brain is definitely dominant.

Needless to say, being left-handed has caused some tragic and humorous moments in my life. My first-grade teacher in the one-room schoolhouse at Paradise felt that using the left hand was a detriment. When ever I started to write with my left hand, she'd smack me with a ruler on the left hand. Experts felt that this kind of trauma could cause people to stutter. Today, they'd have her locked up for cruelty to children.

I always liked to sit at the end of the table. When I got placed in the wrong spot, I always managed to collide with someone else's arm. At my junior prom, a large group of us went out to eat. I managed to hit an arm and spill ketchup on a tuxedo. The waiter saved the day and got it off. Many of my friends called me Calamity Jane at the table.

At my public meetings, when we say the Pledge of Allegiance, I always place my left hand over my heart, instead of the right. In church, everyone else places their right hand over their heart to make the sign of the cross. Guess who uses her left.

Being left-handed makes my writing slant backward. When I first started teaching in an inner city school, one smart mouthed student stood up and acted like he was having trouble reading my writing. I turned tables on him. I had him write the assignments on the board for a week.

Everyone harassed him after I told all my classes about Alfonso being our scribe. I still hear from Alfonso, and we laugh about our first encounter. All the assignments and board writing are done by eager students now in my classes.

Today, a south paw can buy scissors and all kinds of tools to make his life easier. No one teases them because left-handed people are no longer considered oddities.

Tim Dale and Daisy the dog

Special canine cares about just one boy

I'm telling a story about a boy and his dog who bonded to each other 50 year ago.

The dog, named Daisy, was no ordinary dog. The name Daisy makes you think of a female, but Daisy was male dog.

My brother, who is now sixty two, got the dog when he was seven years old. Daisy appeared mysteriously at our door in Kansas City, MO., wearing a chain with a rope attached to it. He had long hair that was matted and was thin. He looked like the small sheltie of today. My brother wanted to keep him, but his owners lived several blocks away. They kept coming to get him. He kept running away. This went on for several weeks.

Finally Daisy's owner said, "You can keep him; I don't want a dog who doesn't want me."

My brother was happy. This dog was devoted to him and tried to protect him from harm. The dog would go on vacation with my parents and Tim. My parents took him on one vacation and he got out of the car and they drove about sixty miles down the road and missed Daisy. They went back and there lay Daisy waiting for them in the shade at the filing station.

Daisy had definite ideas about people he liked and did not like. My friend, Vernilda, was one. He bit her when he got the chance. He didn't like my husband or my Uncle Andy and nipped them, too. He just tolerated me.

Daisy lived a good life until on of the female neighbor dogs came into heat. A dogfight ensued and poor Daisy got his throat cut and died.

My family really missed Daisy, especially Tim and my parents. Daisy was an interesting canine. I am sure that he is sitting on the Rainbow Bridge waiting for my brother Tim to come across.

I talked to Tim yesterday and he said he had never had another dog since Daisy died

Tales take youngster to faraway lands

Reading has always been one of my favorite activities. I read everything I could get my hands on—my dad's crime magazines; my mothers true stories, newspapers, etc. In the two—room country schoolhouse at Paradise, Mo., where I started school, we had our own schoolhouse library. I read most of the books in the library.

After we moved away from paradise and ended up in Kansas City, I attended Central Junior and Central Senior. A branch library was located downstairs at the school. They needed a page to ready the shelves and put away the books.

I worked after school, starting at age thirteen. I ate my lunch in the basement poring over old National Geographic's. I sped away on my lunch hour to exotic places and strange cultures very different from my own.

In the children's section, I discovered the shelves of fairy tales and folk tales and myths. A fairy tale is a kind of fable, and in them you meet witches, queens, giants, princes, elves, dragons and even the little people fairies.

I especially enjoyed the Grimm's first fairy tales, written in 1812, with six more books that followed. Hans Christian Anderson was another fanciful writer of fairy tales. In these tales, you would meet up with Cinderella, Rapunzel and the prince who had been turned into a frog, mermaids, Snow White and the seven dwarfs. All cultures have fairy tales, folklore and legends. Our own American Indian tribe passed on their tales by work of mouth. I especially like the ones about the trickster coyote.

My grandchildren like the Harry Potter stories about fanciful creatures and wizards. I still enjoy Walt Disney full length features and cartoons. I read mystery stories today. Some of the detective magazines that I read in the out house must have rubbed off.

When I went to college, I worked in the library and majored in Sociology. My favorite subject was Anthropology. If my old body could stand it, I would enjoy going on archaeological digs.

Another interest of mine related to fairy tales is UFO sightings and tales of beings abducted by aliens. I like to watch the science fiction channel.

Reading fairy tales and books on the supernatural allows and individual to leave and everyday environments in a book and enjoy fantasizing about what might be. Too much preoccupation with the dark side is unhealthy.

Part of my interest in writing came from reading fairy tales.

Unequal treatment makes her steam

An event which really made me steam was at family dinners before I was married. The women would work in the kitchen getting a wonderful family dinner ready-fried chicken, potatoes and gravy, with all the trimmings. All kinds of cakes, pies and delectable sweets were arrayed on the tables. At the first table with the best of everything were seated the men and boys. Women and girls ate at the second table. All the females did not get first chance at the food. We got what the men left unless our mothers saved something back.

No wonder women were treated like second class citizens when they docilely let their lord and masters go first. We didn't hear too much about women's liberation movements in my day. If there'd have been one in my city, I would have joined.

My father didn't believe in women learning to drive. He taught my brother to drive. I had to wait until I married when my husband taught me. Also, he didn't believe women needed a college education. I surprised him with three college degrees.

Winds of March

The old saying has is that March comes in like a lion and goes out like a lamb.

I can remember some of the Marches in my life, like when we lived in a rural community close to Paradise Mo. The old house we lived in had no inside bathroom fixtures but outhouses were about a block from the house. March winds would be blowing energetically. The long trek to the outhouses was something you put off as long as you could. Strong winds made the roof shake and the doors would rattle. Also cold winds would come up under the holes. The howling wind made you think banshees were outside. One March we had lots of snow and you went to the outhouse in a coat, night gown and hip boots.

In the early 1900's my mother told us about tornados and cyclones blowing up in March. One storm was so scary for her family that they went into the root cellar while the winds whirled overhead. When they emerged from the cellar all the buildings were still standing but the chickens were bare skinned. The wind had plucked out their feathers and drove the feathers into the wooden fences. It was a long time before the chickens grew back feathers.

We also flew our kites in the brisk March winds. My kite got tangled in a tree and I climbed up to get it. I had it in my hands and looked down. I was afraid to come down. My parents told me to get down the same way I got up. I waited around in the tree until it got dark. I was more afraid of the dark than I was of climbing down. That was the end of my tree climbing exploits. March was also the time for awakening of Crocuses and Iris and wild flowers. The winter landscape was transformed by the early signs of spring. Even in 2008 with its winter storms we will see spring soon I hope.

Women's revolution arrives with world conflict

My memories of World War II are limited. I was 9 years old when it started. My dad was 4-F because he had one eye and three fingers blown off by a dynamite cap when he was a child.

I can remember butter, sugar, nylon hose and gas being rationed. My husband's parents lived on a farm and ran a dairy farm, there was no shortage of butter for them I was too young for nylon hose, so I was never bothered by lack of hosiery.

Women left the home during the Second World War and went to work in was factories. My aunt Frances Dale worked in Lake City making ammunitions in Kansas City. She always looked neat in her starched blouses and pants when she went to work. "Rosie the Riveter" was a popular song then.

With this war came a revolution for women. They were needed on the home front for factories and offices. Two-paycheck families became a way of life. Our family mores changed and men and women became equal partners in a marriage.

My dad's antiquated idea of women not needing an education or knowing how to drive a car was outmoded. Women started developing career ideas as they expanded their horizons and became first class citizens and equal partners with their husbands.

The Second World War helped liberate women and began the breaking of racial barriers, with all races serving side by side in the services. We must all accept each other without prejudice if our world is to survive and keep it from being blown up by weapons of mass destruction. I am proud to have lived in the 20th century and to have been a part of this revolutionary change.

The different ways children got to school before the school bus

My mother who lived in Gower Missouri in the early twentieth century walked to school when she was in elementary school. High school years had to be paid by the parents. My mother attended Gower High School in Missouri. She was helped with the tuition by some of her neighbors. She played basket ball and won the prestigious Skaith medal for being the best all around student. She rode a horse into town when she went to high school. It was natural that she should go on to Warrensburg and study to be teacher in one of the local one room school houses after finishing at Warrensburg. She taught one year and met a dashing young man from Paradise, Mo. That man turned out to be my father and they settled in Paradise near his parents.

We still lived in Paradise when I started school. I walked about ten blocks on gravel and sometimes muddy roads. No big yellow school buses for me. I used foot power. Our school house had two rooms one for grades one to six and the other for seven and older. The school house was located besides a local protestant church. We used to play hide and seek around the church and the large trees on the property. One of the perks I thought was when it rained I got to wear rubber boots. I would walk in the ditches beside the road with water that went over my boot tops. I came home with soaking socks and wet boots. I dearly loved it in the spring when a cherry tree hung over the road and we could eat until we were filled up. The owner of the cherry tree ratted us out and I had to help her pick her cherries by climbing her tree. She gave us cherries for my efforts.

When we moved to Kansas City, I was in the sixth grade. I walked to Bancroft Elementary, Central high and Central Senior. The distance was ten blocks. After Graduation I went to Kansas City University. For six years. There was a streetcar line on Thirty First Street. The old car made large noises when it went around a corner, and clanged its bell when it came to a stop to pick up passengers. This mode of transportation beat using foot power. Needless to say I didn't gain weight. All these years of foot power without riding in a car made me into a fairly hardy specimen thanks feet.

CHAPTER 3

HIGH SCHOOL

Central class of '49 takes nostalgic trip

On June 23 and June 24, 1989 the Central High School class in Kansas City had a reunion at the Allis Plaza Hotel for classes 1947-1951. My class, 1949, was the host class.

This was a significant year for Central High, as we past alumni knew it. The Kansas City School District had decided to tear Central down and build a new magnet high school with a large swimming pool.

Alumni were loaded onto tour buses and given a last nostalgic tour of Central before the wrecking balls tore it down. There were 338 graduates who attended this reunion. My husband and I had planned to attend, but illness in the family prevented it.

I talked to a friend who was at the reunion, who expressed the sentiment that "these can't be the people we knew in high school; they are a bunch of old people."

As we talked on, we reminisced about things that were common during our high school years: poodle skirts, street cars and bus tokens, the Hit parade, American Bandstand, peg pants, going to the swinging bridge at Swope Park and to drive-in movies.

The years 1947-1951 saw Harry Truman as president, NATO formed, the Berlin Blockade ended, "I Love Lucy" begin on television and millions of kids watch "Howdy Doody."

After this reunion at Central High School, an alumni association was formed. Each year a new Central graduate is chosen to receive and alumni scholarship and members present it to him.

I received a copy of he reunion booklet and a picture of the people who had attended the reunion.

Seeing people that one shared four years of high school with, makes one wonder where the years have gone.

Excursions on Saturday Night

As a teenager my Saturday nights were spent going to the movies. When I was too young to date, groups of us who lived near Thirty first and Troost would meet and go the the movies there. We rode the streetcar anticipating the treat that awaited us on the wide screen. There were usually four boys and four girls who went. I worked at the library until three. We would then meet and head off to the movies. We would sit there together until five watching cartoons like Daffy Duck, Tom and Jerry, and Mickey Mouse The three Stooges made us laugh loudly and put everyone in the mood for the feature production. We especially liked the horror shows like Frankenstein and shows where vampires and werewolves chased screaming females. It was dark when I came home and the way home was not well lighted. I saw all kinds of boogey men behind every tree when I went to bed, I checked under the bed and in the closets before climbing into bed

When I started dating, we went to the local drive in on Saturday night The movie started at dusk and lasted as late as you wanted to stay. My curfew was eleven thirty. I was late one night and my mother came out on the porch in her nightgown and curlers with bare feet. None of my boyfriends wanted to be eaten alive by that formidable lady. One place where we went was to Singspiration. Here you go to hear the gospel being preached and beautiful gospel music sung. My mother liked the idea of my interest in the gospel at the municipal auditorium. She felt I was getting religion. The truth was I liked the preacher's son. He drove a yellow convertible and would bring me home my mother had had an experience with a preacher's son and she thought they were all minions of the devil. One time he called when I was not home and she told him to stop bothering me or she was going to talk to his father. Needless to say the preacher's son gave me a wide berth.

Another place that double dates and I went was to car races. These races were held on the outskirts of Kansas City. I pretended to like the races because my hero at the time loved them.

As you can see by my story, Saturday nights for me were varied and never dull I remember these Saturday night encased in my memory fondly when I delve into my past memories.

Flash, fun of "50s prove perfect for teen

The 1950's are the years that I remember teenagers coming into their own and having a voice of their own, and buying power. For the first time, teenagers had the money, the leisure and the freedom to carve out their own territory in a prosperous and indulgent society—a place where they could pursue their own youthful hormonally charged version of the American Dream.

Drive-ins were frequented, thanks to cars, and on weekends teens went to see and be seen. The girls wore flats, penny loafers or white saddle shoes and white bobby socks. Boy's clothes came in two types. The "Joe College" style was khakis with buckles on the back and crew cuts or V-neck pullovers. The "greaser "look included the duck tail, tight black jeans and rolled up shirt sleeves to show off the biceps.

My two brothers, Tim and Robert Dale, had motorcycles. They were influenced by the movie "The Wild One" starring Marlon Brando with his motorcycle. My younger brother, Tim, still belongs to a motor cycle club and rides his on excursions with the club in Arizona.

In the 1950's we no longer had jive and the big band era. Rock and roll came storming in. Bill Haley and the Comets, Buddy Holly and Elvis Presley brought this new music forward and the kids loved it. The king of rock and roll was Elvis Presley, who became on of the most popular stars and singers of all time. Fans screamed when he performed his famous "Elvis the Pelvis "twist".

James Dean the idol of many teenagers of this era, and who starred in "Rebel without a Cause" and "East of Eden," died in a car crash on Sept 30, 1955. As one fan said, "Dean was the embodiment of every romantic idyllic feeling my body, heart and mind possessed." Eight thousand letters a month addressed to James Dean arrived after his death, written by sad fans who hoped he had not been killed. A wonderful mystique grew up around him.

Mad magazines came out in 1952 and poked fun at cartoon characters, novel heroines and heroes. One of the covers had a picture of Mona Lisa holding a mad magazine in front of her.

Mary Bechtold

Some games in the 1950's were big fads: very popular for awhile, then gone. One fad game was phone booth stuffing. The object was to see how many people you could squeeze into a phone booth or Volkswagen. At one time, this was a big college thing, but it didn't last long. One of the most popular games invented was the hula hoop, which sold millions in just one year. The hula hoop is still popular today; some people can hula many hoops at one time.

My memories of the drive-in burger joint have dimmed with time, but I remember the hot rods with their noisy engines, with rock and roll blaring. In 1956, there were 130 legal drag strips in 40 states with three million fans. You could find my girl friends and me at the drag races, because that's where the boys and men were to be found.

The 1950's was a fabulous era and I enjoyed every minute of the decade.

Mary and Vernilda

Girls enjoy youth in Kansas City area

The best friend I ever had was Vernilda. We met at Central Junior High School in Kansas City, Mo. She lived three blocks away from me. We did the usual school and girl things together. We stayed overnight at each other's houses. Some of the things we enjoyed were going horseback riding, roller and ice-skating, and Saturday matinees at the local theatre.

We went in groups to our high school football games; we went as much to be seen as to watch the football games. We had other friends who went with us, Clara Moorehead and Joyce Williams. We were not part of the in-crowd like the cheerleaders or the ones the football or basketball player dated.

Vernilda and I liked to go shopping downtown and eat at the Forum Cafeteria. We'd count our money before we got in line to buy our food. Our mode of transportation was the clanging streetcar. This was the way I traveled during my earlier years in Kansas City. No car was waiting in the driveway for me; I walked to get on my transportation.

Vernilda went to work at the Chevrolet plant in Kansas City after high school and I went to college. She went on a date with a man who worked at the Ford plant. He got me a blind date and that is how I met my husband, Eugene.

She married Robert who was in the service. She was married before me and I was the maid of honor at her wedding. When I got married in 1953 she was matron of honor at my wedding. She soon became pregnant with her first daughter Cheryl.

When I took a counseling class at KU, her daughters were the test subjects I used for the class. These girls are both teachers in Kansas City area.

My husband I moved to the Kidder, Mo., area with our two daughters. I would receive a lengthy letter at Christmas telling me about her family. Her family eventually grew to three girls and one boy.

Her children had a 50th birthday party for her in Independence. All her family and friends were there. I got to see many of my old Central classmates.

I still hear from her family at Christmas. I was blessed to have such a good friend to share my early dreams and hopes with.

Thanks, Vernilda, for being my friend

My favorite movies

My favorite movies of the silver screen tie in with my fantasy life when I was a teenager. A lot of my movie attendance took place in my early teens and dating years. In my tween years, I was addicted to cartoons. I especially like Bugs Bunny and Daffy Duck. The Troost Theatre had matinees. You could always find a group of us from Central High watching them. I stopped going to matinees after I started work at fourteen in the Jewish Community Center.

My favorite silver screen movies were the swashbuckling pirate movies. Many of these shows were adapted from novels. I read every novel and history book about pirates who preyed on the seas. My favorite pirate movie was the Black Swan in the 1942. Tyrone Power and Clara Monroe played the hero and heroine. I had a crush on Tyrone Power. I was probably one of the old time groupies. I think I tried to find a real teen age Romeo who looked like him if I dreamed after seeing on of his movies, I took the place of the screen heroine.

Errol Flynn was very lifelike as he played pirate roles, on the seven seas. He was outstanding as he played the Master of Ballantine and Sea Hawk in 1940 and Captain Blood in 1935.

Bob Hope and Virginia Mayo in 1945 starred in the Princess and the Pirate. He wasn't as dashing as Errol Flynn or Tyrone Power but he certainly kept everyone laughing at his antics.

I also liked cowboy movies with John Wayne but he made an outstanding pirate in Reap the Wild Wind.

I think that these movies were good for the families who had grown up with the depression. They were more prosperous now and could see the war in Europe and World War II loaming on the horizon with Adolph Hitler and Germany invading other countries.

When we finally declared war on Germany and Japan pinups like Betty Grable, Hedy Lamar and Rita Hayward were featured in War film. These movies were designed to build up the moral of the American people. Many movie stars went to war to serc their country. I was in high school during the war years and watched the war progress at the movies on the newsreels before the movie was shown. I believe of all the different kinds of movies I saw on the silver screen I liked the pirate and animals movies best. My favorite animal movies were Bambi and My Friend Flicka.

Mary in her loafers

Hard work earned money for loafers

One of the fads that I remember from my teenage days was penny loafer shoes. Money was scarce, and I had to work for many hours at my job to save up the eight dollars necessary for the nice, shiny leather loafers to go with my bobby socks.

We wore our skirts half way between our knees and ankles. They were circular and would swing around to show our legs when we danced to the rock and roll tunes.

Central High School in Kansas City was chosen to appear on American Bandstand. I'll never forget how proud I was to be chosen to represent my school on television. To this day, I still love rock-and—roll dancing and fast music. My own children can't believe I ever appeared on television. They think I lived back in the days of the dinosaurs and cavorted with Fred Flintstone and company.

Mary and Vernilda at Memorial

Liberty Memorial recalls sacrifices of war

A monument is built to commemorate an event that is significant to the people who have lived through it and to remind future generation of what happened. World War I was such an event to the people of the early 20th century. The people of Kansas City built the Liberty Memorial so that future generations would remember the sacrifices that the world had made between 1914 and 1918.

The memorial complex consists of several structures. The 217-foot tall Memorial Tower is surrounded by four stone figures representing courage, honor, patriotism and sacrifice. Two sphinxes—memory and future guard the south entrance. Two museum buildings flank the tower. Names of Kansas Citizens who died in the war are on bronze tablets in the East Building. The great frieze on the north terrace wall depicts progress from war to peace. There are courtyards and stairways which tie the complex together. The main courtyard measure 154 feet by 27 feet. The site dedication memorial wall holds bronze bust of five Allied soldiers.

People like to visit the memorial. These building contained significant historic material and reminders of our country's past. On many occasions, we would visit there before going swimming or boating or to car races or on picnics in summer. In August 1953, I had my picture taken on the courtyard steps. My friend Vernilda Uthe and I posed for a picture on one of the sphinxes at the south entrance.

All of us have aged, including the Liberty Memorial. On Aug 4, 1998 Kansas City voters overwhelmingly passed a ½ cent sales tax for 18 months which can raise $30 million fro restoration and $14.7 million for the endowment of future maintenance. Legislation passed in the Missouri House of Representatives will provide $5million in state funds for the Liberty Memorial.

The tax went into place on April 1, 1999, and funds started accruing in June 1999. Actual construction probably will start in October 1999. At this time, the restored Liberty Memorial is expected to be rededicated on Nov 11, 2001. Now future generation can visit and have their picture taken at this historic site.

First love arrives in uniform during wartime

I met my first love, Don, at a party. My date for the evening was another Don. We all attended Central high School. Don graduated in 1948, the year I was a junior.

Don was wearing his uniform that evening. I noticed him when he entered the room. I would look at him out of the corner of my eye and catch him watching me. One thing led to another and he asked me to dance. He asked for my phone number and of course, he got it.

He was on furlough for a week. I spent most of my time when not in school with him. He was scheduled to go overseas to Germany and to be stationed there for three years. We agreed to date other people during that time of separation. I started college while he was gone. Letters flew back and forth across the Atlantic.

Don was an accomplished artist and sent me many drawings. He also likes to take pictures.

When he returned from Germany, he bought me an engagement ring and we planned our wedding. I had a bridal shower and the wedding time kept growing closer.

Don's parents were divorced and his father lived in Phoenix, Ariz. He planned on us moving to Phoenix, and I would not be able to finish my last year of college.

On evening, we talked and decided to call of the wedding. He would not stay here until I finished college and I would not move until I did.

We parted friends, he went to Arizona and I went on to finish my senior year. I had to return the shower present and my father was stuck with me for the next several years.

My relationship with Don is nothing but a pleasant memory, which I reflect on occasionally. Life moves on and I met my husband, Eugene on a blind date. We will be married forty nine years in August of this year. I hope Don's life had been as pleasant as mine has been.

Life has a way of taking you down many paths until you find the right one.

Lovers considered wedding plans on deadline

When I was 18 and a senior in high school, I met Don at a party. He was home on leave from the service. The Army was going to send him to Germany. We promptly fell head over heals in love. His furlough lasted a week, and we were engaged before he left for Germany.

I WAS GETTING ready to go to college at UMKC. I started in 1949. Don sent me letters every week which I have kept.

Three years passed quickly. I was ready to start my senior year in college. Don came home from Germany. He was more handsome than I remembered. We quickly got reacquainted and enjoyed spending time together.

When I first met him, our interests and plans for the future were similar. The three years of separation had changed us both. I wanted to finish college before I got married. He wanted to get married right away and move to Arizona where his father lived.

MY HORMONES WERE working over-time in conflict with my desire to finish college. We set the wedding date. I bought my wedding dress and had the wedding invitations printed. They were sent out to all our friends and relatives. I had bridal showers and wedding presents delivered.

Two days before the wedding, Don and I had a heart to heart talk. We decided to call off the wedding, and I returned his ring. My father almost had a heart attack. He thought he had the fate of one of his children settled. Now I was back in his lap again.

NOW AND AGAIN I think of Don and what might have been. I think we made a wise decision with our conflicting interests.

I returned for my senior year in college, single, and looking for male prospects. Little did I know the man I would finally marry was just moving to Kansas City and working for Greyhound Bus Lines. I would finally meet him on a blind date. Strange, how fate conspires to shape your life. Eugene told me on the first date that he was going to marry me. I told him he was out of his mind. After a whirlwind courtship, Eugene finally persuaded me to marry him.

ORIGINALLY WE WERE going to be married in December, but I pushed the date to August after I graduated from college. On our wedding day one of my parent's favorite stories is that my father was going slowly down the aisle with me on his arm. I kept hurrying up dragging him as fast as I could go to get to the priest and put the show on the road.

SIXTY YEARS HAVE gone by since that day, Aug, 15, 1953, and none of them have been dull. Two children and umpteen thousand dogs ago, we pledged our vows. I still remember saying, "I'm not marrying you" the first time we met. Just goes to show the old saying, "It's a woman's prerogative to change her mind."

At least in my case.

Man in a uniform moves away

I was a senior at Central High School in Kansas City in 1949. I went to a party after the football game with some girlfriends. I was introduced to a handsome young man in uniform. His name was Don. He had graduated two years before I was to graduate. I spent the entire evening with him and he drove me home. Every evening he was on leave I spent with him, before he left for Germany. While I was near him my heart beat faster. The old female hormones were working.

His time was three years to be served in the Air Force in Germany. I started college a UMKC, and letters and pictures flew back and forth across the Atlantic. I dated other men and he dated women he met in Germany. We had planned to be married when he got home.

I was a junior in college when he got back. He told me he wanted to get married as soon as he got home and move to Arizona to live where his father lived. I had one year of college to finish. He wouldn't stay until I finished.

We had the wedding invitations sent out and the church spoken for. My dad had a fit because he had to explain to his friends why I was jilted. Even though I still felt butterflies when he came near, we canceled the wedding. I went back and finished my degree. I think God had other plans for my life.

My girlfriend, Vernilda introduced me to my husband of fifty seven years. I have had a wonderful life teaching, raising children, running a kennel, teaching in a prison and being a counselor. I have often wondered what my life would have been liked if I had gone to Arizona. I hope Don has had a good life. Life had many roads for us to travel but God points the way down the road he wants us to go.

CHAPTER 4

COLLEGE

Sorority membership enlivens coed's college career

Looking through my college year book is like taking a trip in a time machine back 50 years to 1949. When I graduated from high school, I won a four-year scholarship to the University of Kansas City, which is no more. Our classes were small, and we knew everyone in the liberal arts school.

I became a member of the Beta Zeta sorority on campus. I made many friendships in this group that have lasted a lifetime. We enjoyed participating in campus activities together, such as Burma Friday, where all the sororities and fraternities strived to win competitions for the best skits and performers. There were no campus dormitories at the time, and we all lived off campus.

We were initiated into the sorority with a colorful ceremony. There was no hazing or physical mistreatment with our initiation. We all were made to feel valuable and wanted. I do remember having to carry upper classmate's books and wear assign on my back that said, "Pledge."

One picture that I have came from the 1953 Kansas City Star. Bum Friday was the day that all students enjoyed no classes, casual dress, fun and games, and plenty of food. The day culminated in a formal dance.

Since then the University of Kansas is no more. The grand old building still stands on the campus, but it is now the University of Missouri-Kansas City. It covers many blocks and has thousands of students. It has winning basketball team and staff members and building, including dormitories.

I went back to a class reunion and an updated version of bum Friday. I enjoyed seeing old friends and the expanded campus where I had spent so many happy hours. I caught up on the lives of old friends. I know the members of Beta Zeta now are enjoying the fellowship of their sisters as much as I did. Social clubs are a very important part of young adult's lives.

Ernest

Sophomore crush leads to lasting friendship

When I think of deep feeling from my past, I think of a crush I had on my sociology professor, Dr. Ernest Manheim, who was a professor, at the University of Missouri-Kansas City in my sophomore year in college.

I used to think cemeteries and old bones and past civilizations were boring until I signed up for his sociology class. He had studied ancient peoples and civilizations and made them come alive for his students. I developed a super crush on him and sat on the front row of the classroom absorbing every word.

When the sociology class was over, I was hooked. I signed up for archeology, ancient civilizations and every other sociology class I could get.

Dr Manheim put up with the hero worship and suggested that I consider a fellowship on the master's level after I graduated.

I worked in the sociology department as a fellow after I graduated. He suggested that I take education classes so that I would have a practical minor to fall back on if I could not find a job in the field of sociology.

He and his wife were very kind to me. I baby sat their daughter when they went to university functions. They came to my wedding reception and brought me a very practical gift, an ironing board that I still have and use today.

This kind individual took me under his family's wing and brought me along to adulthood. His liberalism, respect for individuals of all races and intellect, and way of tying the past and present together is something I tried to pass on to my students and my own children. His influence on my life and those of other students made him and outstanding teacher and human being.

My daughter Julie is a teacher, and a lot of her philosophy and life and teaching go back to Dr. Manheim through me.

Dr. Manheim left UMKC and went to New England in his later years. When I lost track of him, he was 100 years old and still teaching. Thanks, Dr. Manheim, for being an outstanding teacher.

Faith wavers, yet survives throughout lifetime

I think the title of my story should be "Found, lost and found again". This is because, as a child, I had a close connection with and belief in God and the hereafter. I attended church and Sunday school as a child and teenager.

In the Protestant church that I attended, in the Sunday school classes, we received a good foundation in the Old and the New testaments. We learned the Lord's Prayer and many comforting psalms. I was baptized at the age of twelve by being immersed completely in water.

I never questioned my faith until I went to college and studied anthropology and Darwin's theory of evolution. I majored in sociology.

One critical experience was a sermon our pastor gave on fire and brimstone. He said that he didn't understand how anyone could believe in God and still attend college classes teaching evolution. I felt as though he was talking directly to me. After that, I stopped going to church regularly.

As I think back over the past and things I have learned, I feel it is impossible not to believe in a high being who watches over us. Just the evolution of man alone throughout the centuries proves this. Ancient cities and ruin have been found that corroborate stories in the Old Testament.

In my early 20's and 30's life moved at a frantic pace. Many different career opportunities and jobs, children and their activities created this hectic pace. I attended church, but tuned out the sermons. My place in the universe was unexplored.

As I began having difficulties with my health and the kennel business, I prayed more and my prayers have been answered. One time in particular, I needed money to pay off a loan. I picked up the mail at the mailbox and went out to burn the trash with the mail in hand; the mail fell into the fire. I managed to extricate the envelopes and there was a check with the money to pay off the loan in the envelope that came out of the fire unscathed. I know someone up above was watching over me. That made a believer out of me. The lost was found again.

When I was married, I joined the Catholic Church and have attended church in Hamilton for thirty years. I enjoy belonging to a church family and being part of the church community.

As I enter the twilight years with my newly renewed faith, I realize that the Ten Commandments are the only way to live. Your life can be healthier and more productive with a strong religious faith. That which I had lost has now been found.

Roscoe and his car

Mary Bechtold

History of outdoor picture show spans 69 years

Richard Hollingshead, father of the drive-in, capitalized on the success of the drive-in restaurant, extending the-in-your-car convenience to include the silver screen. He patented the idea three years after he thought of it. The first drive-in theater opened in Camden, N.J., in June 1933.

The mid—40's saw the roaring bufferterias answer to frustrated moviegoers who wished to stay in their cars and not miss any of the movie or stand in long lines during intermission.

The dawn of the 50's brought the "talk back" system. Starting in Greensboro, N, C., moviegoers pushed a button on the side of the speaker to be connected to the main switchboard indirectly, summoning carhops. The centrally located self-service snack bar eventually won out over car hop service.

The conventional drive-in heyday was 1948 to 1954, when the count rose from 820 to 3,775. Between 1987 t o1990 the number of drive-ins fell from 2,507 to 910. Drive-in attendance dropped off by two-thirds.

On the bright side, in this decade sacral new drive-ins have been built circa 1990, including sites in New York and Alabama.

I dated during the heyday of the drive-in movies in Kansas City. We went to the old Heart Drive In out on Highway 40.

In the summer of 1952, I dated Roscoe. I was not going to school. I worked at Western Auto full time during the week. Roscoe, Ralph, Vernilda and I were inseparable. We went to stock car races, fishing, and boating, swimming, horseback riding and to the amusement park at Fairyland. We rode the Ferris wheel and all the roller coaster we could find.

This was one of the best summers of my life. Foot-loose and fancy free. I enjoyed all the pleasures of summer and good friends.

The drive-in theater was a nice way to spend summer evening with people you enjoyed and double features. We put away the drinks and popcorn, too.

In the 1970's drive-ins began to close. TV and cable television have replaced the drive—ins.

My children, when they were dating would rent movies and pop them the VCR's at our house and those of their friends. I am glad the drive-ins still exists in the United States, although the number is small.

Liberal Arts building

Keepsakes recall memories of famlly

The keepsakes and treasures that I have are related to my relatives and the various decades of my life. My mother's parents used lamps and kerosene to light them. I have a beautiful lamp that is hand carved glass. I very seldom use it, but it comes in handy when the electricity goes off and one cannot see with out these lamps or flashlights.

I still have reading certificates that I received in the late 1940's and 50's. Reading was never a chore for me. I always enjoyed books and could be found with my nose stuck in one. I read all the horse and dog books I could find and then graduated to historical romances. One could visit far away countries when engrossed in an intriguing story.

My other treasured remains of my high school years from 1945 to 1949, are pictures I took of the Central High school campus and friends. I have a bound copy of the Central High Luminary of 1949, the year I was first page editor. I also have copies of my yearbooks. These keepsakes are dusty and the pages turning yellow.

Moving on, one of my favorite keepers is a skull ashtray which is printed with "University of Kansas City," which has grown into University of Missouri and Kansas City.

Pictures of sorority friends are seen in my old albums. College yearbooks picture their graduates as forever young.

Life moves on to marriage years. Some of my favorite keepsakes are the tea set sent to me by my husband when he served in England and the anniversary clock he bought that was made in Germany.

Quilts rank high on my list of favorite things. My mother handmade one, with all the emblems of the 50 states flowers, birds and state mottos. I especially like the Sunbonnet Sue I use in my twin beds.

In the 1960's I had a kennel. My daughter, Julie, bought me small statues of dogs that I have sitting around. My friend, Elsie Moutray, made me ceramic dolls. I have two of these dolls in small doll beds.

One could go on and on about their treasures, but one's keepsakes are a life remembered.

Swooning over swashbuckling pirates

My favorite movies of the silver screen tied in with my fantasy life when I was a teenager.

A lot of my movie of attendance took place in my early teens and dating years. In my "tween" years, I was addicted to cartoons. I especially liked Bugs Bunny and Daffy Duck. The Troost theatre had matinees. You could always find a group of us from Central High watching them. I stopped going to matinees after I started work at fourteen in the Jewish Community Center.

My favorite silver screen movies were the swashbuckling pirate movies. Many of these shows were adapted from novels. I read every novel and history book about pirates who preyed on the seas.

My favorite pirate movie was "The Black Swan" in `1942. Tyrone Power and Clara Monroe played the hero and heroine. I had a crush on Tyrone Power. I was probably one of the old time groupies. I think I tried to find a real teenage Romeo who looked like him. If I dreamed after seeing one of his movies, I took the place of the screen heroine.

Errol Flynn was very lifelike as he played pirate roles on the seven seas. He was outstanding as he played the "Master of Ballantine and Sea Hawk" in 1940 and "Captain Blood" in 1945 starred in "The Princess and the Pirate." He wasn't as dashing as Errol Flynn or Tyrone Power, but he certainly kept everyone laughing at his antics. I also liked cowboy movies with John Wayne, but he made an outstanding pirate in "Reap the Wild Wind.'

I think these movies were good for the families who had grown up with during the Depression. They were more prosperous now, but could see the war in Europe and World War II looming on the horizon with Adolph Hitler and Germany invading other countries.

When we finally declared war on Germany and Japan, pinups like Betty Grable, Hedy Lamar and Rita Hayworth were featured in war films. These movies were designed to build up the morale of the American people.

Many movie stars went to war to serve their country. I was in high school during the war years and watched the war's progress at the movies on the newsreels before the movie was shown.

I believe of all the different kinds of movies I saw on the silver screen, I liked the pirate and animal movies best. My favorite animal movies were "Bambi" and "My Friend Flicka."

What the Fourth of July means to me

Independence Day for me means that I have been able to grow up in a country where I could develop to my fullest potential. My parents lived through the depression of the 1930's working hard like millions of others to deep body and soul together. My parents believed in the Declaration of Independence which stated that all individuals had certain inalienable rights. They felt that anyone who worked hard and set their sights toward an attainable goal could achieve it in the United States the land of opportunity. My great grandparents had come from Germany to Ellis Island with just the clothes on their backs in the early 1800's. They moved westward with the pioneers lured by the free land in the Homestead Act.

I used to listen to my great grandparents talk about how privileged we were to live in the United States. Their parents were made to serve in the armed forces; their children could be arrested and thrown into prison upon a mere suspicion of conspiring against the emperor. Their children worked long hours in the early factories of the Industrial

Revolution. Your rights in Germany usually depended on whether or not you had money or a title.

In the small town where I lived as a child, we had band concerts in the park. These concerts were started with everyone standing in pledging allegiance to the U.S. flag. I can remember swelling with pride when I sang the Star Spangled Banner along with the other folks in the park.

In another country I would never have received a full four year college scholarship and a graduate fellowship. Our country with all of its imperfections is still the only place in the world where men can live and pursue his dreams in relative freedom. Where else can you say that you lied about our country's legislature without being imprisoned, tortured, or killed for disagreeing with those in power. Hurrah for the United States of America!

CHAPTER 5

MARRIAGE

Wedding pictures of Eugene and Mary Bechtold

Twist of fate brought this couple together

In my family, blind dates are the way boy meets girl and love blooms. My mother was a school teacher, and she met my dad on a date arranged by another teacher. If fate hadn't intervened and introduced my parents in the old fashioned dating way, I wouldn't be here. Cupid didn't need a computer dating service for my parents, just a helpful friend.

Oddly enough, I met my husband Eugene on a blind date. My best friend, Vernilda, didn't want to go out with one of the men she worked with unless I went along with one of his friends. She thought there was safety in numbers. Kim, the man she dated ran in to my future husband in Kansas City at the drugstore lunch counter were they both ate near 31st and DeGroffway. My husband didn't have anything to do so he agreed to go. The date was on; we went to the movies.

Vernilda never dated Kim again. My husband never saw the man who arranged the date. Was that fate or wasn't it?

I continued to date my husband who was a Greyhound bus driver. We got married in August, and I have been married for more years than I care to admit. I've been married more years than I was single.

I still see my friend, Vernilda, but none of us have ever heard of Kim, the man she dated.

Paying off the family 'dowry"

My parents were of the old school where fathers worked and mothers stayed home.

My mother graduated valedictorian of her senior class at Gower High School. She went on to Warrensburg College to get her teaching certificate.

She taught in a one room school house for two years. She had grades one to eight. She met my dad, got married and started raising a family in the beginning of the Depression. My parents had the idea that after having children, a woman's place was at home. Men were the breadwinners.

Our lives moved along smoothly until I reached my junior year at Central High in Kansas City. My principal and teachers recommended that I go on to college. My dad was surprised when I won a four year scholarship, with books and tuition paid for. He and my mother agreed to let me go and I lived at home. I worked in two libraries while I was going to school. The four years passed quickly and I graduated from Kansas City University with honors in 1953.

I went on blind date and met my husband, Eugene. We planned to be married in August. One evening my dad asked to meet with Eugene and I explained to my future husband that I had to pay my debt for being home for four years attending college. The amount was $4,000.

We had heard of Indian males bringing so many horses for the bride to the bride's family. I thought this was outrageous to charge a dowry in the 20th century. My husband and I worked on paying it off.

Then, surprise my husband was drafted after we were married for two years. I moved home, got a fellowship and worked on my master's degree. I paid rent and paid off the dowry until Bud got out of the service.

At the time we were paying off the dowry, it really irritated me. Now as I look back on it, I smile and think my husband really wanted me dowry and all.

The most influential person

The most influential person in my life is my husband, Eugene Bechtold. I was twenty-one when I married him. I did not know how to drive a car, take care of a check book or spend money wisely.

After we were married, I got a job and needed a car to drive to work. His first task was to teach me how to drive the new push button Mercury that had come out. I got a lavender and white one. You could see me from far away because of the distinctive colors of the car. He spent countless hours over the weekend in parking lots of deserted business districts teaching me how to drive. I never mastered the stick shift cars. I would grind the gears and make the poor motor sound like it was dying.

When my husband thought I was ready he went with me to take the state driving test. I did everything well but parallel parking and backing up. I took the test five times I finally passed on the sixth. I think the testers were tired of looking at me.

The next lesson I learned from him was a hard one. You balance your checkbook and do not overspend. I was red in the face when the bank called and said we were overdrawn. I had to pay penalties, I was more careful after that to balance the checkbook.

I might have three college degrees, but I came up short in the matters of practical living. My cooking skills were opening a can hoping I did not cut myself and heating up the contents of the can. Gene, on the other hand watched his mother cook. He patiently taught me some cooking skills so I could make a decent meal. You cannot learn everything about cooking from a book.

As the year passed I have become interested in many different occupations from running, to teaching inmates and helping them get their GED's in prison. My husband's greatest gift to me was giving me the freedom to venture into new areas and applaud when I did well. What else could anyone want from a husband?

Driving Lessons

My first experience with driving lessons came when I married my husband Eugene. He had a new stick shift Ford. I could hardly wait to get behind the wheel. Fate intervened and that didn't happen. My husband was drafted in the Korean War and stationed in England for two years.

My dad didn't believe in women drivers. I lived at home that two years and the ford was jacked up in the back yard. Would you believe that can ran when he got home? My driving lesson was put on hold and I continued riding public transportation. I practiced on the old stick shift and didn't do a good job of shifting the gears. My stops were abrupt and I ground the gears. My husband's patience grew thin. He was a Greyhound driver with a good safety record.

One night on television I saw big beautiful mercury with push buttons instead of gears. I thought I need that and I will pass the driving test. We went to the car dealers and I got new purple and white mercury with lovely push buttons. I aced the written part of the driver's test but, I didn't bank on the policeman I had to take for a ride. I took my first test in North Kansas City. I didn't pass because of parallel parking. Undaunted I went to Liberty and who do I get same OLE policeman again, I passed the entire driving test. He made the remark "Always go forward and stay out of parallel parking spots."

I got a teaching job and drove my Mercury to work for six months with no difficulties. One night I decided to go to the Antioch shopping Center at night. I came out and somehow backing up hit a concrete light pole. The new car had to be repaired. After that when my husband was off he drove me to a vacant parking lot in North Kansas City, I learned to

Parallel Park. Believe it or not I would rather go forward than backward. I am superstitious.

War changes couple's direction

My husband and I were married during the Korean War. I had just graduated from college and got a job as a secretary at Katz Drug Company. My husband drove for Greyhound Lines.

Being called to the service was the farthest thing from my husband's mind. He had osteomyelitis in his leg when he was six years old. The doctor scraped the bone and removed about five inches from his upper right leg. His status was 4F during World War II.

Surprise! He was called up by the draft board for the Korean War. He passed the physical, and became on of Uncle Sam's finest.

They sent him to Fort Bliss in Texas. He was given limited duty and kept thinking he'd get out of the service. Every Army doctor who saw him said he shouldn't be there, but didn't know how to get him out.

He was trained as a radar operator and sent to Lakenheath, England. We had planned to move to Alaska where I was going to be a teacher, and he was going to be a bus driver. The Korean War change all this.

What a doggone year

At the age of twenty-five, I had been married four years. Two of those years my husband was in the service. He was a radar operator in England. I was living with my parents again. My father thought he wouldn't have any child at home but my brother, Tim who was ten years younger than I was.

I had been given a full tuition scholarship to work on my master's in education. My dream of being a famous archeologist was not going to help me make a living. I was studying in a second field which was proving to be more practical than going to Egypt to study pharaohs and their burial places.

My husband came home from the service and we started looking for a home. We bought one in Gladstone, Mo., and moved in. The first occupied house in the whole housing complex had a resident. I had taken a teaching position in seventh and eighth grades in my own alma mater, Central High.

No new home would be complete without a dog, I thought. One of my students kept telling me about these small puppies that his dog had. I feel for the idea hook, line and sinker. When the puppy was 9 weeks old, he delivered the dog. It was a large boned puppy with big feet. He was very loveable but would not stay in our fenced yard. He would get out and go down to the neighboring school and beg for food in the lunchroom. What a commotion he caused. I finally had to give him away to a farmer, who was pleased with him.

This was the year I drove my new push-button Mercury to the shopping center in Antioch and backed up. I hit a big light pole and made a big dent in my back bumper. It was the only car in the shopping center at the time. It took me years to live that one down. I still go better forward than backwards.

I thought I needed protection since our housing addition had only two houses that were occupied. Eugene was gone many nights as a Grey-hound bus driver. I saw an ad in the newspaper, "German Shepherd for Sale," just what we needed.

I bought the dog while my husband was gone. He came home late one night and started to unlock the door. The German shepherd reared up and looked him in the eyes. My husband leaned on the doorbell and I had to go rescue him from my protector.

The dog, named Otis, was a wonderful companion and he did not like to be left alone. If you were not home, he ate everything in sight, even the concrete on the walls of the basement if that was all he could find. We felt Otis needed a new home and put an ad in the paper. An older man in a Volkswagen bought him and drove off with Otis sitting in the back seat.

Many dogs have come and gone since the two dogs that I have written about. These dogs were among the most memorable. These are some of the things I remember about being twenty-five.

Early Television

After listening to programs on the radio, watching and hearing live performances on the television was like having a movie theatre in your own home.

My husband Eugene and I bought our first home in Gladstone. It was complete when we added our own television set. Western shows were my husband's favorite. Gunsmoke with Kitty and Matt Dillon was top on his list. I liked Bonanza and Big Valley. The scenes were magnificent and you felt like you were living in the Old West. I enjoyed the Rifleman with Chuck O' Conner and his son.

I Love Lucy was one of my favorite shows. I always enjoyed the comedy of Fred and Edna along with Lucy Arnez and Desi. We never missed the Ed Sullivan and his variety show. All the women and girls loved it when Elvis Presley sang on his show. Band Stand was another show on television that I could not miss when I was at Central High School a group of us went there to appear on it when it was in Kansas City.

Fred Allen and Gracie Burns were tops in comedy on television. I listened to them on the radio before we had television. They seemed to be a famous couple who really loved each other.

T.V. land on Dish Network had played a lot of the old Television Shows. My husband watches 'Bonanza, Gunsmoke and Big Valley. I watched the old Green Acres when they played rerun on it. The Partridge Family was another show that my children liked.

The old shows of the 60's and 70's had higher moral values that some of the reality and comedies that we see on television today. I look at CSI Miami and other shows with forensics. These shows give you and opportunity to work your mind.

You could get addicted to television. I watch two or three hours per night. Television is with us to stay.

Mary's problems with cooking

When I was growing up I learned the basics of boiling water, cooking eggs, and how to do the dishes. All the materials used in our house were fresh. Chickens were slaughtered by wringing their necks. I always got the job of steaming the headless chicken and picking pin feathers off. I loved fried chicken but not the process of getting it from the live chicken to dead cooked chicken.

My mother was a stay at home mom who had our meals waiting when I came home from school. I started working at fourteen in a library after school and on weekends. My time for cooking was almost non—existent.

Time flew by with my working and going to school. Along comes the wedding date and I am married, my poor husband cooked better than I did. He taught me some of the cooking basics. He had watched his mother cook when he was young and had osteomyelitis.

My mother in law was the best cook. Marvelous concoctions would arise in her kitchen. Her fried chicken and biscuits and gravy were a wonderful treat. She enjoyed watching people eat and exclaim over her food.

I learned to cook prepared foods from boxes and cans. We invited our relatives up to eat with us. I decided to cook a roast and potatoes. I got the Better Homes and Garden Cook book out and followed the directions. I thought anyone who could read could cook. Surprise! I overcooked the roast and burnt his potatoes. My relatives with false teeth had trouble eating.

My mother in law said "Poor Bubbie, he must be starving." My mother came back with a retort saying "He looks plenty fat to me." I can read books and recipes but I still have to watch what I cook. I am the best consumer that Schwann has of frozen foods and packaged dinners. I may have gotten A's in graduate school but, I would have gotten F's in cooking school. All those women who cook up delicious meals on television have my admiration.

Dwelling place becomes home with addition of two children

When I lived in Gladstone, Mo., I lived one mile from a new housing development called Carriage Hill. Many months went by as I went to Carriage Hill to admire the exhibition home. I didn't think we could afford to buy a house that looked like that and had so many square feet. The house had a courtyard in front of the door with a brick sidewalk. There were magnolia trees and gorgeous flowers.

I had gone to school at UMKC with the realtor's son. He said, "Why don't you see if you qualify for a loan?"

Much to my surprise, we qualified and the house was ours. The house had a formal living and dining room with an entrance hallway that led to a family room with a fireplace and sliding patio doors. We had a huge kitchen with a dining area and all kinds of built-ins and appliances. There were three bedrooms and three baths. Decorating the house with French provincial furniture was fun.

We were lonely in that house with only my husband and me and a Pomeranian dog. One of my favorite purchases was a German regulator clock. I still have that clock.

My years in that house were lonely. We kept feeling our family needed children. While we lived in Carriage Hill, our daughters, Marijean and Julie Bechtold, became members of our family when they were on two and three days old.

Gladstone was growing by leaps and bounds at the time. We bought a farm a mile south of Kidder and that is where we lived until we sold the farm in 1988. We just moved down the hill and build another house.

The Gladstone area was nice while we lived there and I will always remember my Carriage hill house. That was a very happy time from me when our family expanded from two to four.

Volunteer Bureau

When we adopted Marijean, I still lived in Carriage Hill with people all around me. The City of Gladstone was growing by leaps and bounds. The Clay Platte Health and Welfare Council were formed to help with some of the rising problems like the need for a mental health center north of the river. We also worked on the growing school population and not enough schools and dogs running loose. If these dogs were taken off the streets, where were they be housed. I was asked to be the Director of the Clay Platte Health and Welfare council. My job was to preside over meetings and do leg work to help solve some of these problems. I only worked part time before we moved to the Rural Caldwell area. We had solved one problem before we had moved. The major problem that we solved was set up a mental health office in the North Kansas City Hospital. It was just one or two rooms the council provided chairs, lamps, desks and a secretary. A psychologist was hired and patients started filling the waiting room. More personnel were added our residents did not have to go to Kansas City to see a mental health specialist.

Years later after I lived in Caldwell County, I was called and asked to come to a meeting where the early founders were to be recognized for the work that they had done in the establishment of this clinic that had been so needed. At the dinner we attended, they called my name and I was recognized for my work. This was one of my finest hours. My husband children clapped with the others in the crowd.

Greyhound Lines

"Leave the driving to us." How many times have you seen the picture of a Greyhound bus and a Driver flash across the television screen advertising Greyhound line?

The roots of Greyhound began in 1914. There were a lot of small bus lines competing with the train to get people where they wanted to go and on time. Bus transportation provide people with a way to move to other areas, see the country, live in small towns and work in cities, and go to see relatives in other cities at an economical cost. The smaller bus lines united and expanded during the Depression and the War years, tweny-seven companies formed the corporation. The corporation had a headquarters in Phoenix, Arizona. My husband, Eugene was hired and worked for Southwestern Greyhound line, origination in Kansas City, Mo.

My life has been intertwined with Greyhound Lines since 1953. My husband worked for Greyhound Lines then. He was on what was called the extra board. That meant when any schedule for Southwestern Greyhound lines had to many passengers for one bus, they put a second one on. The extra board driver got together when their wives went to work and would wait for a call to report to work. Holidays came and went and the buses overloaded, out the driver went that meant time and half for working on holidays. Of course wives and children went to many dinners and celebrated the holidays by themselves.

Many times living on an isolated farm and kennel, I had to handle things by myself such as a two day ice storm where all our heat was cut off. Eugene was in a nice warm hotel room in St Louis while we were shivering on the farm.

Families were given free passes on buses. My daughter, Julie and I traveled to Washington DC on the bus and home. We had a scary trip coming home in Pennsylvania. Some young men behind us were drinking and bothering passengers. One tough cookie said to his neighbor and pulled out a sharp knife, "If the bus driver comes back here, I'll slit his throat." Thank goodness the driver kept driving. We transferred to another bus in Indianapolis and left the driver and the noisy group. The dangerous men had a car waiting for them in Indianapolis and drove off.

Most of the people who rode the Greyhound Bus were hardworking people visiting their relatives or going for visits on trips all over the country. When gas was rationed, many people rode the bus because it was either that or the train. I guess they could have walked or rode bicycles.

Eugene became an officer on the Greyhound Bus Union, trained drivers how to drive and had a regular run to St Louis before retiring. Greyhound fed and clothed us for thirty-five years. We have many friends and acquaintances as a result of Greyhound Lines. We go to Greyhound retirees meeting twice a year. My husband still has his uniform and hat that he wore 15 years ago before he retired hanging in our closet. We have a memorial brick with his name on it in the entry of the Greyhound Museum in Hibbing's, South Dakota. The museum contains all the models of Greyhound buses that were driven over the years and other Greyhound memorabilia from Greyhound enthusiasts. The Greyhound retirees motored to South Dakota for the dedication of the museum in 1999.

Moving involves woes.

When my husband and I were young, we were going to move to Alaska. I was going to teach school and he was going to drive a bus across Alaska. That never happened but, we did move to a remote area off Highway 36 one mile south of Kidder, Mo. We were the first house off the highway down a gravel road on the edge of a 180-acre farm. We built a new house in November of 1967.

The house was ready to move into in January 1968. The day we picked to move was cold and below zero and snowy. The moving van was filled with our furniture and belongings. We moved the tropical fish in our cars, but Jack, my big, beautiful 10-inch Jack Dempsey fish died on the move. He was frozen solid. I had had him for 10 years and felt like he was a member of the family.

Our house sat on top of a hill and all I could see was white on the ground and ice on the trees. The wind was up that day and it whistled and banged around the house. Air crept in around the windows in the two north bedrooms. I thought to myself, "this is how it would have been if we had moved to Alaska, only worse."

The time came for my husband to go to work driving a Greyhound bus. My daughters were two and eight months old. When he left for work, I felt isolated. I had two children to take care of a house to straighten up and at night I could hear the coyotes howl and owls hooting. We all wore several layers of clothing, because it was cold even with heat.

We have moved several times, but never in the dead of winter, and into an isolated house. I love living in the country now, but I sure felt alone at first after living in a city with neighbors all around me.

Cabin Fever

I woke up in the middle of the night, hearing ice clatter on the windows. I got up and fixed breakfast, turned on the radio, no school because of icing on the gravel roads and highways. My daughters were happy NO school. It kept icing up the trees and sidewalks. Kennel helpers couldn't' get to work so I got dressed up and went out to the kennel to take care of three buildings of dogs. I had to watch to keep from falling it was so slick.

In three hours I was ready to go inside and fix lunch. Thank goodness we had kerosene heaters in the dog houses because the electricity was off. Our furnace would not run. Four three days of bitter cold we were isolated. My husband was in St Louis snug and warm in a hotel.

We dressed in several layers of clothes. We brought in mattresses into the living room. Our lights at night were kerosene lamps. My daughters entertained themselves with playing Barbie's and games. They were sure glad to see that big old yellow school bus pull in the driveway. After three days I was glad to see the kennel helpers and life going back to normal.

I felt alone like I lived in Alaskan Wilderness. This was the time that I had cabin fever in the worst way. All that livestock and two children who were depending on me, I felt like some of the prairie women must have lived back in the 1800's When Eugene walked in after driving his Greyhound bus home and said "How did you like the ice." I felt like beating him over the head" fortunately no pipes burst. This was the worst bout I ever had with cabin fever.

Rural life lends warm, caring environment

As the holiday season rolls around, it is time to be thankful and count our many blessings.

I am thankful for living in a rural area for thirty years and being a part of an area where the people are warm and caring and interested in each other. I feel like I am part of an extended family.

Good health is another thing I'm thankful for. This gives me the ability to do the many things I do and enjoy my life as a productive mother, grandmother and teacher.

My faith in God is another thing that I am thankful for. He has always been there for me and my family in the rocky times.

Another plus to be thankful for is the contact I have in my life with the children I work with in the elementary school where I am a counselor. Each day, I am privileged to see life from the eyes of a small child. This helps me to keep from growing old in my mental attitude.

I was blessed in the parents that I was given. They taught me the value of a dollar, the one must work for what he gets, love and moral values. My mother is still living and can counsel me in the ways of life.

Lastly, I'm thankful for a husband who lets me be myself and let me go to school after we were married. He realized the value of an education for a woman. I appreciate his letting me change occupation and interests as I aged. I wish all women could be as blessed with a life's partner as I have been.

Young wife fears for self, children, when left alone.

SCARED-This word conjures up feelings of a racing heart, blood pounding in my ears and my adrenaline kicking in. This has happened to me twice in my life.

The first time it happened was a dark snowy night about 2 o'clock in the morning. My husband was a Greyhound bus driver who was gone four or five nights a week. This particular night he was out of town.

We lived on an isolated farm at least three-fourths of a mile from our nearest neighbor. I heard a pounding on the door. My dog barking her head off. She was jumping at the door and barking. The only one home was two small children and I. What to do.

I had the screen door latched. It was a man and woman with no overshoes on in the snow. I peered out. They were stuck and wanted to come in. No way was I going to let them in. I called my nearest neighbor, and he agreed to pull them out of the ditch. They stumbled back they way they had come. Needless to say I got little sleep the rest of the night. We lived not far from and isolated road that people used for a lover's lane at night not realizing it wasn't graveled or paved.

The other spooky event occurred on a Sunday in the fall, hunting season. I looked out over the fields and saw a hunter with a big gun walking all over the fields we had posted with" No Trespassing" signs. I walked over to where he was hunting and told hem to get out. He just laughed and kept on hunting. I called the conservation agent, and he waited for my hunter to come back carrying game he had killed out of season. He was arrested, fined and given a court date.

I'll never forget going to the courthouse in Kingston, Mo., to press charges. Our hunter did not pay his fine until he saw me come into the courthouse. I found out later he was a convict who pretty much did as he pleased. He kept himself and his hunting equipment off our farm after that.

Happily Ever After

I was an avid reader of all the fairy tales in the Central High Library where I worked after school. This job gave me an opportunity to peruse the section where the fairy tales were kept. These stories always ended with "and they lived happily after'.

My life was idyllic in our new house in Kansas City North. Teaching school and driving a new car was like heaven to me when Eugene got back from the service. There was something missing. I wanted to live happily after. However children in my classes were not the same as having them at home to care for and love. We had been married ten years but no little ones. We decided on adoption and went to Catholic Charities and adopted two little girls one was a year older than the other one. Life became hectic our neighbors held various baby showers for us and life settled into a routine. I looked around at the neighborhood and saw row after row of houses. I could see all my neighbors in their close backyards.

We decided we wanted to move to a place where we had more space. Eugene was raised in the country and I lived in a small town until I was ten when we moved to Kansas City. We started looking around the areas north of us that were not so populated. We looked around Cameron and Hamilton and the Kidder area. We found 180 acres and had a new house built upon the acreage. We moved in the dead of winter, it was blustery cold with snow on the ground.

We got settled in, it was then time for Eugene to go back to work. I with one baby and a two year old were left alone while he was driving his Greyhound Bus to St. Louis. The wind whistled and the coyotes in the woods howled. My "happily ever idea", of moving didn't seem so great. I missed looking out and being able to see people.

I stuck it out through the winter and spring came. Everything looked beautiful with the grass and flowers. We planted apple trees and iris. I began to get acquainted with my neighbors and they invited me to join a club of women. I was slowly integrated into the area and became comfortable with staying alone. My disappointment with country living lessened. I began to feel that I had moved into A "happily ever after "place. I have been here forty years and was once more in a "happily ever place".

Family fellowship figures in making holidays memorable

One of the happiest holidays I've ever celebrated was the Thanksgiving that was held at my home in Kidder, Mo., when the Bechtold Kennels was alive and well. All of my nieces and nephews were there. My brother Bob and his family and all my children were there. My mother was there also.

Ole Tom turkey tasted better and all the trimmings seemed grander than they had ever been before.

The fellowship was good, and we were all thankful for the many blessing that we had received. Our health was good, and our families had prospered, although we lived many miles apart.

My kennel dogs received and extra treat that night because of the good fortunes that they and their offspring had brought to me and my family. My family and I looked over old pictures and talked about past times that had happened earlier in our lives.

My brother and I talked about searching for toys before Christmas and un-wrapping them to see what they were. We carefully rewrapped them.

We also watched Christmas Eve after we went to bed to see Santa (Mom and Dad) putting the toys under the tree.

When my children were small, I had trouble finding hiding places for the toys. I had to put them in a gunny sack and hide them in the kennel and the barn, suspended in a feed sack.

Another hiding place was the trunk of my car. My grand-daughter comes over frequently, and I still hide the Christmas presents in my car. Old habits die hard.

Another fond memory for us was riding on sleds and snowy weather. My mother made snow ice cream after the first snow. It really tasted delicious to us. We didn't have television and learned how to entertain ourselves through the long winter evenings.

My grandchildren are always saying they are bored. My mother always found some work for me to do when I started yelling I was bored. I found something for them to do and they don't get bored nearly so easily.

My brother Bob and I talked about cutting paper figures out of the catalogs and giving them names and making house and furniture for them. I still like to fantasize and make believe.

One of the best memories that I can pull up is of Christmases at the kennel when my daughters were small and tucked into their beds and I was sitting on my divan watching the Christmas lights flick off and on. The tree was over flowing with presents, and my children were dreaming of hearing Santa Claus and reindeer landing on the roof that had no chimney.

After my relatives left, my husband and I cleaned up and got ready to put the decorations away for another holiday. The day had given us a treasure trove of old memories and a set of new ones until the next time we were together

AUG 1953

Mary, Eugene and friends

My Regrets

This title covers a lot of memories. I always thought when you were married life would be wonderful. My first dark cloud arrived when my husband was drafted. He was rejected as a soldier during World War II. He was drafted for the Korean War. He had osteomyelitis when he was a child and this was the reason why he was rejected during World War II.

He was sent to Fort Bliss, Texas for training. I packed my bags and moved out of our apartment. My father was happy to give me away at the wedding. Now after less than six of marriage, he was seeing me coming through the door with all my bags and baggage my husband's car was put up on blocks to await his homecoming in our back yard. We settled into a routine. I went back to college and kept working upon my master's degree.

Letters flew back and forth across the Atlantic. He became a radar operator in England. I wrote the president saying I'd like to go to England and teach the G. I.'s who needed to get their G.E.D. at the base where my husband was stationed. I got a letter back saying I was eligible to go. I was to send credentials. My mother was happy to have one of her chicks at home again. I didn't go and stayed home to work on a Master's Degree.

Two years passed rapidly and Eugene came home. We immediately filled out an application for a house under the G.I. Bill. I went to work teaching for the Kansas City School District. He went back to driving a bus for Greyhound. I have always regretted not going to England and spending those two years with him. This is my story which tells why Happily Ever After does not always last.

Fiftieth Wedding picture

CHAPTER 6

TEACHING

Mental Health Satellite Clinic is in Operation

Clay and Platte County have begun using a satellite mental health clinic and a family and children service facility at 230 Northeast Evansdale roads, social workers said today.

Mrs. Denise Backlund, social worker for the Mental Health center, said the first patient for the newly-established facility began receiving treatment today.

Also busy today was the Family and Children Service center operated by Miss Bonnie Gaines social worker. She and Mrs. Backlund are available for a half day each Friday.

The new facilities are functioning with little financial aid, Mrs. Mary Bechtold, executive director of the Clay-Platte health and Welfare council said.

Though the Weston Missouri Mental Health center provides the staff-social workers and psychiatrist-cost of maintaining the office must come from contributions, she said. The staff is supplemented at present by four volunteers.

The Mental health center Mrs. Backlund said provides direct patient care, educative and consultative services and psychiatric service for children and adults.

Volunteer Women Help Disturbed children

In a rage a dark eyed tanned little boy of six, rushes at the nearest person. He screams and pinches at those who are unfortunate enough to get in his way. He utters one word which sounded like momma. He refuses to talk to adults. This child has never been in school. Why? Because he is so seriously emotionally disturbed that it is impossible for one teacher to control him in a classroom of 39 children and protect the other children from him.

There are many children like James in the United States who cannot be educated because there are no public school facilities provided for them. It is too expensive to hire one teacher for one child which is the ratio needed by a severely disturbed child. How can an education be preceded for him?

This is the same question that plagued mental health specialists, educators and the parents of disturbed children. The Department of Child Psychiatry, Heed and organization of parents and the Kansas City Missouri, School system, answered this question with the creation of the Day Care school which opened in September 1965 as the first classroom for severely disturbed children in the area. Seven children ages 6-10, enrolled in the school are too disturbed to attend regular public school classes.

The classroom is unique because it represents the combined discipline of education, psychology, social work, psychiatry and medicine. The seven children receive their psychiatric treatment during their school day. The parents are also treated in group sessions during the week. In this way, the entire environment of the child is being controlled and changed. The teacher and the clinical team meet to discuss the child's progress.

Twenty-nine women volunteers, working as teacher moms, of all races and religious denominations, are involved in the project. They work on an individual basis with the pupil morning from 9:00 to 12:30 Monday through Friday. Their main job was to establish a warm relationship with the child so that he could begin to relate to people. The women's ages' ranged from 21 to 70. The only requirement made of the teacher mom was that she has children of her own or experiences in working with them.

The director of volunteers for the Kansas City Mental Health Foundation, Miss Margaret Dart, sent out letters to churches in the

Greater Kansas City area describing the need for volunteers to work with disturbed children.

The Methodist churches turned the letter over to their Wesleyan Service Guilds and the circles which made up the Woman's Society of Christian Service. Six members of the Wesleyan Service Guild responded to the call. The seven teacher moms were all from different Methodist churches and will be continuing with the program in its second year.

One teacher mom, a middle aged black woman, won the trust and love of the seven year old white boy she was working with. This child had brain damage, had been left alone extensively in the first year of his life, was slightly mentally retarded and was fearful of people. At first Charles sat in the corner and covered his eyes and refused to look at her. Within two months, his smiled and ran to her and said in a broken voice, "I love you."

The changes in the children were due to the devotion of these women. They served without pay; their reward was love.

In January 1966, all the children were doing some type of school work. They had learned to follow simple directions, pay attention in groups and to enjoy school. Their growing awareness of other people was communicated by smiles, hugs and sharing of food. They no longer held on to their parents when school tome came, but rushed to get their teacher moms.

For these seven children, these unselfish women who followed the Christina principle of helping one's neighbor were the beginning of hope.

Mental Health Project

After leaving the principal of the School for disturbed children, my husband and I submitted our name to adopt children. The investigation process is a lengthy one. I was approved to become a volunteer director for Citizens in the Northland Area wanting to bring about changes to help citizens living there. One of our priority projects was a new mental health center in our area. After working for months on this project, I was anxious to see mental health in our area My months of work finally became a reality. We were given space at the North Kansas City Hospital. All of the materials for the office were donated, desks, furniture, lights, chairs, typewriters, lamps. The dream of the organization had become a reality. We were off and running. Money from a grant was to pay the salaries of a therapist, psychologists and secretaries. Publicity in the Kansas City Star brought in many clients.

Many years later this became a large clinic with many psychiatrists, psychologists, and social workers a large reception was given for the individuals who were instrumental in making the clinic possible. My husband and I, and our two children attended this event. I was asked to stand and be recognized as a vital part of the clinic's original birth. This was one of my finest moments when everyone clapped for me.

My turning point

My story begins ten years ago with my first year of teaching in an integrated junior high in Kansas City, Missouri. My teacher training courses in college had not prepared me for the problems and needs of the culturally deprived child. Education courses reflected middle class philosophy and equipped me only to understand children from the same middle class background as my own. The course were slanted toward the student who lived in the suburbs with two parents was well acquainted with books and had plenty to eat.

My two classes' of 2 1/2 hours each were composed of 76% black. I taught history, English and spelling. All of the people pictured in the textbooks had white skin.

One short dark skinned boy with piercing black eyes attracted my attention. His clothes were wrinkled dirty and secured with safety pins where buttons or zippers were missing. His hair always had lint in it. The look in his eyes reminded me of the eyes of a child who stood with his face pressed against the window of a pet store watching a puppy wag its tail. My student's look was that of longing for something he could not have.

He seldom completed his assignment. In class I saw him quietly put his head on his desk and sleep away the class period. He did this day after day regardless of what activity the rest of the class was engaged in.

Finally, I reached the end of my patience. My teaching supervisor had paid an unexpected visit. All the students were busily at work: the room hummed with activity. As I explained the class projects to her, a loud snore startled us. We looked around; his head resting on his arms, the culprit was lost in sleep. I marched to the rear of the room and shook his shoulder insistently. He sat up and made a pretext of working on the assignment.

Fifteen minute later, he was fast asleep.

Once again I shook him. He jumped up and looked as though he were going to strike me. Suddenly he dropped his fist.

"Do we bore you that much?"

"No ma'am. I was up late last night taking care of my sick brother."

"I took care of my old grandmother too," a voice called from the back of the room

The students roared with laughter at the remark.

A likely story, I thought as I calmed the class. He always has an excuse ready.

Rueben's naps became a source of irritation to me. I woke him every few minutes. For punishment, I kept him after school to do the assignments he hadn't finished. I ridiculed him in front of the class.

Nothing worked. He slept more and more, and it became harder to rouse him.

Three months of school passed. The leaves turned color and fell to the ground leaving the trees barren and defenseless against the cold.

On the first day of December, I automatically walked to the back of the room to rouse Rueben. His seat was empty; it remained that way for the next three weeks. He must be playing hooky, I thought. A child like that doesn't have any sense of responsibility and doesn't want to better him.

One afternoon I drove to Rueben's home to catch him red-handed with no excuses for skipping school.

I knocked on the door. As the door swung open, I expected to see Rueben. Instead a slight barefoot girl peered around a small crack in the door.

"Is your mother or father here," I said, standing tall to command more respect.

"I ain't got no Dad and my mother's in the hospital."

"Is your brother, Rueben, here?"

"No, ma'am, he's in the hospital too."

Two preschool children peered out behind her skirt. They clung to her as if she were their only protection. They were barefooted with matted hair and runny noses.

"May I come in and talk to your babysitter?"

"I'm taking care of them till Maw and Rueben get home. We ain't got any money for a babysitter. I guess you can come in."

As I stepped inside I looked at the bare room an old dirty pink divan sat in one corner, a television in the other.

The two small children were nothing but skin and bones. I could see the kitchen from the living room. Dust lay in the corners. Boxes of crackers, empty cans and dirty pots and pans littered the kitchen counters and sink. The entire room smelled of un-emptied garbage.

"What is the matter with Rueben and your mother?"

"The doctor said they hadn't had enough to eat. We've been kind of hard up and they've been letting us eat their share of the food."

"Have you any food now?"

"No.'

"Well you will have. Just lock the door and I'll be back in a jiffy with some groceries."

"You're not at all like Rueben said you were. He thought you were a mean old bag who was always picking on him.'

I could feel the crimson spreading all over my face.

Why, I thought as I drove to the store, didn't I try to find out the reason Rueben was so sleepy. At that moment I resolved to find out why each student behaved as he did. No more external punishment without knowing what caused each child to act as he did.

I bought enough groceries to last one week and contacted the children's aunt who agreed to look after them until their mother got home.

While Rueben was away, I made arrangements for him to receive free lunches at school. A church group in the area agreed to keep the family supplied with food.

Visiting the children, I learned that thirteen year old Rueben had been working all night in a laundry to buy food for the family. No wonder he was sleeping in my class.

Rueben returned to school with out acknowledging my visits. He tried very hard to stay awake and keep up on his assignments. He made a passing grade at the end of the year.

For seven years, I remained in the same classroom at Central junior high. The first week of school never passed without a visit from Rueben.

I still receive Christmas cards from Rueben and his family. I can not thank him enough for the lesson he taught me: to look beyond a person's external actions and try to understand him as a total human being in his environment.

Because of this experience, I became a more effective teacher and closer the to the students Rueben taught me to project myself in the life of the student and understand his actions.

The turning point in my life began with the sleepy boy and ended with the realization of the dignity and worth of all people, regardless of their background, color or ambition.

Books pile on happiness

I believe the happiest times in my life have been associated with a school or a library. Books are lying all over my house—biographies, love stories, horror, and non fiction, to mention a few. Looking backwards makes one nostalgic. The people that one is close to at one period of your life move away, marry, or lose contact except by mail or and occasional telephone call.

My life is now one of the happiest periods that I have experienced. I am retired and enjoyed the first few moths of retirement—shopping, visiting neighbors, and playing with grandchildren—but I soon got bored and wanted something else to occupy my time.

My entry into my present occupation came about year and a half ago. I heard Carla Franks, the director of volunteers at the Western Missouri Correctional Center talk about the need for volunteers at the prison. I signed up and was assigned in April, 1991 as a volunteer and attached to the education department.

I thoroughly enjoyed working there. I worked three hours a day, four days a week with an inmate who didn't even know his alphabet in the beginning. He progressed to about the third-grade level before I was given a different assignment. Another fascinating job I was given was to work with a accident victim who needed some help with his speech.

I enjoyed working as substitute librarian when the librarian had to be absent. I helped many a prisoner find information and books. What I couldn't find, the inmate clerks helped me with. We talked about all of the current topics seen on television and in the newspapers. Many of the insights made me look at things in a different way.

A paid teaching position opened up in the education department In December of 1991, and I was asked to apply for it. I am now working nine hours a week with adults who want to receive their GED and better themselves when they leave us.

I'm happiest when I am helping someone else and learning new skills.

I can truly say this is the happiest time of my life

Communication skills aid woman throughout lifetime

Talent can be defined as that gift which one has and uses. Elvis Presley's talent was his musical ability; Stephen King's was his ability to write scary fiction stories. My talent lies in the field of communication—both written and verbal. I began my career as a writer in high school. I was a page editor of the 1949 Centralian and was an editor of the high school newspaper, the Luminary. I liked seeing my words in print.

My teaching career began in the Kansas City, Mo., school system at Central Junior—the same school I attended. I taught social studies and English. Our Missouri state teaching journal, School and Community, became a vehicle for the articles I wrote. There were many things I thought could be done to improve the school system one of them was the need for an elementary counselor in the grade schools. There were none at the time I was a teacher. I became one of the first elementary counselors in the Missouri area. Here's where my verbal skill came into use. I had my time divided between seven elementary schools I worked for the Hickman Mills School system for two years with this experimental program. The program was so successful the first year that they hired two more elementary counselors. I also wrote articles for The Instructor and Catholic Digest and had my master's thesis published in the Journal of Experimental Education. I still write and publish articles about things that I feel passionately about.

My verbal communication talents have been developed by a variety of occupations. The one taking the most skills was my elementary counselor's job where I presented an elementary counselor's program to preschoolers for fifteen minutes. It was difficult to keep three and four year olds interested and playing to get the message across.

Working as a teacher in a prison with convicted felons was another challenge, helping them get their GED. It was hard to keep the line between being conned and showing respect for them. Another challenge was having inmates in class who had to go to school because they were below the fourth grade in educational skill.

I was the director of a volunteer bureau in the northland area of Kansas City. One of the greatest needs this area had was for a Mental Health Clinic in the Northland area. Our dream was finally realized when the clinic opened its doors in North Kansas City. I went to a recognition banquet and was recognized as being a founder of the psychiatric clinic that is located there.

When I owned and ran a kennel for fifteen years, I sold all of my doges to individuals all over the country on the telephone. Most of the people on the other end of the telephone were just voices. I got to know them as people through our verbal communication on the telephone. In the fast pace world we live in, verbal and written skills are important. Through the use of the computer, I am getting acquainted with writing for e-mail publications. They are brief and need to have words that will catch the reader's attention. This is a major challenge to an individual who started with her high school publications

Students, teacher learn about life from each other

Pleasant memories for me come from the 1960's. My husband had returned from the Korean War. After serving two years in England as a radar operator, he got his job back as a bus driver for Southwestern Greyhound lines.

I went to work as a teacher for the Kansas City School District. My first teaching assignment was at Central Junior High School.

This was during the first years on integration. We had an integrated staff, as well as integrated students. Our principal was Girard Bryant, a Black American who had his PHD. Mr. Bryant was a mentor to the new teachers. We had classes of 49 students. Mr. Bryant was one of the most compassionate men that I had ever met. I learned many things from him about the Black American culture and how to deal with students from lower socio-economic environments.

I think I learned as much from the students as they learned about curriculum from me. We spent many hours discussing life and what could be done about it. I learned that children are resilient and can endure much. I had to adapt my textbooks and teaching materials to the reading level, which was that of the fourth grade. The books were written at the seventh grade level. After adapting the material, the students learned quickly.

We went on many trips. Manor Baking Co. was their favorite. We got free eats rolls, bread, donuts. I visited many homes and never met a parent who wasn't trying to help their child, even thought they had many handicaps to overcome.

This was the time when I learned to drive and got brand-new Mercury with pushbuttons. The old gearshift and I did not get along. My mercury was lavender and white.

We bought a new house in Meadowbrook in Gladstone, Mo. My students gave me a dog—a little dog turned out to be a big boxer who annoyed the neighbors and raided their trashcans. He went to a good farm home. I had a housedog next, a little Boston terrier.

Time passed quickly when we lived in the house in Meadowbrook. One memorable event at the time was an epidemic of measles at Central Junior. All of the students contacted the two—week measles. The cases died down. One weekend I got sick. My throat was sore and I broke out with a rash. I had developed the measles with a high fever. I had to say at home for two weeks. My students thought that was funny.

I inherited a student named Clifford who was having a difficult time at home and was getting into all kinds of trouble. He was given into our custody to be transported to Boys Town. He became a model citizen, went to college and is now teaching. He had children and grandchildren of his own who are college graduates.

I have had many happy times, but these are very pleasant memories.

Warm fuzzy feelings surround celebrations

Valentines Day always brings back warm fuzzy feelings and the feeling of being loved and cared for when it arrives each year. Looking back into past years of my life brings many happy memories and faces into focus.

The best valentine I ever received was a homemade one that Harold, a seventh-grade student made for me back in 1963 when I taught at

Central Junior High in Kansas City, Mo. There were forty three students in my morning class. Schools were newly integrated at the time. Our textbooks were written at the seventh-grade reading level, and three-quarters of the class read at the third-grade level.

Harold had a cleft palate, stuttered and could barely read. His clothes were torn and dirty. Children made fun of him and he was the brunt of many cruel jokes.

I sent Harold out of the room one day and proceeded to give the class a lecture on putting themselves into someone else's shoes. Gradually the cruel remarks about Harold ceased.

On Valentine's Day Harold brought me a homemade valentine saying "Thank You, teacher. I want you to be my valentine." He told me he had printed every word himself.

I lost track of Harold, but I still remember the warm feeling that valentine gave me. It meant more than expensive valentines I have received because it came from the heart.

Another valentine that I cherish came from a student named Clifford in my eighth-grade class in 1964. Clifford was your typical at-risk-kid. He was mouthy, cocky and primed for trouble.

I couldn't leave my classroom because I knew some of the bolder students would be extorting money from the weaker ones. When I left the classroom, I lined up and took three or four trouble-makers with me.

For some reason, Clifford and I hit it off. Finally at a meeting of the teachers of Clifford and his mother, they expelled him. I was the only teacher who said positive things about him.

He returned after his suspension and got into trouble with the law. He asked me to appear as a character witness for him at the hearing. I went, and he was placed on probation.

Valentine's Day came and went. In with the other valentines that I received was one from Clifford. He could draw and the card showed a funny teacher saying the student has some good qualities. The second drawing showed the student saying "Thank You."

I still hear from Clifford, who did not go to jail, but went on to college to be a teacher who influences the live of others.

Valentine's Day this year will find me looking at the valentines I receive from the students I work wit has a counselor and reminiscing about past valentines

St. Louis trip remembered

When I think of trains and train rides, I think of Kansas City and the 1960's and integration. At that stage of my life, I had just graduated with my maters degree in sociology. I was full of enthusiasm and just knew I was going to help solve the world's problems.

Every year the Missouri State teachers met either in Kansas City or St. Louis. If they met in St. Louis the schools in Kansas City each elected two delegates to represent them in St. Louis. I taught at Central High School for three years and was a representative delegate for two years.

We rode the train, which left from Union Station in Kansas City, to St. Louis. You could meet fellow teachers and exchange gossip, teaching tips, and enjoy elegant food on beautiful china and enjoy many cups of coffee.

The Union Station was a beautiful building with elegant marble. The place bustled with people and trains coming and going. I liked to watch the people and invent ages, lives, and scenarios for them I guess that was the writer in me even then. If they could have read my mind they might have been astounded by some of the lives I'd invented for them.

The two days we spent at the teacher's meeting were always full. You had to take notes so you could relay the information at the faculty meetings.

The last trip I made on the train to St. Louis as a teacher delegate stands out in my mind. The tracks ran through a farmer's cattle field, and there had been a break in the fence and cows had gotten out and were all over the track at midnight.

By the time the farmer was located, cows corralled, we had been there an hour.

My husband worked the extra board for Greyhound during these trips, and my father fell heir to picking me up. This was at two in the morning. I'll never forget him saying, "I thought when you married, my pick-up days ended but I guess I was wrong."

Salty talking parrot keeps Peddler Company on road

As I think about various peddlers and hucksters I have know, one is outstanding.

He was my mother's Uncle Riley. When I was about 10 years old, I can remember them arriving to visit us in Kansas City in the 1940's. He drove a panel truck filled with all kinds of tools and trinkets and medications with wondrous healing properties.

If you needed something, he could always reach into that truck and pulls it out, kind of like a magician waving a wand and producing a rabbit out of a hat.

Another interesting thing about this truck was a mean parrot that would just as soon bite you as look at you. He had a colorful X-rated vocabulary that would beat a salty sailor's. I believe Riley would have fitted in better with life in the late 1800's driving a wagon and traveling the west.

Manner trucks and horses were among my favorite peddlers because they always brought good thing to eat. My mouth would water as I heard the clop-clop of his horse's hooves.

Before refrigerators were invented, we had ice boxes. Trucks brought ice to our house so we could keep the food cool. Milk wagons came by bringing their daily allotted bottles of milk. My husband's family owned a dairy in the 1930's and 1940's.

In the 1950's I taught school nine months, and during the summer I peddled an assortment of items. The one I remember the most was a reducing table. I was a sales person who called on leads given to me by the company. They expected us to dress up and wear hose and heels while carrying their forty-pound reducing machines. I think I sold four before I gave up from exhaustion. Working for them helped me be a good advertisement for their machine. I demonstrated these to women with their husbands looking on and making comments.

Another one of my ventures was selling a vacuum cleaner. I had to demonstrate it to people who just wanted their houses cleaned up. One call I made was to an old geezer who had wolfish tendencies. I was lucky to get me and my vacuum cleaner out in one piece.

I also did surveys for a drug company. I made an appointment with the doctor and filled out the survey. The doctor and I both got paid for our time. I enjoyed doing this. At least I was not lugging heavy objects.

I admire people who sell things and hold sales positions. In later life, I sold puppies to pet shops all over the United States; this was much

Mary Bechtold

easier than my earlier sales ventures. It takes special people to sell things. My hat is off to them.

Fall is my favorite time of the year

When I think of fall days one of my favorite memories is seeing hundreds of beautiful butterflies gathered at the back of our house and barn in the warm sunlight. They were yellow, red, blue and almost all the colors of the rainbow. This was God's harvest of beautiful creatures to feast our eyes on.

We were also blessed with apples red and golden. The trees surrounding our house would have beautiful red and green leaves. We had more then enough apples to share with our neighbors.

Our pond would fill up with geese winging their way south to warmer climates. Their visit was short. While they were there they spent their time honking.

The fall meant that students were beginning a new year and the teachers were getting a new crop of children. I always liked the smell of a freshly polished classroom and new books. School buses were running up and down the gravel roads carrying their precious cargo of children twice a day.

Hayrides were popular at this time of the year. You needed a jacket because nights were cool. Our church sponsored the hayrides and my husband and I got to ride along with them.

Only one thing spoiled my remembrances of fall. You would hear bang, bang in our woods and know that hunters had sneaked onto our property to hunt in the woods.

I think fall was my favorite time of the year because it was the end of the growing season and crops were harvested. I went to school for 18 years of my life. I taught school for almost 20 years. I still feel the urge to find a classroom and go teach.

CHAPTER 7

COUNSELING

Start of Counseling Career First Elementary Counselor in Kansas City area

While I was teaching at Central High in Kansas City Missouri, I discovered I had more luck with some juvenile delinquents if I knew something about their previous school histories I scanned the school files and cautiously approached my most disruptive students. I asked them what they really liked to do I had the students to write papers about how they liked to spend tier time outside school. They read the papers in class and made a class newspaper out of the stories. Slowly their behavior in class improved. Discovering that I had to know the whole person, I took more guidance classes in my education master classes.

One Sunday I read a classified ad in the Kansas City Star. "Adventuresome teacher wanted to start one of the first Guidance Programs in Missouri. I answered the ad with a resume and was interviewed. I got the job working as an elementary counselor for seven schools in the Hickman Mills School District I also got to develop an elementary guidance program. I worked two full days in one school and half days at the other schools. I woke up early every day and hurried to get there I enjoyed the work so much. Students were referred by the teacher for counseling on a one on one basis. I gave individual intelligence tests. Time flew by. I kept folders on the individual students I worked with and worked up reports on the children who needed to be sent to a psychologist at the Psychiatric Receiving Center a psychologist at the

Psychiatric Receiving Center approached me with the idea of starting a classroom for disturbed children at the center. This became a new focus for me as I ventured into a new world.

I found that I liked being an elementary guidance counselor more than working with severely disturbed children and being under scrutiny by all kinds of visitors. I had always wanted children and I had the opportunity to adopt one. I had to stop working so I would be ready to stay home with the child. My life now had a new focus.

Guidance for Elementary Grades

"Unmarried, sixteen year old is found shot to death in her home with her seventeen month old son standing unharmed beside her."

To many newspaper readers, accustomed to reading of crime and violence, the story was not of particular significance.

For the author, the above mentioned story was a painful experience because of memories of the girl who had been my student two years ago.

The girl had been in my eighth grade class; handicapped by a third grade reading ability and poor writing and study habits.

School for her was an unhappy experience with little self-satisfaction in her low grades. She frequently was truant as apparently she found more ego satisfaction in companionship with dropouts.

It is not surprising that she became pregnant before the end of the school year. This is typical of girls in underprivileged neighborhoods, products of their environment.

Welfare and social workers are aware of this process because many of the children they aid have the same background.

It is difficult to rise above one's surroundings without special help. This girl who followed her mother's example represents a failure by the family to provide her with proper moral standards and values and failure by the public school to take over the function that the family fails to provide.

The young mother might have been saved if she and her family had had help and guidance by school personnel in elementary schools she attended.

Junior high school, where the first full time guidance counselors are provided in so many large cities, was too late for her as it was here that her education was terminated because of pregnancy.

At present, there should be one guidance counselor for every 200 pupils if the school system is to have triple A rating. The ratio between guidance counselors and students should be lower for schools in under privileged areas because of a high truancy rate, high rate of disciplinary cases, many underachievers and many non motivated students.

Noted writer in the fields of delinquency and education believe work with potential dropouts and delinquents should begin in elementary school. It is here that children's personalities and ideas are the most malleable.

All elementary schools in lower class neighborhoods should have professional certified guidance counselors. There should be also one social worker from the state Welfare Department and visiting teachers assigned to work closely with these elementary guidance counselors.

The visiting teacher, counselor and social worker should visit with the families of these children so the family and school can co-operate for the best interests of the child.

If a family is unable to buy the required school material for the child or feed him properly there should be an independent fund set aside for this purpose.

The Kansas City school system has such a fund to provide underprivileged children with needed supplies.

Class loads should be reduced in underprivileged neighborhoods so teachers may have more time with their pupils individually and each child can be aided to develop to his maximum potential.

Teachers in this underprivileged area should be especially chosen for and placed by a school system in this area. Teachers in these schools should be mature, emotionally stable, tolerant and aware of community value and problems in the area where they are assigned.

Perhaps school systems might rotate older personnel so that what might be considered the less choice assignments should not go to inexperienced personnel. Experienced teachers in these areas would give the newer teacher a feeling of security and lend an atmosphere of stability.

It is easier to prevent tragedies from occurring than it is to deal with the event itself. By the time under privileged children reaches junior high school it is more difficult to adequately help them.

Guidance and delinquency prevention programs of secondary schools would be more effective if begun in elementary school where changing the personality and influencing character development of the elementary school pupils is more successful.

Guidance programs along this line have been instituted in New Your City and St. Louis. Although still in the formulative stages, the programs in both cities have increased understanding and co-operation between the family and the school and reduced the dropout rate considerably.

Sociologist and psychologists ponder juvenile court statistics. Educators talk about increasing discipline problems, devil may care attitude among students and dropouts.

If anything can be done to help underprivileged children, schools must begin their guidance programs in the elementary school and work toward the prevention of juvenile delinquency through the proper guidance of parents and their children.

A cause for counseling

School is related to juvenile delinquency in three ways. It may produce delinquency; it may help to prevent delinquency or it may deal with delinquent behavior encountered within it walls.

Many feel that the school is the most important strategic community agency in the effort to prevent delinquency since the school reaches practically all children at relatively early periods of growth when children are the most malleable.

For many maladjusted and potentially delinquent children high school is just another frustrating and unhappy experience. Much need to be done in revising the over-all school curriculum to relate it to the life experience of your so—called delinquents.

The counseling program needs to be revitalized to help potential drop outs and disturbed delinquents realize how remaining in school will aid them in their future life.

Counselors also should work closely with delinquents to make them feel they are apart of the school and are wanted.

The counseling program can help to combat delinquency by developing programs to fit the school community by establishing the best possible school environment, and by giving the so-called delinquent a feeling of belonging and a sense of achievement.

The counselor deals with the child as a whole in the situation as a whole and co-ordinates all specialized information which psychologists, psychiatrist and physicians can contribute to schools its teachers, parents and welfare workers.

Clinically a delinquent is a juvenile who habitually resolves his personal social problems through aggressive behavior which the dominant society finds bothersome and contrary to value identification. Legally speaking a delinquent is a child between the age's oaf seven and 17 who had committed a crime, has had a juvenile court hearing and has been pronounced guilty.

As the reader can see by the two definitions the psychologist, psychiatrist, sociologist and lawyer look at delinquency from a different view point. The counselor should be widely read in all fields and have a broad understanding of the problem of juvenile delinquency. He also must be able to distinguish the true delinquent behavior from the normal adolescent rebellion against adult authority.

The counselor must establish and preserve a positive attitude toward the delinquent as a child needing help. The counselor can't maintain an effective rapport with the juvenile If he identifies with the multitude attacking juvenile delinquency.

The counselor must be aware of tell-tale signs identifying the potential delinquents. These factors can be divided into three categories: personal, home and family environment and school.

Some of he factors are: associates with others who are or have been delinquent, feels disliked or unwanted, poor home discipline, family belong to group, lives in multi-family dwelling, dislikes school is truant from school frequently family is mobile or migratory. For more information about theses factors, the reader should consult the Glueck Predication tables and the K. D. Proneness Scale and Check List.

Another way the counselor can help to prevent delinquency is to use and be apart of child study and diagnostic resources.

In areas with high delinquency rates the counselor in secondary schools should work closely with the case workers of the juvenile court and the welfare agencies. If the counselor is aware of the child's environmental conditions outside the school and works with e community agencies serving families the guidance program for potential delinquents can be much more effective.

The counselor effective in combating juvenile delinquency will be aware of the implications of research in his field and will attempt to implement these promising practices and will strive to evaluate his

Mary Bechtold

effectiveness in spite of the rash of subjective and personal opinions that may be in the air as the best ways and means of handling juvenile offenders. The counselor should review the case from time to time as new evidence and insights are developed.

The guidance counselor playing the adult authority role may use his special training and skill in establishing a therapeutic relationship with a potential or active delinquent in the school. The guidance counselor or in this role will give the delinquent a model for him to imitate and will be effective in making a positive change in his behavior.

Influences in the school, home and community that contribute to delinquency must be identified realistically. The counselor must understand the factors that contribute to poverty in his own community and work constructively with others to overcome it while helping pupils to forty themselves against its damaging influences.

The counselors can also assist delinquency-prone pupils by job placement. Since economic factors are frequently one cause of delinquent conduct, financial security through part time employment is often an essential consideration in the rehabilitation of delinquent youth.

The counselor has the strategic role to play in the guidance of all youth, whether he is a member of the delinquent two percent or one of the "normal" adolescent populations.

Elementary Guidance—Then and Now

In November of 1963, I wrote an article for School and Community entitled "That Ounce of Prevention—Guidance for Elementary Grades". I based this article on the need for earlier prevention than junior high in children's lives if the school was going to make significant changes in these children's lives.

I began my teaching career with the Kansas City School system at Central Junior and Central Senior. Our classes of common Learning had 40 pupils in them. Our textbooks were written at the eighty grade level. Two thirds of my students were lucky if they read at the third grade level. I adapted my lesson plans and watered down the textual material. My students responded by doing he work when they could understand it.

Children who can't learn many times compensate by disrupting the class. If one can't get attention by doing good schoolwork, eh achieves it in other ways.

In order to change the classroom behavior of my rowdy students, I started to study them one by one. I looked over their cumulative records, visited their homes, kept them in after school and talked to them individually. The same patterns kept emerging, single parent homes, no father figures, gang memberships, resentment of authority figures, and minor scrapes with the juvenile court system.

I felt that I could have helped these children more if I could have started to work with them in elementary school. School periodicals were saying the elementary counselors were being trained in teacher's colleges. I went back that summer to get in Master's in Elementary Guidance.

Hickman Mills had an opening in September 1964 for one guidance counselor for seven schools on an experimental basis. My job description was evolving as I worked that year. I worked that year with students that were referred by the teachers on the referral slips that I left in each building. I tested children on individual intelligence tests, counseled the students referred, sent student to Kansas City Mental Health centers for complete psychological workups, referred parents and their children for counseling outside the school. Another one of my functions was a referral source for parents and teachers for consultation about classroom problems.

Thirty years later, I had an opportunity to go back into elementary counseling. I was employed by North Davies R III in the 1994-1995 school years. My job description as an elementary school counselor has changed in the past thirty years to keep up with developmental changes in our society as well as our country's lifestyle.

To be fully accredited, schools in Missouri may employee elementary school counselors. The emphasis on the program now is on prevention of problems before they arise. The counselor teaches classes to all the grades such as understanding yourself and others, getting along with your family, knowing how drugs affect me and others, decision making, careers and the kinds of occupations the student might be interested in, how to study more reflectively and sexual discrimination.

I do counseling with at risk students, students in small groups, counseling with children who refer themselves or are referred by teachers, report child abuse and plan workshops to help parents become better parents by acquiring new tools through workshops. I am also available to teachers and parents as a resource person.

I now am able to see the promise that I felt the elementary counseling program has from the beginning. From my perspective of wanting to see an elementary counseling program implemented, I have come full circle to seeing how helpful the program can be by working with the child when he is younger and more malleable. Students who are headed in the wrong direction, class clowns, non workers, and bullies, shy and resentful children are still young enough to be helped before their bad habits become ingrained. I have been fortunate enough to see a program implemented and see how it works.

Why a full-time elementary counselor?

Through personal experience I have come to believe that counseling in elementary schools is a must. If our school or district doesn't have at least one counselor, you should campaign for one. Suggest that adding a counselor to your school staff would be a good use of ESEA funds. In your campaign you can stress why counseling before children reach junior high age is so important and you can describe some of the services a counselor renders.

Need for guidance

Need for guidance in the early school years is attested to by the following facts: Statistically antisocial tendencies manifest themselves in children between the ages of seven and ten; the problems that turn children into school dropout begin to develop whiled they are still in the grades; and weaknesses in subject matter that handicap students in high school and college begin to develop long before those levels are reached.

Other factors, both in and out of school, which increase the need for early guidance, are:

Population explosion: In a too crowded classroom, often staffed by inadequately prepared teachers, the withdrawn child may be overlooked and the aggressive one over disciplined while the average student goes unchallenged.

Population mobility: The child who has left familiar faces behind and must adjust to new surroundings, new children, and new teachers often needs special help.

Working Mothers: When both parents are employed outside the home, children may suffer from lack of companionship and adult supervision, and from weakened family ties.

Broken homes: A child who is reared in a home with one parent, or has a stepparent, or must share his natural parents, on some court-ordered schedule unquestionably, need understanding and counseling not required, by the child in a home untouched by divorce or separation.

Mental illness: Emotional disorders have their roots in attitudes of the past as well as in situation of the present. Guidance personnel, alert to sign of damaging emotion in children, may help to change the conditions which evoke such emotions.

What guidance does?

Counseling services at all levels—elementary, junior high, and senior high—assist students in making a better overall adjustments to school, to themselves, and to society. The desirable development of the individual so as to increase his chances of success in adult life is the goal of these services. Emphasis is on early identification of a pupil's intellectual, emotional, social and physical characteristics, development of his talents, diagnosis of any learning difficulties, and early use of community resources to meet his needs.

Guidance, like other school functions, requires the cooperation of all members of the school staff. All are concerned with preventing problems or detecting minute ones before they grow.

A counselor's duties

Through the responsibilities assumed by counselors vary, my own duties are sufficiently definitive to use for campaign purposes. They can be roughly divided into three parts: acting as a resource person, testing and counseling children.

As a resource person, I

1. Interpret to teacher's parents and administrator the results of group intelligence tests and achievement tests.
2. Discuss with teachers children who have problems and help teachers who have such children develop techniques for aiding them to solve problems.
3. Give talks at PTA meetings, service clubs, and wherever there is interest in learning about the counseling program.

My testing responsibilities are:

1. Testing children who may be candidates for special education classes.
2. In the spring, testing kindergarten children who, according to their teachers, have emotional problems or are not of average ability.
3. Testing children new to the district.
4. Administering individual intelligence tests to children whose scores on group tests are very low or very high or are open to question.

Some of the direct counseling services I render are:

1. Counseling children who have minor personal problems that interfere with school work.
2. Working with underachieving children.
3. Giving diagnostic reading tests to children with reading problems and make specific recommendations for correcting difficulties.
4. Meeting with parents of children for whom the district provides no school services, for the purpose of finding ways to get special help.
5. Studying children considered emotionally disturbed, giving personality tests to determine the severity of the problem and conferring with the parents.

6. Working with psychiatrist and various agencies in behalf of individual children.

7. Interpreting to the teacher of an atypical child the findings of psychiatrists and the recommendation of therapist.

8. Assisting teachers with children who consistently require some form of discipline.

Silent Partner to a parent's Brutality

The nine year old was nervous and high strung. His teacher had sent him to the counseling office because he was hyperactive and aggressive toward others in the classroom.

Foremost in my mind was "What is causing the child's difficulty in adjusting to school routine?"

I examined the cumulative recorder card carefully before our interview. His intelligence and achievement test scores showed that he was capable of doing superior work.

This variable eliminated, we next concentrated on learning as much as we could about how he felt abut such things as his classmates, his parents, his brother and sisters.

I tried a word-association test on him when I mentioned the word father, his eyes dilated and he whispered "strict".

When I gave the word brother, he said "run away." On the Michigan Pictures Test, he told a story about a little boy and his father. He said the little boy was beaten and worked over with a rubber hose because he had spilled some shoe polish.

After I had been seeing the child regularly for a month, I noticed a pattern in the anecdotal records his teacher had been keeping, his behavior was much worse on Monday and Friday than on other days.

The child had told me he had a stepfather who took care of him while his mother worked.

One Monday the boy came to see me and asked if he could talk. He talked for over and hour. He unfolded a tale of horror that sounded as if it had come from a "chiller" movie.

He had been beaten over the weekend because he forgot to put the lid on the shoe polish. The step-father became angry when he found the shoe polish and took the child into the basement and beat him.

I had our nurse look at the child and she found black and blue marks on his body. The teacher when questioned also reported that he had had bruises on his face and a black eye.

The child also said his stepfather had spanked his three week old baby sister with a newspaper for crying.

When I asked him what his mother said, he quoted her as saying "If he is stupid enough to do things to make his stepfather angry he should get beat up."

I reported the gist of the preceding interview to my immediate superior who suggested I contact the Juvenile Court. I contacted a worker who asked me if I had witnessed the beating incident and if so I would sign a complaint? Of course, I hadn't seen it. We then let he matter drop since I was hearing the story from the child.

A few months went by; his teacher told me that he had broken his arm. The child told me his arm had been broken when his stepfather threw him on the floor. This happened on Saturday but the parents had not had the arm set until Tuesday.

I was in exactly the same position that I was when he told me about the beating with the rubber hose. I was not a witness. If I signed a complaint, I could be held liable if the charges were proved to be false.

The father would be told that the school had filed a complaint. This would not have made for a congenial relationship between family and school. The juvenile worker told me it was their policy to leave the child in the family setting if at all possible.

In my search for assistance, I turned to the Youth Bureau of the local law enforcement agency who said that they would investigate any evidences of child brutality without involving the reporting school officials.

By the time I contacted the police, the child's broken arm had healed and now I have to wait until the child is mistreated by his stepfather again before I call the police.

I cannot help but worry about the child who lives in this type of home environment. How can he become anything but a warped personality if he's lucky enough to live through the beating to maturity!

PTA's and all school groups should be working for legislation that would protect doctors and professional people such as school psychologist from liability suits by the parents of the "battered child."

A uniform procedure should be worked out so that each professional person who comes in contact with a child who has been brutally misused by his parents would know immediately what steps to take to protect this mistreated child and prevent recurrence of the same situation.

Instances of child mistreatment and brutality are on the increase. My conscience will not let me be a willing accessory to a child's abuse if I can take the necessary steps to call it to the attention of proper authorities.

Job after Prison

After I left the prison, I saw an ad in our newspapers "Part time Counselor needed" I called and they wanted to see me and read my resume. This job was for the Coffee Jameson School district. I didn't know what I was getting into. Their counselors were being hired because the district needed them for recertification. It was a small school only sixty students in the elementary and high school. I was to work two days week. I didn't know I would be developing a program for the elementary school from scratch. The staff at the elementary school was helpful and I liked the students. I would take an entire class and do individual counseling of students referred to me by teachers. Role playing was something you could do with an entire class. We did role playing on subjects such as getting along with others: what happened when you smoked, how to be respectful to teachers friends and parents, how to not succumb to drugs, One particularly favorite role playing was how to understand how other people felt when you were insulting or bullying them. We were visited by counselors and counseling students from Missouri Western. They came to visit numerous times.

As an experiment I took the preschoolers and worked with them on role playing. We worked on such subjects as, do not interrupt the teacher do not hit or make fun of other people. They were with me a half hour but, I felt their attention span was too short for more time with me

Later on in the year found out that I had the elementary guidance program to write. I did this on my own time in the summer. I got it done and the district was certified.

My husband started having problems with his heart. I got a call at the school that was an emergency. I had to take him to St. Louis Hospital. I resigned at the end of the year, from the school.

I missed all the children and teachers. I enjoyed the three years that I spent at Coffee. This was a thoroughly enjoyable experience. I sometimes see some of the adults that I worked with as well as children.

CHAPTER 8

CHILDREN

Julie with horses

Calamity Julie has many a mishap

When I think of incidents that were not funny years ago, I think of my daughter, Julie, when she was growing up.

She had just gotten her driver's license permit and I had gotten a new Ford Station wagon. She borrowed it to go two miles to the Kidder

Kurve for gas. She came home without the gas can, with the neighbor bringing her.

My station wagon was one half mile up the road and looked like it was climbing a telephone pole. The car was a total loss. That was not funny then, but it is now in the annals of family history.

When she was ten she liked to read, she got a new radio that was battery operated for Christmas. She climbed a tree to sit and read and listen to music. The radio fell out the tree and had to be replaced.

Many incidents happened with her horses. One day she was riding and got a phone call. She handed me the horse's reins and I was to hold the horse until she got off the telephone. For some reason the normally friendly-to-people horse reached out and bit me. That really hurt and I was so mad that I was steaming.

When she received a phone call another time she was again riding. She tied the horse to the propane tank. In her struggle to get away, she overturned the tank. Fortunately, it did not explode.

Those were not the only incidents involving Julie and her horses. Her horse got out on the road and she went after her in the car. Somehow, the horse broke the windshield of the car. She had a date that night and let us to care for the car's windshield.

One other incident did not involve a horse. She decided to hard boil and egg in the microwave. She forgot to pierce the egg. That was one hard microwave to clean I left that to Julie.

Julie is a responsible adult now. She helps her parents and other people in many ways. I used to call her Calamity Jane. I am so glad we have been privileged to see her grow up and become a responsible adult.

Adoptions brighten couple's world

"Every cloud has a silver lining" means that you should never feel hopeless, because difficult times always lead to better days.

One of the darkest clouds in my life was the fact that my husband and I had been married 10 years and had no children. My brothers were married and had children. My closet friend, Vernilda, was married and had four children.

Eugene and I enjoyed our life and our respective careers. We liked our life but, we felt like something was missing to make our family complete. My career was counseling children and working with them five days a week. I couldn't take them home.

We talked to our parish priest and he urged us to adopt children. We applied to Catholic charities and were approved after home studies and investigations.

Our first child, Marijean, came February of 1966. She was three days old. When we picked her up, she had dark eyes and a head of coal black hair. We were told she couldn't lift her head up. The first thing she did was to lift her head up and look around. Life after that became a series of night feedings and visits to the pediatrician. Our dog didn't adapt well to this tiny intruder who made so much noise.

Baby showers and people admiring her in the supermarket were common. All the kids in the neighborhood wanted her to come out and play. She crawled, walked, talked and did everything early.

One and a half years later at Christmas, we got a second daughter, Julie. She was the best Christmas present I ever received. She was blond, bald and beautiful.

After that, life became busy with kindergarten, brownies, baseball, riding lessons, dancing lessons, boys, prom and college. The years passed quickly.

We moved to a farm when they were small and one daughter had sheep for 4-H and the other had horses and dogs. Julie's passion for horses still exists to this day. She has five horses now.

My daughter Julie expressed it best: "God matched us as parents and children and that's the way it was supposed to be." I could not have had biological children that could have fulfilled my life more than these two girls have. My two grandchildren are 13 now.

One's purpose in life is to leave something of yourself behind in your children and their offspring when you die.

In my case, not having biological children just opened the door for the silver lining in our lives in so many ways. Our cloud disappeared and the sun burst forth with a new glory.

Four generations

Children tie together Christmases past, present and future.

Whenever, I think of the story of Ebenezer Scrooge, I remember the ghosts of Christmas past, present and future.

My Christmas tree lights are flicking off and on as I reminisce and start thinking of Christmas pasts that no longer exist, except in my memories.

I have fond memories of my childhood and going to my great-grandmother's house in the Smithville area. I liked looking at her large, Victorian house, with all the beautiful whatnots.

All my great-uncles and aunts, as well as my grandparents have passed on, but they live on as I think about Christmases past.

I liked watching the women prepare the traditional Christmas feast. The men were always served first, and women and girls ate at the second table. The ladies, however, saved some of the goodies back for the women, so we wouldn't get the running gears. I always felt that people should all eat together.

As time passed, I grew up, married and went to eat Christmas dinner at my mother's house. She lived in Gladstone, and my brothers and our families gathered there for the holidays. We enjoyed good fellowship and food as we gathered.

I now am the grandmother, and my family gathers at my house for the traditional holiday feast. We all eat at the same table—men and women alike. I don't think my dinners taste as good as I remember tastes and smells from the past.

I think that one of my best memories of Christmas was when my children had gone to bed at Christmas and had visions of Santa Claus and Rudolph dancing in their heads. I sat there watching the lights flicker. I had to hide Santa's present in my barn, tied up in a gunnysack so my nosy children couldn't find them. We had Sears & Roebuck and Montgomery Ward Christmas catalogues and they were well marked by my daughters, showing what they wanted. I thought I could hear sleigh bells tinkling as I went out to sneak their presents in. It was beginning to snow that evening.

Now, my children have children, and they are putting up their own trees and hiding present from nosy children who wonder what they are getting for Christmas.

As I look at pictures I realize how fortunate I am to have shared the lives of my daughters and their children. My Christmas past, present and future all come together in them.

Megan

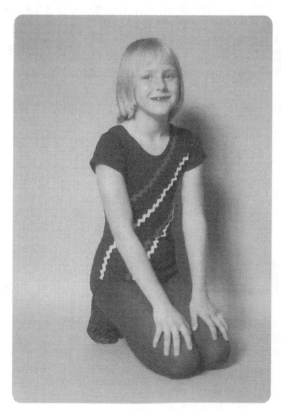

Julie

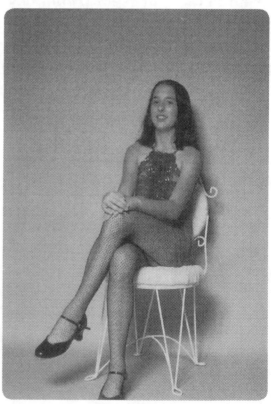

Mari-Jean

Dancing Feet

Whenever I think of dancing, I remember the little girls dressed up in their dancing costumes in the early 1970's. They tap-danced, did fancy turns to jazz music, and strutted their stuff at the local summer fairs. The acrobats even walked across exercise boards and twisted their bodies in various positions.

Marijean, my oldest daughter took to dancing like a duck to water. She continued lesson at Meri's dance studio until she graduated form Hamilton High School. She was one of the members of the dance team who went with the marching band. When she was ten, she dressed in a red dancing costume and did a tap dance solo at the Kidder picnic.

Julie, my younger daughter switched from tap to acrobatics and walked on the balance beam and did tumbling exercises. She continued acrobatics until she developed another all consuming interest—riding horses and showing them she used some the skills she acquired as an acrobat to show horse in 4-H completions. She has so many trophies and ribbons they fill one showcase.

They say that parents have their children do things that they would like to have done as children. When Julie's daughter, Megan was born I was thrilled another child who could take dancing lesson. When Megan was in preschool, she started her dancieng lesson. I was one proud grandmother, when I saw her in her red costume at the dance recital they put on for parents. Like her mother, she only danced for two years. She fell in love with horses and started to ride and enter competitions. I think dance lesson and acrobatics help build a child's agility and self confidence.

Back in the late 1930's and 1940's I went to square dancing and round dancing get-togethers with my parents. I love to hear the callers at the dances and the sound of the fiddles. All the children would get together and try to imitate their parents I come from a dancing family. Many of my relative could do the Irish jig. I love rock and roll and Elvis Presley tunes.

McDonald's Scare

Do you remember in earlier years when McDonald's was under fire from people who were waiting to harm the employees when they closed late at night? My daughter worked at the McDonald's in Cameron. She worked the night shift. I expected her home by 2:00 a.m. One night 3:00 a.m. came and went, no Julie. I threw a robe over my pajamas and drove off to McDonald's

The lights were burning brightly at Mcdonalds. I could see people inside. I drove around and around the building. People kept looking out and pointing at me. The employees looked frightened. They gestured and pointed to me as I drove around and around the building.

The parking lot was almost deserted except for the employee's cars. I got out of the car and walked up to one of the doors. The employees scattered to the back and the doors were locked. As I peered in the windows, who; should be looking back at me but, Julie. She went to the back and the other employees looked relieved to find that it was just an overprotective mother. They cancelled their call to the police.

Julie came out and I followed her on the highway. She left me behind with a sudden burst of speed. I was so rattled that I passed the road to our house I drove a mile to the next road. At night everything looked alien to me. I drove three miles before I got to a road which took me home. When I got there, Julie had gone to bed. I thought I would never live this incident down. It was the talk at the high school for a while.

Twins

Fraternal twins join farm family for awhile

My experience with multiple births has been limited to twins. The definition of twins is of two off-springs born at the same time. In the early 1970's my children were three and five. I had worked as the director of the Clay Plate Health and Welfare Council. In this position, I worked closely with the Director of Family Services in North Kansas City. After we moved to Kidder area, the Director of Family Services would come to our farm pond and hunt for frogs. One of his favorite foods was frog legs.

On one of his trips, he told me about fraternal twins who were in foster care and needed to be placed. They were three and needed temporary placement until they were adopted. I agreed to take them. Family services brought Norman and Terry to stay with us. They were beautiful children of Nordic descent. It was summertime and all four children played outside. I had to watch all of them closely to keep them away from the pond. I went in the house for a second. When I retuned, Norman was down by the pond taking his clothes off to dive into the

157

pond. He said," I'm going swimming." He spent considerable time in a chair in "time out" for that escapade.

We pastured cows, and kept them behind our house, fenced off with electric wire and barbed wire. Another time, Terry touched the fence and got zapped. I rushed out and she said, "I only wanted to play with the cows and the fence bit me."

They lived with us about six months before they were adopted. We were all sad to see them go, and our house seemed emptier after the left. Life went on. I often think of them and wonder what they are doing as adults.

Julie on horse

Greatest gift of all for her mother

In December 1967, I received the best Christmas present of my life. I was working as the volunteer director of the Clay Platte health and Welfare council in Kansas City. We lived in Gladstone with our 1 ½ year old—daughter Marijean.

It was a day like any other Dec 18. I had the Christmas tree up and the presents under it. The phone rang; it was Catholic Charities. The social worker told us to pick up our new daughter.

We made arrangements to pick her up Dec 21. We had three days to get ready. We needed baby furniture, clothes, presents—all the things a new baby would need. We shopped at breakneck speed.

Before we knew it, it was time to get our new daughter. That morning was a cold, snowy day. The trees were glistening with their white cover, and the world looked bright and new.

When we got to Catholic Charities, we were ushered into the office. There, in a baby carrier, sat a solemn little being looking at us. She was perfect from the top of her blond head to the bottom of her tiny feet. Blue eyes looked at us quizzically. We wrapped her up and took her to her new home. She looked at everything as we carried her into our home and made her a part of our lives.

Christmas that year seemed brighter because of Julie, our new daughter, our Christmas miracle. I have gone through many holiday seasons, but none better than the day Julie entered our lives. We were privileged to watch her grow from a tiny baby to a young woman with a family of her own.

She enriched my life with her love of horses and animals. Many incidents that occurred with these animals are fun to share with the children I counsel. They enjoy these stories as much as I enjoy telling them.

She has grown into a fine; sensitive woman who cares about other people and is dedicated to her job as an elementary school teacher. I think the world is going to be a better place because of her work in shaping young minds.

I get to watch my granddaughter, Megan, grow up. She looks exactly as Julie did when she was growing up.

As the year 1996 draws to a close, I can count my blessing as I think about the Christmas miracle so long ago.

Mary, Julie, Mari-jean

Harried mother of two

Have you ever known a harried mother of two daughters, fifteen and seventeen? I ran a business as well and tried to keep up with them. Needless to say I ran myself ragged.

Julie told me she had to stay at school and work on a float. M.J. the other sister told me she was going to an unsupervised party where the parents were not at home.

I took M.J. and she and I went to the house about 7:00 where the party was being held. Lights were on all over the house. Radios were blaring and I could see teenagers everywhere. I marched up the driveway lined with cars. I knocked on the door. Someone said come in.and I went in. They were not expecting an old cougar. The young people dove behind chairs out of sight. They did not want me to see them and tell their parents. There was what I thought was a pornographic movie playing; my daughter was on the sofa watching the movie with Budweiser in her hand. You should have seen the look on her face. Pure astonishment! You would have thought I was the wicked witch of Ender. I spied Julie and had her and her friend come with me. We made a grand exit with everyone staring at me. Julie was mad and flabbergasted to see me appear. She told me she was too old to be checked on by her mother. Surprise!

I learned a lot of my tactics from my mother who would chase off my boyfriend in her nightgown with bare feet.

One of the teachers at the high school thought I should not have done what I did and told the children in his classes that. I wonder what liberal planet he grew up on.

I think I scared every student in the school. I only did what I thought was right. I did not believe in unsupervised parties. I wonder if I was named the wicked witch of the West.

Megan on horse

Grandma Pinocchio

Have you ever heard of a Pinocchio nose? People joke about nosy people having them. I have a page on face book. A lot of relatives and friends have pages on there also. I like to read the home page and their pages and see what is going on in their lives and what they are thinking about.

About a week ago I was reading my daughter's page. And what do you think I was seeing? At the very top of the page it said "when you are coming home from work" and her daughter says "stop at the Cameron police station." This had been written the night before. I could not imagine what business my granddaughter had with the police. I called my daughter's roommate. She did not have a clue about the message. She preceded to text my granddaughter in her college class and told my grand daughter to call me. Mystery solved. The police had some stolen CD's of Megan's and wanted her to pick them up. Grandma's anxiety was alleviated and all was well on the home front. This is one incident I would have liked to avoided My Pinocchio nose made a mountain out of a mole hill. This will not stop me from reading face book's home page. Life goes on with many more interesting incidents ahead for me to see.

Three misses

I am going to tell you about three near misses that have incurred in my lifetime so far. The first happened when my father went to work on the road with the Koss Construction company building roads in Kansas. He left my mother and two brothers and me at home on an isolated acreage in Grandview, Mo. We had no car. We had no means of transportation except the schoolbus which stopped at the door. Our only way to go to the store was to ask the neighbors one half a mile away to take us. If we missed that bus we could not got to school.

We had two near misses while we lived there. My mother went outside to feed the chickens and left me babysitting my two year old brother. I turned my back on him and he got a hold of a bottle of coal oil. It was in a soda pop bottle, he drank the whole bottle. I suppose he thought it was soda pop. I rushed out to get my mother. We had no way to get him to the doctor. Mother kept feeding him whole milk. He finally threw up what he had drunk. I went to the dairy outside our house about one half mile away. They took us to the doctor and my brother was fine.

I had a way of getting into mischief. There were rails for a train outside our house we amused ourselves by seeing who could stay on the tracks the longest before jumping off when a train was getting close. Our guardian angels had to work overtime saving us from the blasting freight trains.

There was a high water tower down the road from us. It was very tall. My brother dared me to climb it. Fool that I was I did it. I got to the top easily Boy did it look like it was a long way down from the bottom I was afraid to come down. The sun went down with me still up there. My mother said 'If you want down, you can get down the way you got up'. I crept down slowly at dusk shaking all the way down. Needless to say I got the board of education for this stunt.

Pictures of four generations of horse Riders

Eugene Bechtold

Vivian Dale

Mary

Julie and Megan

Mary Bechtold

Independence Day celebrations bring a variety of activities

I believe that our past helps to shape us into what we become. Adventurous souls left England and the other European countries looking for freedom and a better life than they left behind. This country fought and won its freedom from an oppressive king. Ellis Island welcomed immigrants coming to make their fortunes in a new land.

My ancestor's came from Ireland and Germany. They moved westward with the tide of settlers wanting to stake their claim to land in the West.

As I draw former Fourth of July celebrations from my stock of memories, I think of growing up with park bands playing patriotic songs. There were family get-togethers with food—chicken, watermelon, muskmelon, potato salad, etc. We ate until we could hold no more.

Firefly collecting was a great sport when you put them in a jar to watch them light up. As the sun went down and the heavens became dark, firecracker displays would light up the heavens. We watched these celebrations of our country's birthday with wide eyes. I was always afraid of fire-crackers and never wanted to handle them.

When my own children were small and school was out, we always had the Kidder picnic to look forward to. You could go a mile away from home where you could eat your lunch or dinner and look at craft exhibits or flea markets. Children could win toys in various game booths or ride the carnival rides.

Marijean my daughter, always danced for Meri's dance studio as a solo or with a group. She loved tap dancing and jazz and performing.

Julie, my younger daughter, liked acrobatics, and performed with Meri's dance studio with acrobatic groups.

She also competed in 4-H horse shows at the picnic. It was a great treat to ride your horse over the show ground and give kids rides.

The Kidder picnic has been discontinued and my children are grown and have children of their own. My memories are rich with Fourth of July's past.

I am very fortunate to have been born in a country with such a diverse heritage that has allowed me to pursue and fulfill my dreams of how I wanted to live my life.

Pagan event turns popular

Halloween, which originated as a pagan festival for the dead, has survived in popular culture as a night of trick or treating by the children and others dressed in costumes of fantasy and the supernatural.

All-hallows Eve is observed the night of Oct 31 followed on Nov1 by All-hallows Day or All Saints Day. The ancient Celts observed it to celebrate the onset of winter and the beginning of the Celtic New Year. It was a solar festival marked by sacred fire and fire rituals.

Numerous folk customs connected with pagan observances for the dead have survived to the present. In addition to the souls of the dead roaming about the devil, witches and numerous spirits are believed to be out and at the peak of their supernatural powers.

In Ireland and Scotland, the custom of extinguishing one's home fire and re-lighting it from the festival bonfire has continued into modern times.

The custom of trick or treating has several origins. The Irish went from door to door to collect money, cheese, eggs and apples in preparation for the feast of St. Colombo Kill. Soul cake begging or offerings of one's self helping in exchange for promises of great riches or protection against bad luck are ancient forerunners of modern-day trick or treating.

When we live in Gladstone, Mo., a residential suburb, we stocked up on candy in preparation for Halloween and spent Halloween answering the door to little trick-or-treaters. I liked looking at the children in their costumes with little pumpkin bags in the late 1950's and early 1960's.

When my children were small, we moved to the Kidder area on a 180-acre farm, with the nearest neighbors about one mile away. My Halloween nights changed dramatically. In the last 25 years. I have probably had a total of 20 trick-or-treaters.

When my children wanted to go trick or treating, we dressed them up and drove them over the countryside, where they would unload and ring the doorbell and yell, "Trick or treat'.

Both girls have grown up and are going trick or treating with their own children and are answering the doorbell to little spooks and goblins trick or treating.

I was born in the wee hours of Nov1, All Saints Day. I'm glad I missed being born on Halloween and being mistaken for a spooky changeling of the Halloween spirit.

Mary Bechtold

Pets enjoy holidays along with owners

When I think of past holidays I remember Christmases and Thanksgivings past. My mother lived in Kansas City and we all went to her house to enjoy a holiday feast. My two brothers and their families and mine would get together and enjoy holiday feasts. We would visit and get caught up on happenings in our lives during the past year. We all enjoyed watching the children unwrap their presents.

My mother is now in her 90's and I'm in my 70's. We go to Thanksgiving and Christmas dinners at my nieces and nephews houses. My daughters live in other states and are lucky to make in home for one holiday. Their children are teenagers and they like to have their celebrations at home with their friends.

I spend a lot of time with my three small dogs that enjoy the holidays as much as we do. Leftover turkey and ham finds its way to their food bowls. Animals sense your moods and offer a great deal of comfort and companionship to their owners. My daughter, who is an animal lover put presents and treats for her dogs and horses under her tree, I have wrapped presents for mine also.

I enjoy the hustle and bustle of the holiday season. I like to go to the stores and watch the children looking at the myriad of toys, books, puzzles and DVD's that say, when you gaze at them, "Wouldn't you like to have me?"

I am sitting here looking at my Christmas angels and Christmas tree with the flashing lights.

The mail brings lots of catalogs with gift ideas. I enjoy looking through them. I buy many of my gifts from them. No wonder so many of them find their way in the mail to my house.

This year, I will be attending a Christmas dinner at my niece's and other dinners of the organizations that I belong to. What a happy time that will be.

See inside for stories about Mom, Dad, country schools, the Great Depression and more. For information about cover photos, please see Page 2.

BY THE *St. Joseph News-Press*

New paper article of Julie

Prizes won at the Kidder picnic

When my family moved to Kidder, Mo. One of the highlights of the year was the Kidder Picnic in the summer.

For three days we enjoyed the park in Kidder where the picnic was held. There was a snack shack where delicious hot dogs, hamburgers and barbecue sandwiches were sold. The local woman made and donated pies. We also stuffed ourselves on homemade ice-cream.

Carnivals would come and set up shop in the park. My daughters always enjoyed riding the merry go round, the Ferris wheel and other flying swings. They also wanted money to shoot at targets and win stuffed rabbits and bears. One carried a bear home that was bigger than she was.

Both of my daughters were in Meri's Dance Studio. Marijean performed on the stage in a red dancing costume. She also did acts for the talent shows. She did this many times over the years.

Julie my other daughter did acrobatics. She loved horses. She competed in every horse show. Julie rode her horse the mile up to Kidder on a gravel road to the show with her parents following in the car.

She competed for prizes in the arena. She won many trophies over the years. One of the top things that she enjoyed was giving the other children rides on her horse.

I enjoyed the baby contests and shows for the cutest little Mister and Miss. My husband like the horseshoe pitching games, another favorite was the bands that played cowboy music while the Ferris wheel whirred.

Today the Kidder Picnic goes on. My daughter Julie is in charge of the horse show. The children compete for prizes like saddles, bridles scholarships and other horse equipment. Thinking about the Kidder Picnic takes me a long way down memory lane into my past.

Quick slap upside head fixes bad attitude

Discipline in this day and age is not corporal punishment. Rewards are used for good behavior and privileges are taken away for unacceptable behavior. Time out is used with small children.

When I was growing up, discipline was meted out quickly, I can remember being kindergarten age and wanting to stay with my grandparents. When you stayed with them, you got everything you wanted. I would tear up my aunt's dolls; eat so much candy it would make me sick.

My mother had been a school teacher and she felt that you needed to go to school. When I cried to stay, my dad picked me up and gave me several pats on the rear. I went home and went to school. I feel my parents did the right thing.

When I was older my brothers Bobby and I would fight and holler when we were going somewhere in the car. My dad said, "You have been picking at each other . . . now fight it out." Bobby and I looked at each other horrified. We tapped each other a few times. We never teased each other as we were riding down the road again.

We were never disrespectful to our parents. If you did retribution was swift—a quick slap upside the head.

As teenagers, we always had our curfews. If you violated that curfew, you could expect to see my mother in curlers and bare feet in her nightgown.

The latest I ever stayed out was three in the morning. I said, "I'm going home with him." She dashed out and grabbed me by the ear. My date screeched his tires and took off like a bullet.

My daughters liked to pick at each other in the back seat while I was driving some where. I got angry, pulled over to the side of the road and we got out and I gave them three swats on the rear. Funny, how you pattern your self after your parents.

I had a habit of leaving my belongings everywhere. My mother got tired of it and picked my things up and hid them. That stopped my leaving thing all over the house.

My daughter Julie also likes to leave things everywhere. I told her to pick up her room. She went in with me and said she couldn't see anything on the floor. I took a trash bag and started picking up goodies. She said, "Hey, I can see them now." She proceeded to pick up the remaining items. I kept the confiscated toys for a few days before returning them.

My other daughter Marijean, tried playing sick when she was in elementary school. I was ready for her. She had to stay in bed, no telephone, no television. She could read. After one day of bed rest she was ready to go back to school. I had played the same trick on my mother, only my fate was worse. I was dosed with castor oil.

My parents were good to their children, the discipline was not harsh. They wanted us to grow up to be decent citizens, respect our elders and other people and obey the laws of the land.

Shade Tree Mechanics

During the Great Depression years we lived in a farming area. My father grew up on these farms and spent many hours helping keep the farm machinery going. We couldn't afford to have our old Model T worked on so, he raised the hood and by trial and error got it going.

My brother watched my father work in his cars and passed this talent onto the children. As the only daughter, I wasn't interested in what was under the hood. I could not drive a stick shift. The push button Mercury solved my dilemma. There was only on mechanical monster my father tackled that defeated him. He worked on a coal furnace, kicked it and had it removed for a wonderful furnace that used electricity. We were glad because we didn't have to keep coal going into the furnace to keep warm.

My daughter, Julie had talent with being a shade tree mechanic. She started at and early age overhauling her clippers and saddles. Today she can chop down trees, overhaul mowers when they do not work to mention a few of her talents. She puts up electric fences to keep her horses in. When I need help with something mechanical I call upon her. Necessity and curiosity let her to work on her own machinery and appliance. My father would have been proud of the talents if he had lived to see what she could do.

Sweet Valentine

When we think of February, we think of Valentine's Day with its cards, boxes of candy in the shape of hearts and cupid shooting his arrows into lovers.

February with its promise of spring soon to come means something else to me. My daughter Marijean was born on February 27. She was a late Valentine's Day present. When we brought her home, childhood experts told us she wouldn't be able to hold her head up. I looked in her bedroom that night and she had her head up looking around; she knew it was not the hospital.

All her life, she has been curious about the world around her and other people. We lived on a farm and she could hardly wait to go to school. When the kindergarten bus came, she was jumping up and down waiting for the big yellow bus. I didn't have any trouble getting her to go to school. She liked dancing lesson and appeared in many dance recitals and enjoyed doing something that came naturally to her.

She was a cheerleader, FFA princess and homecoming princess in high school. After graduation from high school, she went to college, where she studied interior design. She likes to watch the decoration channels and is interested in antiques today. She has another birthday coming up as I write this story. She was my best Valentine's Day present.

One Valentine's Day, my friend Ginnie's husband bought her a dozen red roses. The truck did not have heat, so he drove home; when he got home the roses were blighted with frost. It was not the roses, but the thought that counted.

Another year, I sent my daughter, Julie a plant for Valentine's Day to her school in Colorado. Her student thought it was from her secret admirer. She never did tell them her parents sent it.

Visit from an animal guardian

One foggy morning a ghostly guardian was with my daughter Julies as she drove to college. Julie was passed by a speeding Mac truck that had almost side swiped a car in front of her. Suddenly, in the gray fog, a fuzzy, dirty little dog was weaving back and forth across the pavement. Julie with her characteristic concern for animals slowed down and turned around to go back and look for the pathetic scruffy canine.

As she drove the other way, the fog became thicker. When she reached the spot she spotted the elusive dog darting back and forth. She stopped the car, got out and tried to catch the elusive dog. Just when she thought she had him cornered, he would fade into the mist. She must have tried to catch him for twenty minutes. He just seemed to disappear.

As she looked at her watch she knew she was going to be late for class, she climbed into her car and headed for her college. As she drove by the car that had been ahead of her it was crushed beneath the speeding Mac truck.

Julie might have been beneath the huge truck except for her ghostly four legged guardian who detained her by darting back and forth across the road. Who is to say how many of our deceased four footed friends watch over us after they depart from this life. I believe they live beneath a rainbow bridge watching after us until we join them on our way across the rainbow bridge to heaven.

CHAPTER 9

EUGENE

Stonemason builds trade that unites history of two countries

The stone for the New Your Stock Exchange was quarried in Germany, where my husband's grandfather, William Bechtold was born. His grandfather was a stonemason by trade. He helped load stone on boat bound for the good ole U.S.A and New York City.

When the boat was loaded, he stowed away on it. He didn't land at Ellis Island where legal immigrants embarked, but slopped off under the cover of night at one of the eastern seaports.

He put his talents to work and helped build the New York Stock Exchange building. When this job was finished, he worked his way westward by plying his trade in the areas where he stopped to work and build up his funds. He finally settled in the area around Boonville, Mo., where the German Catholic population lived.

Many examples of William's work still stand at Boonville. He built the old jail there. On farms around Boonville, some of his tables and benches in stone still stand. He made stone foundation for houses and stone cullers.

My nephew visited the German branch of he Bechtold family, and the original houses that his grandfather lived in still are standing.

The First World War was a time of mixed feeling for William Bechtold. He loved his adopted country, but he felt certain loyalties for Germany, where he had been born. Feelings ran high as many Americans viewed the German immigrants as possible spies. The same thing happed to the Japanese Americans in World War ll.

William Bechtold had five sons. The descendants of these children live all over the United States, and many are still in the Boonville area. His story is the story of an individual who left everything behind to go to the New World and make a new life for himself with nothing but his two hands and the determination to succeed. His sons, like their forefathers learned a trade and did well in the new country of their birth.

I have always been fascinated by William's story and am pleased that I can put it in print.

Bechtold Family

German ancestors bring traditions

My husband's family and my own family have German ancestors who immigrated to America to make a better life for themselves and their off-spring. With them, they brought their old country traditions and festivals. Christmas was a day for celebrating the birth of Jesus Christ, who was born 2,000 years ago.

On the first Sunday after Nov 26, German children receive the Advent calendar from their parents. The calendar had bright little pictures with numbers and small paper windows. These calendars hang beside the beds, and children can open up a window each morning. Candles, bells or chocolate can be found inside the window.

Christmas came to the barbarians in Germany, brought by St. Nicholas, a fourth century bishop of Asia Minor.

Santa Claus was born to replace St. Nicholas, and wore a red suit and traveled in a sleigh drawn by reindeer.

The Christmas tree originated in Germany also. Again, folklore has it that Martin Luther put up a Christmas tree for his ill daughter in her nursery, and decorated it with candles.

In my husband's family, as in many German families, food played an important part in the Christmas celebration. Candy, fruitcakes, plump geese and turkeys were all readied for the Christmas celebration.

One activity the Bechtold family always remembered was going out on the farm and finding the right evergreen to put in the living room for decoration, getting out the ornaments and decorating the tree.

In the Dale family, we always went to the store with my dad. My mother had to go back and put out the gifts so we would think that Santa had been there when we returned on Christmas Eve.

In my family, I had to hide my Christmas presents from my children. The trunk of my car and a gunnysack in the barn made good choices. They never found them there.

Another tradition we had was getting new ornaments that were hand made by my children. I am still looking at ornaments on my tree today that they made. I also have ornaments that came from the first tree that we ever had.

Of all the Christmas traditions and memories that I have stored in my mind, that of family get-togethers at Christmas dinners with the Dales and my family stand out the most. Long—departed family members march back and forth in my treasury of Christmas memories.

Last, but not least, of the Christmas traditions is the midnight Mass on Christmas Eve which helps you focus on Christmas real meaning: the birth of the Christ child.

Man makes last-minute decision to head for U.S.

The common man in most European countries led a bleak existence in the late 1860's. Letters would come from relatives who had immigrated to the United States painting a glowing picture of life there.

Kings and queens and court royalty were the ones who led fantastic lives. Young men and women became restless and wanted freedom and prosperity like their relatives had found.

William Bechtold was born in Germany. His profession was that of stonemason. A boat load of stone was quarried in a mine nearby the town where he lived and was to go to New York City. He helped load the stone onto the ship and, as he loaded it and idea came into his mind. He thought, "I don't have any money but I'll hide below deck until the ship pulls out." When the ship was out on the ocean, he was discovered. He worked as a deckhand to pay for his passage.

When the ship pulled into the New York harbor, he saw the Statue of Liberty. Like all new immigrants, he went to Ellis Island.

When he was released, he found a job as a stonemason working on the foundation the New York Stock Exchange with the stone he had loaded. When he completed his work on the job, he and a group of immigrants he had met decided to seek their fortunes in the west. They got as far a Boonville, Mo.

It was a river town like Freudenburg, the town he a had come from in Germany. He bought a farm, got married, and started a family. Many generations of Bechtolds lived in and still live around the Boonville area.

William left his mark on this area, too. He helped build the old Boonville jail, which is still standing. On the farm where he lived, stone benches and tables are still standing as examples of the work that he could do.

My nephew, Paul Hartley, went back to Germany to visit Freudenburg where his relatives had lived. He saw shops and streets where William had walked. One picture he took shows a store with the name Bechtold on the front.

As so many immigrants did, William came to the United States with a trade and clothes on his back. He was successfully integrated into the vital life of a growing industrial nation.

Man makes last-minute decision to head for U.S.

The common man in most European countries led a bleak existence in the late 1860's. Letters would come from relatives who had immigrated to the United States painting a glowing picture of life there.

Kings and queens and court royalty were the ones who led fantastic lives. Young men and women became restless and wanted freedom and prosperity like their relatives had found.

William Bechtold was born in Germany. His profession was that of stonemason. A boat—load of stone was quarried in a mine nearby the town where he lived and was to go to New York City. He helped load the stone onto the ship and, as he loaded it an idea came into his mind. He thought, "I don't have any money but I'll hide below deck until the ship pulls out." When the ship was out on the ocean, he was discovered. He worked as a deckhand to pay for his passage.

When the ship pulled into the New York harbor, he saw the Statue of Liberty. Like all new immigrants, he went to Ellis Island.

When he was released, he found a job as a stonemason working on the foundation of the New York Stock Exchange with the stone he had loaded. When he completed his work on the job, he and a group of immigrants he had met decided to seek their fortunes in the west. They got as far as Boonville, Mo.

It was a river town like Freudenburg, the town he had come from in Germany. He bought a farm, got married, and started a family. Many generations of Bechtolds lived in and still live around the Boonville area.

William left his mark on this area, too. He helped build the old Boonville jail, which is still standing. On the farm where he lived, stone benches and tables are still standing as examples of the work that he could do.

My nephew, Paul Harley, went back to Germany to visit Freudenburg where his relatives had lived. He saw shops and streets where William had walked. One picture he took shows a store with the name Bechtold on the front.

As so many immigrants did, William came to the Untied States with a trade and clothes on his back. He was successfully integrated into the vital life of a growing industrial nation.

Eugene and two sisters

Telephone party lines

Cave men sat in their caves and jabbered at each other with sign language or speech, which the majority understood. Man has been a social being since Adam and Eve were exiled from the Garden of Eden. They lived together since there was safety in numbers.

Before the telephone, American settlers used the Pony Express to get messages from New York City to San Francisco, California. Imagine if you can how pleased a settler in California was when he received a letter from back East. Gold at Stutter's mill caused a flood of settlers flocking into the area to fine their fortunes.

Alexander Graham Bell in 1876 talked on his "electrical speech machine" or telephone and said these historic words to his assistant" Come here Watson, I want you." The possibilities of what could be done with his invention became limitless. By 1884 long distance connections were made between Boston Massachusetts and New York City, New York. The Unites States of America was working its way into the modern world.

My older relatives and my husband's family, the Bechtolds, shared telephone party lines and so many rings told who was receiving the call. Other people, the neighborhood busybodies, listened in on other people's conversations for recreation. Imagine trying to impress you sweetie or plot a crime with half the neighborhood listening in.

During prohibition, a bootlegger, who made the best liquor in Boone County, lived at the end of a lane. He had no telephone. The individual's with phones would watch for the federal agents looking for illegal whisky makers. The people with phones would call ahead and the man closest to the head of the lane with the telephone would run over to the bootlegger and warn him. When the Feds arrived at the illegal whiskey still, everything was on the up and up, no evidence to show any kind of illegal activities. Everyone would be busy working with animals or farm related task. After the agents left, everyone went back to making booze. Everyone who warned the whiskey maker got free alcohol and his buddies had a happy Saturday night.

We no longer have party lines and we value our privacy, but we are still communicating in new and better ways thanks to Alexander Graham bell. The party line gave way to radio talk shows like Walt Bodine, in Kansas City, Many subjects were discussed by those who called in on the phone and expressed their pet peeves. We now have television show where individual air their dirty linen for everyone to see and hear.

Communication all over the world is fast with E mail. Chat lines on the Internet and E-mail have developed from Alexander Graham Bell's telephone and the party line. I go to my computer, switch it on and I send a message, forward pictures to a friend in Australia. People are no longer confined to national boundaries. We can chat on the internet with people all over the world. Our world is one gigantic party line.

Youth puts 'Tom' in tomboy

Eugene Bechtold didn't grow up in the days of game boxes and television heroes. He lived on a farm in Boonville, Mo., with lots of animals and ways to entertain himself when he wasn't doing chores on the farm.

In the 1920's and 1930's stories of gangsters, moon shiners and kidnappers were on the radio and in the newspapers. He didn't want to learn to read the stories of Peter Rabbit or fairy tales. He learned to read to know about mobsters, like Pretty Boy Floyd, and the FBI and Elliot Ness cleaning up the country and ridding it of mobsters.

He wanted to read all he could about the kidnapping of Charles Lindbergh's son. He bought comic books and detective novels telling about crimes of gangsters and detectives who caught them.

Ma Barker and her sons were written about and he devoured these magazines. He admits he never would have learned to read it had not been for them.

Eugene had a Red Ryder BB gun, and pretending to be a G man shot out the glass windows in the barn, he must have thought he was Elliot Ness. Needless to say, his dad was most unhappy and he was grounded and lost his BB gun.

Cowboy magazines and cereal boxes all showed pictures of Roy Rogers and Gene Autry. He wanted t o be a cowboy and fight Indians. At recess, the boys at school would shoot at each other with play guns and swing across the creek like Tarzan to get away from their pursuers.

Eugene admired Charles Lindbergh and had toy airplanes and did learn to fly after he grew up, so he fulfilled one dream.

He thought he might like life on the river, so he and one of his friends who worked on the river and helped repair banks, camped out and lived in a tent. Their food was the fish they caught and fried in an iron skillet. Now, he can look back and think how much he enjoyed doing some of these things, living his fantasies.

Dance Floor carried to the schoolhouse

When I think of dancing before the 1950's, my mind automatically drifts back to the one room schoolhouse.

My husband, Eugene, grew up on a farm in Booneville, Mo., where he attended a one-room schoolhouse until he went to high school. This schoolhouse was used for many neighborhood get-togethers.

The parents built a special dance floor to fit into the small schoolhouse. The desks would be moved for the dance floor. Local fiddlers, guitar and banjo players would tune up for the do-si-dos.

My mother—in-law could dance all night and be up at the crack of dawn to milk cows. My father-in-law didn't dance, but my mother-in-law took her whole family to the school house for a few hours of fun and recreation.

179

Dances were a family affair. When the children got sleepy, parents laid them on coats stacked in the corners and covered the up. Older boys and girls made their own sets and imitated the dancing of the adults. Many young lovers met at theses dances and practiced their courting techniques there.

Pioneers going across the plains westward would put their wagons in a circle, rifles close and bring out the musical instruments and bow to their partners in and square dance. My husband's grand—parents immigrated from Europe and came westward to Missouri and brought their love of music with them. Many different nationalities went together in that one-room schoolhouse in Booneville to socialize and enjoy themselves.

Boys swung like Tarzan

My husband, Eugene, went to a one-room school house for the first eight years at Boonville, called Mount Sinai.

There was a woods behind his school. All of the boys congregated in these woods at the noon recess in warm weather. The boys would use the vines hanging from the trees to play Tarzan. They would swing as far as they could and leap or fall off beating their chest hollering "Me Tarzan. Where's Jane?"

Another imaginary game that they played was Cowboys and Indians. They harvested the thin reedy weeds and put a pole in the middle. All of the reeds went inward and stacked on the pole making a tepee. Berries were used to stain their faces for the war paint. Imagine their mother's annoyance in trying to get the blackberry stain out of their clothing. Grapevines were also used when they wanted to tie up their captives.

Big bags of marbles were the school boy's prized possessions. They traded marbles, wagered them and spent many happy hours shooting them at recess. Whenever the lessons got boring, they sneaked out the back door for a fast game of marbles. They could get in the right spot under the windows and not be seen by the teacher. If she missed them they pleaded diarrhea and an extended stay in the outhouse.

Cops and robbers was another recess favorite. The boys divided up into two opposing teams—the cops and the robbers. The woods behind the school resounded with shots from cap pistols. My husband thought he was the ultimate police officer when the local undertaker gave him a real .32 automatic used by a man who had committed suicide. The gun had no bullets, but it made him and impressive policeman as he faded in and out behind the trees. Image his parent's horror, when they discovered the bullet-less .32 in his possession.

Dog-pulled pony cart thrilled farm children

The pre-1930 vehicle that comes into my mind is the little pony cart that my husband's family owned. My husband and his sister lived on a farm in Boonville, Mo. This must have been the farm where Noah's ark originated. They had carrier pigeons, horses, cows, geese, turkey, wild chicken and rabbits. They were dairy farmers who milked twice a day and delivered the milk in town.

This pony cart was a small sled with a harness for "Doll Puppy," the name of the hound dog who pulled the sled, and was my husband's sister's favorite dog. He kept the preschool children occupied as he transported them all around their spacious lawn. With no cartoons to entertain them, these children spent many happy hours driving their homemade pony cart.

When the two children went to school, the pony cart was parked, and the hound escorted them to their school. He waited at the end of the lane at the close of school wagging his tail.

Several years passed and one winter day the children missed their hound dog. He was no where to be found. They searched everywhere trying to find their friend. Finally, Alrita discovered him hanging on a fence about two miles from home. Someone had stolen and chained him. He managed to escape, but his chain became his executioner as it got caught in the fence.

Today my grand-children ride in a red wagon and motorized cars that are battery powered.

Musketeers number four at Boonville School

Everyone has heard of the book and the movie, "The Three Musketeers." In my husband's case, it was the four musketeers: my husband, Charlie, Roy and Francis. They went to school together at the one room schoolhouse in Boonville, Mo., in the Depression years.

They sneaked out the schoolhouse door to play marbles, Cops and Robbers, Tom Mix and Tarzan the Ape Man on the vines at noon in the woods that surrounded the school-house.

My husband's closest co-conspirator in his childhood years was Charlie. He took Charlie to pick up his date and he picked up Charlie instead, when her father answered the door and intimidated him. Charlie was going to leave before Gertrude came out the door.

To enhance and make cops and robbers more realistic, Eugene borrowed his dad's revolver and carried it to school when they played Cops and Robbers. Thank goodness he forgot the bullets or the four musketeers might have been killed with the real bullets.

Charlie and Eugene enjoyed cruising Boonville, exceeding the speed limit and outrunning the local sheriff. Needless to say they both liked liquor before their 21st birthdays. As my husband said, they didn't know what a delinquent was in his day or he would have been labeled.

Charlie was the friend my husband lived with on the river cutting wood and selling it to support them. They were a modern version of Tom Sawyer and Huckleberry Finn. They bought a jeep and we went to see the sights of our great country.

After feeding their wanderlust, they moved to Kansas City and got jobs. Charlie went back into the service in the Korean War, leaving Eugene alone. Without his best friend, Eugene went on a blind date and met me, his Kismet. We were married and the Four Musketeers faded into the past. They still see each other when we return to Boonville. I enjoy sitting and listening to them relive the past when they were the Four Musketeers.

Eugene and Alrita

Boomerang Christmas gift?

My husband, Eugene, has fond memories of the Christmas present that he bought his sister, Martha Ann, in 1935. His parents had been paying him for helping with chores on the farm, and he had been saving his money. He had loved trains ever since he was a small boy. He looked longingly in all the stores at the trains with their tracks and engines. He thought he'd like to have this as a present for himself. He knew if he liked it, she'd love it.

He bought the train and wrapped it up and put it under the tree with his sister's name on it. Martha Ann, who was only 6 at the time, looked at the present and shook it many times before Christmas.

Eugene and his sisters enjoyed going out and selecting the 10-foot tall Christmas evergreen each year. Money was scarce in the Bechtold household, as it was in all household during the Depression. Their family ate well, however, and the children received lots of love and attention.

Finally, Christmas morning dawned bright and early. Nature had cooperated and provided the Bechtold household with a Christmas snow.

183

The Bechtold children had been up since daylight wondering what Santa had left and what was in the brightly colored packages under the tree.

Martha Ann opened all her presents-dolls, baby beds, blankets and dishes. But low and behold, there was a windup train with an engine, freight cars and a caboose with three feet of track. Who was there to help her put it together? You guessed it! Eugene.

Eugene and his sister spent many happy hours playing with the train. Eugene was the engineer and Martha's dolls took rides in it.

Eugene at age 8

Pageant plans fill many one-room schoolhouses

Two Christmas programs stand out in my mind. Both of theses programs are events that happened in other people's lives and were told to me.

The first program took place in the early 20th century when my mother was a young child attending school in a one-room schoolhouse in Clinton County and either riding her horse to school or walking.

Every Christmas, the children presented a program of Christmas songs. Mr. Schaefer, an older gentleman who love children, went to all the schoolhouses, driving his big truck filled with toys. He unloaded the toys and carried them into the schoolhouse. Each child was allowed to pick one toy. My mother's best Christmas present from these visits was a 24inch Kewpie doll.

My mother's parents did not celebrate Christmas with a tree or presents. They had candy, cheese, nuts and oranges or apples. Mr. Schaefer's visits were especially meaningful to my mother, since gifts were not exchanged at her home.

The one room schoolhouse in Boonville; which my husband attended in no longer standing. I have listened to the stories my husband has told me about his holiday programs in the one room schoolhouse.

The school board hired a teacher who was interested in drama and plays. Each season, she prepared the children for a pageant to be presented to the district parents. My husband, Eugene was 8 years old at his time. The school had a notable stage that was left up permanently in the middle of the room. The teacher put her desk on the stage. In this way, she could see everything that took place from her command post.

The piano was sitting in the corner of the room and one particular pageant was built around Christmas songs. For each song, the children dressed in costumes to represent the character portrayed in the song. My husband wore and old bathrobe and represented one of the three wise men. Other less fortunate children were dressed as sheep, donkeys and other animals in the stable.

When the night of the Christmas play arrived, it was snowing heavily and the people came in sled drawn by horses that were shod. They also came in wagons drawn by horses. It was too slick for the cars of those years.

Lights blazed in the little red schoolhouse as each child sang and played his parent in the Christmas play. After the last song died, the family's exchanged greeting and loaded up their children to return home.

The little red schoolhouse fell silent as the school was closed for the Christmas holidays.

Plenty of room for Christmas

The little red school-house, what fond memories it evokes.

I have listened to the stories my husband has told me about his days in the one-room schoolhouse at Boonville, Mo. The school board hired a teacher who was interested in drama and plays. Each season she prepared the children for a pageant to be presented to the district parents. My husband was eight years old at the time.

The one-room schoolhouse had a notable stage that was left up permanently in the middle of the room. The teacher put her desk on the stage. In this way, she could see everything that took place from her command post.

The piano was sitting in the corner of the room this particular Christmas pageant was built around Christmas songs. With each song, children dressed in costumes to represent the characters portrayed in the song. My husband wore an old bathrobe and represented one of the three wise men. Other less fortunate children were dressed as sheep, donkeys and other animals in the manger.

My husband's father and my husband went out to select the largest tree, cut it, and bring it to the school house on a wooden stand; the teacher and the children decorated it with popcorn strands, candy canes, and ribbons. Names were drawn. The teacher gave little brown paper bags with candy and oranges. The teacher received a gift from each child.

When the night of the Christmas play arrived, it was snowing heavily and the people came in sleds drawn by horses that were shod. They also came in wagons drawn by horses. It was too slick for the cars of those years.

Lights blazed in the little red schoolhouse as each child sang and played his part in the Christmas play. After the last song died, the families exchanged greeting and loaded up their children to return home.

The little red school house fell silent as school was closed for the Christmas holidays.

Couple keeps postman busy

From 1948 to 1956, I was perfecting the art of letter writing. I kept the postman busy sending letters back and forth across the Atlantic Ocean.

I met Don in 1948 at a party with some Central High School seniors in Kansas City, Mo. We clicked, and he asked me to write to him when he went overseas to Germany. We spent the entire week before he had to go to Germany getting acquainted and doing things we both like to do.

He spent four years in Germany; we had planned on getting married when he got out of the service. Things changed in four years, and we went our separate ways when he came home.

My husband of 51 years and I were married in 1953. We had not been married very long before he was drafted for the Korean War in 1954. He served two years in England as a radar operator at Lakenheath. I wrote him almost daily while I was finishing a master's degree at the University of Missouri at Kansas City.

Time flew by, and he came home and resumed his life as a Greyhound bus driver. I became a teacher in the Kansas City public schools. His picture in his uniform is part of this story.

Writing is something I still enjoy. The computer has opened us vistas all over the world for letter writers.

I get messages and e-mails from people in New Zealand and Australia. Pictures come in to show me how they live. You feel like you have a friend you've never met who lives oceans away from you.

I am not sending out the volume of letters that I did in the late 1940's and 1950's, but I still hear through the postal service from old friends.

Quick history of Halloween given

Halloween conjures up memories of witches, hobgoblins and things that go bump in the night.

Halloween is the name applied to the evening of Oct 31 preceding the Christian feast of Hallowmas of all Saints Day. The observances connected with Halloween are thought of having originated among the ancient Druids who believed that on that evening Saman the lord of the dead called forth hosts of evil sprits.

The Druids customarily lit great fires on Halloween to ward off the ancient spirits who revisited their former earthly homes. Later the Romans added to Halloween the custom of honoring Poman, the goddess of fruits of trees. This is where the use of hollowed out pumpkins to resemble grotesque faces lit by candles placed inside began.

I was born on Nov 1. I just missed being one of the Halloween spooks. I still enjoy Halloween parties with their apple cider, candied apples, hayrides and barn dances. I show Washington Irving's tale of Icabod Crane to my students then.

My husband and his cronies at the one room grade school in Boonville especially enjoyed Halloween parties for parents and students. Picture if you can grade school students in their knickerbockers trousers and costumes in the early 1930 are stationed at the two punch bowls: one with pure apple cider and the other laced with alcohol that they had sneaked in from the local bootleggers.

All the parents and kids they didn't like got the pure apple cider. Their buddies got the doctored apple cider. Every Halloween at the little red schoolhouse same format same culprits never go caught. If that had been me first time I would have been sunk. No wonder my husband says he was a juvenile delinquent before people knew what they were.

Back in the days of the horse and buggy my grandfather and his cronies were riding home from Starfield one dark and eerie evening they looked over to the right and what did they see in the twilight mist rising above the graves was shimmering white face glowing at them. They would hear thuds and bangs through the gravestones and weeds. They put their horses into gallop and sped into town.

On the way back they checked out the graveyard they clambered off their horses and advanced cautiously. The same white face beckoned to them. When they go up to the face there stood a white faced cow placidly eating grass. What an interesting Halloween ghost! My mother's family laughed at this tale whenever they hear it. My grand children enjoy it too.

Youth puts 'Tom' in tomboy

Eugene Bechtold didn't grow up in the days of game boxes and television heroes. He lived on a farm in Boonville, Mo., with lots of animals and ways to entertain himself when he wasn't doing chores on the farm.

In the 1920's and 1930's stories of gangsters, moon shiners and kidnappers were on the radio and in the newspapers. He didn't want to learn to read the stories of Peter Rabbit or fairy tales. He learned to read to know about mobsters, like Pretty Boy Floyd, and the FBI and Elliot Ness cleaning up the country and ridding it of mobsters.

He wanted to read all he could about the kidnapping of Charles Lindbergh's son. He bought comic books and detective novels telling about crimes of gangsters and detectives who caught them.

Ma Barker and her sons were written about and he devoured these magazines. He admits he never would have learned to read it had not been for them.

Eugene had a Red Ryder BB gun, and pretending to be a G man shooting out the glass windows in the barn, he must have thought he was Elliot Ness. Needless to say, his dad was most unhappy and he was grounded and lost his BB gun.

Cowboy magazines and cereal boxes all showed pictures of Roy Rogers and Gen Autry. He wanted t o be a cowboy and fight Indians. At recess, the boys at school would shoot at each other with play guns and swing across the creek like Tarzan to get away from their pursuers.

Eugene admired Charles Lindbergh and had toy airplanes and did learn to fly after he grew up, so he fulfilled one dream.

He thought he might like life on the river, so he and one of his friends who worked on the river and helped repair banks, camped out and lived in a tent. Their food was the fish they caught and fried in an iron skillet. Now, he can look back and think how much he enjoyed doing some of these things, living his fantasies.

Mother, mother-in-law creates lasting, delicious memories

My most significant food memories come from my mother's kitchen. When I lived at home in Kansas City, I always remembered the tantalizing smell of doughnuts that she made in hot grease and dipped in sugar. She would take fresh snow when we lived in the country, and make snow ice cream. The ham and bean smell that permeated our kitchen in the winter made coming home from school a pleasure.

My mother was also a wonderful cake baker: she made delicious apple cakes and pineapple upside down cakes. Christmastime was always a fine time, with fudge and divinity candy that she made.

I am afraid that I didn't inherit her talent for cooking. Truly good cooks add a pinch of this and a pinch of that to the recipe. Mrs. Bechtold, my mother in-law, was an add-a-little-of-this-and-that cook. She cooked large meals, since she lived on a farm.

Every weekend at this farm in Boonville, eight chickens were killed, dressed and fried. She never knew how many people would be putting their feet under her table at Sunday dinner.

She always cooked a big pot of potatoes with their jackets on every morning. She enjoyed watching people eat her food. If she knew you liked something, she'd have it for you the next time you visited.

My husband loved angel food cakes, and for his birthdays, he always had an original 24-egg-white one baked by a neighbor.

I appreciate good cooks and all of my relatives, past and present, who made my taste buds sing.

Embarrassing situation holds humor in later years

We can imagine our earliest ancestors as they sat in their caves at night with the sound of wild animals on the prowl in the jungles and thick forest. The shaman or religious leader would pass on stories about ancestors and founders of the tribes. Stories would be told about the trickster, ole coyote, or Mother Earth and heroes of the tribe.

Folk stories are tales that are handed down by word of mouth from generation to generation. Before the printing press was invented, storytellers wove their tales and they were passed on by word of mouth, sometimes accompanied by a musical instrument.

As a child, I can remember listening to my elder talk. I still enjoy listening to other people telling about their adventures.

My husband, Eugene has told me many stories abut his relatives and how they came to the United States and emigrated westward. His grandfather was a stonemason in Germany in the late 1890's. He was loading stones for shipment to the Unites States, hid on the boat and came to America. He helped to build the New York Stock Exchange. He wanted to see what was over the next hill and mountain, and ended up in Boonville, Mo. He built the jail in Boonville and many other structures.

The Bechtolds loved their land and protected their possessions. My husband tells about on of his grandfathers, who heard a noise and rushed out with his gun. He stopped a robbery in progress and had a heart attack and died on the spot. All his relatives felt they too felt the need to watch their property so they too could keep what belonged to them.

My husband's family Paul and Lizzie loved animals. They raised Boston terriers. One particular male was a house dog that slept with my husband. This dog was not too good a friend. When Eugene came home late at night beyond his curfew, that dog would bark and wake up the whole house.

The Bechtold family always attends mass on Sunday. A funny thing on Saturday was, when it was time to go to catechism, Eugene could not be found. One of his favorite hiding places was the drainage ditch. They dug him out and off he went to his lessons.

A funny thing in the Dale family was, my mother always answered the telephone when I was gone. Romeos she didn't like were told not to call again and she never told me they called. One night, I had a date with Roscoe and we stayed out past my curfew. When we finally got home very late, my mother was waiting for us. She came out with her hair up in curlers and very mad. I bravely told her I was going home with him. He literally ran to his car and peeled down the street, leaving me to face the music.

One event that made an impression on my mother as a child was the story of a bum that hid under the bed and jumped out and slit throats of a whole family who had returned from church. She still looks under her bed after being gone and so do I.

I will end this folk tale narrative of Bechtolds and Dales with a story about one of my daughters and I when she was teenager. I was waiting for her to come home so I could go to bed, and a loud knock sounded on my door. When I opened the door, there stood a policeman with my daughter in tow. His police car still had the red light flashing. She had been speeding and an inspiration came to her to tell him, I was sick. As he looked me over, he said, "You don't look sick." He put us both in the back of the police car—me in my nightgown and bare feet. She got a ticket and I got a lecture.

I later saw the patrolman on the road. He recognized me and waved.

Traveling man's adventures fascinating, but scary

As a child I always loved to listen to my elders talking as they cooked dinner or cleaned up the dishes. You could learn a lot of interesting things if you kept your mouth closed. Someone was always saying "little pitchers have big ears", meaning me.

I heard many tales about life in earlier times. One particularly daring man started smoking when he was six, wouldn't go to church and hid in drainage ditches so he could stay home. It wasn't surprising when I overheard the tale of how he used the new BB gun he got for Christmas.

He enjoyed shooting cats when they were sleeping or drinking their milk. He also took his BB gun and went down to the overhead bridge above the railroad tracks. When the freight train pulled out, the boxcar doors would be open and he would shoot the bums riding in the cars hitching a free ride. There was nothing they could do to protect, themselves or to get even with him. They stood in the cars frustrated, shaking their fists at him. He was sitting on the bridge laughing until the tears rolled down his face.

Another railroad pastime of this same boy was challenging his sister to the game of chicken. They tried to see who would be the first to jump off the track as the engine came roaring toward them. He sure liked to live dangerously. His sister gave up first always.

His adventures left my hair standing on end. I'd have been too scared to do anything he did. He made the statement, "I was a juvenile delinquent before they knew what juvenile delinquents were."

It was inevitable that our hero would succumb to the lure of the rails. He hopped a freight train bound for St. Louis to visit his grandfather. When he retuned, he told of how the men who rode the rails helped each other and close escapes for the railroad employees who searched the trains looking for nonpaying passengers.

I never heard the sound of a train whistle without thinking about this adventurous relative of mine. The stories I heard fascinate me still.

Legislation aids recovery of nation under economic collapse

The stock market crash in October 1929 marked the beginning of the Great Depression. Unemployment increased, and the economic security of many people was threatened. Farmers lost their land, homeowners their homes and workers their jobs. In the years following the stock market crash, thousands of banks closed, and many Americans lost their savings.

Roosevelt's overwhelming victory in the 1932 election, coupled with the urgency of the worst economic collapse in U.S. history, opened the way for a flood of legislation in 1933. Almost immediately after taking office, Roosevelt called on Congress to convene and began what was known as the Hundred Days, Several bills provided mortgage relief for farmers and homeowners, and offered loan guarantees for home purchasers through Federal Housing Administration. The Federal Emergency Relief Administration expanded existing relief grants to the states and resulted in assistance for more that 20 million people.

Meanwhile, the New Deal was taking shape. One part of the program was to promote recovery to the needy. A third part was to furnish permanent reforms, especially in the management of banks and stock exchanges.

The relief laws especially showed Roosevelt's recovery plans. He had a bill passed setting up the Civilian Conservation Corps. It gave 250,000 young men meals, housing, uniforms and small wages for working in the national forest and other government properties. Another law set up the Federal Emergency Relief Administration, which made grants to the states for relief activities. The WPA gave people work on roads, dams, public buildings and other federal grants.

My husband remembers the CCC from the Great Depression by the type of work that they did in the Boonville area of Missouri. He visited some of the camps where the men were working. They cut down trees, planted new trees and made pathways in and out of park areas. The men were between the ages of 17 and 23, and were both married and single. They received $30 per month.

The WPA projects In the Boonville area were regulated by the Democratic Commissioners. One of the commissioners lived with my husband's family. He went with the commissioner as he checked to see how the projects were going.

A rock-crushing project at the rock quarry employed lots of men. Rock was dynamited, and rocks were cut down into small pieces with pickaxes. This was used to gravel the roads in the area.

These projects always had more men than they needed. This way, the individuals working earned money that kept them and their families from starving. These men, between the ages of 21 and 65 were of all races, religions and colors.

My husband's mother liked to cook and enjoyed watching people eat her tasty food. The workers on the rock crushing project stopped there frequently for food. Many tons of crushed rock could be found on or near this farm on roads and feedlots where it was needed.

People cared about and helped each other during the Depression, where every one was struggling to survive. Compassion and living the Ten Commandments were important in that day.

Husband, father-in-law makes good impressions

My father-in-law, Paul Bechtold, was one of the kindest and most thoughtful men I have ever known. When my husband and I were first married, he used to come and visit us. He knew I liked books. I didn't have bookcases, so he built me sturdy bookcases to keep my books in. That was over fifty years ago, and I still use them in my computer room. I also needed a table to hold my tropical fish tanks. He built me on so sturdy it held up two ten gallons tanks full of water.

Paul was a farmer most of his life. He was a jack-of—all trades and could repair or make anything. His farm was a virtual Noah's Ark—Boston terriers, ducks, sheep, horses, cows, pigs and chickens lived there.

The most interesting thing was the fact that they raised racing pigeons. I don't know where he raced his pigeons. They would let the pigeons out in another town and then time whose pigeons go back the fastest.

Paul and his family ran a dairy and sold and delivered milk in Boonville, Mo., for years until he retired from the farm and moved into Boonville. Running a dairy is a seven day a week job. He kept busy at all times.

Paul was a good father. He went to church, lived the Ten Commandments and presented a good role model to his children; His children respected him and grew up to be good parents and law abiding citizens.

My husband, Eugene patterned himself after Paul as a father. Both men did things with their children. Eugene knew our daughter, Julie loved horses. He bought an old car to pull a one-horse trailer to horse shows. He worked for Greyhound as a bus driver in Kansas City, and he planned his work around horse shows so he could take her to shows. She usually won trophies in them. She still has these trophies sitting on her shelves today.

Paul got a pony for my husband and his sister to ride when they were under age five. They have pictures today of them on the pony.

Our daughter, Marijean, loved to dance. Eugene never missed going to see her dance in recitals.

Paul Bechtold, my father-in-law, cheered me on when I got my Master's so I could teach. He also encouraged his children and grandchildren to be the best they could be.

I'm fortunate to have had two such wonderful men in my life and my children's lives.

Eugene Bechtold

Soldier misses one war, participates in next

As I think back over my life in the 20th century, one thing which affected my life, both as a young student and a wife, was World War II. During the war itself, I was a student, from 1944-1949, at Central High School in Kansas City, Mo. I did not meet my future husband until 1953.

My most vivid memories of the Second World War are of radio broadcasts and newsreels that I saw at the movie theaters.

My husband Eugene was the right age to fight. As a child, he had osteomyelitis, and this gave him a 4F classification. He tried to enlist all over Missouri and got the same answer at each post: 4F he stayed home and worked on the farm.

The Great War finally ended, all his friend came marching home and he moved to Kansas City.

He and I met on a blind date. I had just graduated from college. He ran until I caught him. We got married Aug 15, 1953. We had just set up housekeeping and he got a note from his draft board—greetings from Uncle Sam. The Korean War was on. He passed his physical.

He was shipped off to boot camp in Fort Bliss, Texas. After training, he was shipped off to Lakenheath, England as a radar operator. Left to my own devices, I went back to school to complete my master's degree. He was gone two years.

I missed the opportunity of a lifetime when I didn't join him in England when he was there.

While he was in England, a military doctor told my husband that he should never have been drafted. He missed the big war and combat duty in Korea. Our lives were altered by this trick of fate after World War II was over.

My Regrets

This title covers a lot of memories. I always thought when you were married life would be wonderful. My first dark cloud arrived when my husband was drafted. He was rejected as a soldier during World War II. He was drafted for the Korean War. He had osteomyelitis when he was a child and this was the reason why he was rejected during World War II.

He was sent to Fort Bliss, Texas for training. I packed my bags and moved out of our apartment. My father was happy to give me away at the wedding. Now after less than six months of marriage, he was seeing me coming through the door with all my bags and baggage. My husband's car was put up on blocks to await his homecoming in our back yard. We settled into a routine. I went back to college and kept working upon my master's degree.

Letters flew back and forth across the Atlantic. He became a radar operator in England. I wrote the president saying I'd like to go to England and teach the G. I.'s who needed to get their G.E.D. at the base where my husband was stationed. I got a letter back saying I was eligible to go. I was to send credentials. My mother was happy to have one of her chicks at home again. I didn't go and stayed home to work on a Master's Degree.

Two years passed rapidly and Eugene came home. We immediately filled out an application for a house under the G.I. Bill. I went to work teaching for the Kansas City School District. He went back to driving a bus for Greyhound. I have always regretted not going to England and spending those two years with him. This is my story which tells why Happily Ever After does not always last.

Eugene in tower

Eugene at desk

Barracks

Bechtold operated radar anti-aircraft base in England

During the 1950's, Korea wasn't our only threat. The Cold War with the Soviet Union had begun and to prevent an all-out war and to provide

197

defense for not just the United States, but all countries, the U.S. set up air bases around the world.

Eugene Bechtold, now 78 of Kidder was stationed on a base in England.

"I never went to Korea myself. When I got out of radar school, I went to England," Bechtold said. "Lakenheath, England was where I was stationed."

His term of service began on July 25, 1954. He was discharged in November of 1955.

Eleven years earlier, Bechtold tried to enlist in the army during World War II.

"When I got out of high school, all of my friends were either drafted or volunteered in the service," Bechtold said. "World War II was still going on, it was 1943. I thought, well, I want to go too, but I wanted to be a pilot in the air corp."

The Air Force has not been formed by that time. "So I went to take the test to be an officer, a pilot a navigator or a bombardier. I passed those test, but when I went to take my physical I couldn't pass it. They told me that I could maybe get into the ground forces, so I reenlisted. I went through all of the tests again I still couldn't pass."

Bechtold had a bone disease in his left knee when he was six years old that kept him form being able to enter the armed forces.

"When the Korean War started I was drafted. I couldn't pass the test thought."

A couple of years later, he was tested and still couldn't pass his physical. At the end of the Korean War, Bechtold was once again called up. "They called everybody up that could walk and so I went to take my physical down on the plaza in Kansas City. He had a stack of paper about the size of a Sears and Roebuck catalog that had followed me all theses years. He flipped through the books and examined me and told me that, nowadays there was a place for everyone in the military."

Bechtold passed this time and moved on to Basic Training at Fort Bliss and then went on to radar school. During that time the Korean War was ended and the DMZ line was created.

"We got married and we were getting ready to move into a nice new apartment and low and behold, Uncle Sam calls," said Mary Bechtold Eugene's wife.

Mary Bechtold said that she has a chance to teach GED classed in England and now regrets not going. "I regret not going it was the chance of a lifetime."

At the base in England the army provided anti aircraft protection for England, with 75 mm Sky sweepers that could be used against low-flying aircrafts.

"They were still concerned with Russia," he said. The air force base also housed B-47 Bombers that could bomb East Germany or Russia if they were needed.

"We had live ammunition and bombs," he said, the radar facility that he helped to operate was not far from where the munitions were stored.

"We provide protection for this airfield with the 75 mm guns. My section was the long-range radar. We had range up to 180 miles. WE could bring in a plane and give it to the guns at 10 to 12 miles out. We were low-flying aircrafts. The high flying stuff was left for the fighter jets."

The base was used as a decoy for a larger base, Mildenhall, 3 miles south of Lakenheath, during World War II. During World War II the base was equipped with fake barracks and was more out in the open than Mildenhall was.

However, during World War II, Hitler's bombers rarely made it north of London. The Lakenheath base was also used as a prisoner of war camp toward the end of World War II.

"Later on during the Korean War, they made the Lakenheath base into a regular air field," he said. "The runways weren't quite as long as they should have been, but it was adequate. The bombers had to use parachutes when they landed and they couldn't carry large load when they took off. They'd load them up with the bombs and then refuel them in the air."

Many of the bombers made testing runs to North Africa and then returned to the England base.

"I think we did a good job, because nothing ever happened," Bechtold said. He said that the planes were set out so thaw the Russians could see where they were and the only thing that was kept secret was the radio frequencies.

"Anytime they had the good will tours when the Russians would come over and visit, we had to make sure that anything they might need or want was locked up," "Bechtold said.

Bechtold was a draftee and after his term, went back to his life as a Greyhound bus driver.

Eugene Bechtold was in the 60th Battalion. "The battalion has a history. It was wiped out a couple of time in World War II," he said.

CHAPTER 10

KENNEL

Spurred on by a dream

In 1989 I was getting ready for bed. I heard a thud in the bathroom. I jumped off the side of the bed and found my husband unconscious on the floor. He woke up a few minutes later and didn't want to go to the doctor.

We went to bed and I couldn't sleep for several hours. I remember thinking I can't run this kennel and brokerage business by myself. I dreamed and I heard someone talking "don't despair; it is time for you to continue your mission of helping others, children and adults with your counseling degree. You must fulfill your purpose that God intended for you. Don't be afraid. I fell into a deep sleep comforted by the dream.

We were able to sell the kennel property and dogs and moved a half mile down the hill from it and put up a new modular home there.

I decided to volunteer at the Cameron Library in the minimum security prison at Cameron. I enjoyed the work. One thing led to another and I took a full time job as a GED teacher in the Education Department. The work was interesting and I enjoyed seeing the inmates that got their GED in my classroom graduate.

One evening I was reading the Cameron Shopper, out jumped an ad "Elementary counselor needed part time". I worked there for three years and helped start their elementary counseling program.

Of all the jobs that I have had I think I enjoyed this one the most of all. I had fulfilled part of my mission for God. I still see my students who have frown up to be responsible adults and contributing citizens. I am very glad that I had that dream in a time of despair.

Life events return, repeat during slumber

Almost everyone has experienced one or more dreams that contain anxiety or outright fear. These experiences can be quite traumatic or become recurrent.

For some, unpleasant dreams or nightmares repeat in actual content. For others the content may change while the theme remains the same, such as scenes of falling, making speeches in front of an audience or being pursued.

My dreams that I remember began as a teenager when I lived in Kansas City and worked at the library located in central High School. I walked home from the library on damp, dark fall evenings down a hill. The fog would roll in and obscure the view ahead and behind you.

I dreaded every block of the six block walk. I just knew I heard foot steps behind me. I would stop and the footsteps would stop. Even now that I am in the twilight years, I wake up heart pounding walking down that hill with footsteps resounding behind me.

In recent years since I sold the kennel 12 years ago, I dream about cleaning the dog kennels and other related tasks.

One kennel job was taking the papers out of the cages and burning them outside. Once I went to get the mail and received a large check. I got out the matches to burn the trash and dropped the check with the trash. I started the fire, but was able to fish the check out unscathed.

Frequently I dream of cleaning dog pens and burning trash. In that trash is lots of green dollar bills which I can never rescue. I wake up trying to beat out the flames.

When I was an elementary school counselor at Coffee Mo., the students thought my dreaming about cleaning dog pens hilarious. Most of their dreams were about bogey men hiding in the closets, ghosts or on horseback or aliens abducting them.

We always had Dobermans at the kennel. Dusty my daughter Julie's dog assisted me one night when the kennel dogs were barking loudly. Illegal hunters had treed a raccoon at the pond. I let Dusty out and she put them over the barbed wire fence. The next morning I saw jean material caught on the wire.

I still dream about the raccoon hunters and in my dreams I look for people with spots missing out of their jeans.

The Kennels in Kidder

Twenty Five years ago I lived on a farm outside Kidder, Missouri with my husband and two daughters. Our livestock consisted of two hundred and fifty dogs. I bought and sold other people's dogs and puppies and shopped them all over the United States. This was a busy year with the children in school my daughter Julie and I traveled all over the East Coast to see where my dogs were sold in pet stores. Most of the dogs went to Doctor Pet Centers whose headquarters were in New England. One of our most memorable trips was to Boston, Massachusetts. We got to meet people like Ross Johnson the CEO of that company in Boston. He took us out to eat at a restaurant in 'Boston that overlooked the harbor. The fascinating thing about this restaurant was the fact that it turned around.

We rented a car in New England and went to see the Atlantic Ocean. We got brave and ventured out on the Atlantic Ocean in a rowboat. It was a mind boggling to think of all the settlers who climbed off ships and settled the area. On a bus tour, we visited the church of Paul Reveres midnight ride and also saw where the Boston Tea party took place. The tour made us review our United States History. One of the pet shop owners from New Orleans came to buy dogs for her shop and drive them home. She had an air conditioned truck to transport them in. We became friends and I continued to sell her dogs until her husband received and ambassadorship as the U.S. ambassador the Austria.

You would meet all kinds of people who raised dogs. A lot of farmers found that dogs made lucrative crops. Other people raised their dogs illegally without supervision from the Agriculture Department. I tried to avoid buying dogs from unlicensed people. One unlicensed man brought his dogs to sell when his licensed had been revoked. He parked in the driveway and agriculture inspector arrested him after he brought his dogs in. He had to call his wife to come and get his little boy since they were taking him away.

The old kennel up the hill from our house stands lonely and forlorn now. No dogs live there now. Ever so often when I go by I can see and hear in my mind all the dog doors opening and the dogs running our on the runways barking at everything that moved. The old buildings could still tell some interesting stories.

Bechtold kennels growing by leaps and bounds

They're affectionate, fun to watch and play with, and they'll never ask for the keys to the car or bring home a bad report card. Some people would rather have one or more of them than a child, and Mary Bechtold of Kidder has capitalized on that to become a successful business owner.

We're talking about dogs . . . . Pekinese, Pomeranians, Dalmatians, Lhasas, golden retrievers, elkhounds you name it, and Mary has probably raised it at her farm home, with the help of her husband, two daughters and staff of three full-time and three part-time employees.

What began as something to do for half a day when her oldest daughter started to kindergarten sixteen years ago has blossomed into a kennel and dog brokering business. This has Mary traveling to the east coast and shipping one hundred fifty dogs through KCI airport every week.

"I got dog fever" recalls Mary. "It's like going to Alaska and digging for gold. I started seeing money in all those puppies."

It wasn't instant success for the dog-raising business. It took plenty of reading and trial and error. "Dog breeders and brokers are a lot like horse traders. We're attracted to each other," laughs Mary explaining that she asked a lot of questions of other people in the business.

Soon after starting to breed and sell registered dogs, Mary decided she wanted to ship and broker dogs. "I didn't know you had to have a license from the Missouri Department of Agriculture." A helpful inspector from that department told her after her first shipment that she would need a license and proper handling facilities. That's when the Bechtold property began a transformation that still continues today. Over the past five years Mary and husband Gene have built two puppy rooms, an adult doghouse and other holding facilities. Their operation now boasts a special ventilation system designed by Don Rains, not retired as a MU Extension engineer, and scaled down from a hog house. It also contains a germ light, which has cut the incidence of kennel cough in the Bechtold business.

Dogs cannot be shipped with kennel cough. Neither can they be shipped with a variety of other problems, so heath care is important to the Bechtolds. When Mary buys dogs from breeders, she keeps them in a special holding area instead of mixing them with her own animals.

Each pup is examined and has to have a health certificate. Before they're shipped out, Mary's veterinarian, Dr. Jerry Rainey from Cameron, takes the animal's temperature, looks at its eyes, skin, teeth and listen to its heart. "It's a more complete exam than most brokers have done," reports Mary. She wants to assure that she doesn't get animals returned or have to place many and she thinks it's important to maintain a reputation as an honest broker with healthy animals. Any pup that does die is taken to the Department of Agriculture's diagnostic lab in Cameron so the problem can be traced. If it is from a breeder Mary buys from, she works with the breeder to see that the defect is corrected before buying any more animals.

In addition to the thorough exam dogs are given shots for kennel cough and parvo and are routinely wormed. Those records accompany each dog to its final destination, which might be a pet store or a chain in Miami, Boston or Atlanta, and they will sell at retail for between $300.00 and $1,500.

People who make that kind of investment in an animal intent for it to be an important part of their lives and Mary has had contact with many of the owners of dogs she raises or brokers. "I'm thinking about writing my doggie memoirs someday," she laughs.

One of her customers had trouble relating to people and was so enamored of the dog Mary sold her that when it died, she had it cremated and it remains placed in an urn so that it can be buried with her. In the meantime, she ordered one exactly like it.

"I get pictures through the mail of my dogs and even Christmas cards signed with paw prints." One of her former pups in now the mascot in a race car wile another on rides in his owner's bib overalls and carries the moniker "Killer".

Lately Mary has been traveling to some of the outlets she sells too, to put on seminars on health care. She enjoys that.

But despite the financial success the variety and satisfaction inherent in the business, she's longing for day she can go back to school and pursue her longtime goal of counseling. For several months she's attended a women's program at he University of Missouri and Kansas City designed to help with career changes.

"I hate to give up a lucrative business, but I also hate to stay in the harness". Mary says wistfully. It's easy to see that inner conflict when you see her walk up to a pen of dogs and talk to them affectionately. "You have to like animals to do it," she concluded.

Kennel ships seven thousand dogs a year

"I first got dog fever before I even had a place to keep them," explained Mary Bechtold, owner of Bechtold Dog Kennels in rural Kidder. "When I first got started I knew very little about the business, but I bought some books and taught myself all about dogs."

Bechtold Kennels opened for business in June, 1970 and since that time its business has grown considerably. Beginning with just a few dogs, Bechtolds presently ships approximately 7,000 annually to pet stores and individuals throughout the nation.

Pomeranians, Yorkies, Peekapoos and Pekinese breeds are raised at he kennels. Presently, 50 adult dogs and 35 puppies are housed at the Bechtold facilities. The kennels also buys 125 to 150 puppies weekly, to be sold to it customers.

"Most of the dogs that we buy here are from this area," stated Mary. "I buy primarily from about 80 people some of them are small raiser with just one or two dogs, and others are into the business a lot more extensively.

Bechtold kennels is licensed by the United States Department of Agriculture (USDA) to sell and ship dogs. "The people from whom we buy the dogs also have their agriculture licenses," said Mary. "I learned quickly about the licensing shortly after I got into the business. I had just shipped a couple of dogs to New York City when the authorities from the Doartment of Agriculture came to visit me. I didn't get into any trouble but I did learn that I mush have a license to be in this business."

According to Mary's report, anyone who has more than three bitches (female dogs) and one male dog is required by the federal government to be licensed by the USDA. The USDS also requires that such kennels keep records pertaining to where each dog is purchased and to whom it is sold.

All the dogs that are sold by Bechtold Kennels have had two parvo virus shots; had one distemper shot; been wormed at least twice; and had shots to protect against kennel cough and Bordetalla Pneumonia. Every dog shipped from the kennels is also registered by the American Kennel Club.

Buying the Pups

The puppies that are bought by the kennels are usually eight weeks old. While this is a general rule, Mary explained that she buys no puppies that weigh less than two pounds, regardless of the age. Many of those from whom she buys the puppies deliver the animals up at location in St. Joseph, Chillicothe, Brookfield and Macon.

"The first thing that I do when I get the puppies here is to examine them, and to see if the they have been well taken care of," related Mary. "Then I decide what I need to do to get them ready to sell. There is really a wide difference in the type of care that the various dogs have received. If I find that the puppies' from a particular person are consistently improperly cared for, then I will not buy any more from the person."

After Mary has determined that the dogs are up to her standard, they are bathed. This process includes cleaning the ears and trimming the toenails of each animal.

The dogs are then examined by a veterinarian, Dr. Jerry Rainey, Cameron. "He (Dr. Rainey) started with me when I first got into the business," noted Mary. "I have learned a lot about dogs from him the past 15 years especially in the very beginning when I was the sole worker."

If the dogs are healthy, a health certificate is issued by Dr. Rainey. Once they are ready to be sold. They are kept at the kennels for an additional two days before they are shipped. In all, the puppies spend six days at Bechtold Kennels as they are prepared for resale.

"I could sell twice as many dogs as I do now if I had adequate space and help, the market is there," stated Mary. "If I could get someone really good who would stay in the business, then I would be able to handle more dogs. But the way it is now, I can't see expanding much beyond what we are presently doing.

The staff

Donna Bain, manager of the kennels, has been employed there for four years. She started as a kennel helper and worked up to her present position two years ago.

Her job includes: handling all telephone communications of the business; sending out the American Kennel Club registration papers to the pet stores and individual: overseeing the part-time help and making sure that everything is running on schedule and overseeing the tagging of the puppies.

Julie Bechtold, Mary's daughter is the only others fulltime employee. Mary is presently teaching her how to buy dogs and exposing her to all aspects of the business. Other part time employees include Shawn Evans, Debbie Pollard, Sandy Haskell, David Moore, Dennis Adams, Michele Howland and Sandy Silkwood.

In addition to dogs, Bechtolds sell approximately 30 cats (Persian, Himalayan, Siamese and Registered Siamese) monthly. "About the only difference in the cats and dogs," explaining Mary, "is that he cats just require a little different type of care."

Dog kennel offers warmth when electricity goes off

As I look out my windows at the icy landscape, with the trees and their branches all covered with shiny Jack Frost ice, I think of other wintry landscapes of the past. In the 1970's, I lived at a kennel with grade school children and lots of dogs. One winter was particularly snowy and icy. The electricity was always going out in our house. We heated our kennels with kerosene heaters. If we got to cold, we could always go and sit in the doghouse, where it was warm.

My dogs always waited until after one o'clock in the morning to have their puppies. I would get up in my flannel night gown, put on a warm sweater, coat and big boots. My appearance always caused a big commotion in the doghouse. Two hundred dogs would have to bark at this strange apparition in the doorway. I would stumble my way back to the house where the electricity was still off.

One icy night, the lady who drove the dogs to the airport in the early morning hours forgot the air bill and vet certificates. I jumped in my car about two 2:00 o'clock and chased her to Holt, honking all the way. I attracted the attention of a policeman. I had to get out and explain why I was honking and dressed in a night gown, coat and boot's He checked my driver's license, and helped catch the driver, with siren blowing. The dogs did get out on time.

We had a steep driveway that had to be plowed and dug out. We hired the neighbor and his tractor to dig us out. Pet stores wanted Christmas pups to be shipped out of KCI. You had to drive to the airport and be there in the wee hours of the morning. One wintry evening I drove a load of dogs to KCI. I made it, but trucks and cars were sliding off the road. Coming home was worse; I put the jeep in four-wheel drive and prayed. My guardian angel must have been riding with me. I slid once and managed to get back on the road. I could see cars off in the ditch everywhere.

We still have heaters that are not powered by electricity in case of emergency. I keep my kerosene lamps full and ready to go. Raising dogs in not easy in winter weather, it is not for the faint at heart. If you are alone on ice and snow, you can fall and break something and freeze to death before you are rescued.

Now I sit in my warm house and remember slipping and sliding as I walked to the doghouse and drove to the airport. I'll bet the policeman who helped me catch the driver was glad when I go off the road.

Mary holding pet

Mary holding puppies

Dogs become pet project

In my lifetime, I have held many jobs. I worked in a library shelving books, taught school when integration was beginning in Kansas City, sold reducing tables and encyclopedias, and interviewed doctors for pharmaceutical companies.

By far the most interesting occupation I've ever had was that of being in business for my-self when I was a dog breeder and broker for twenty years. I think this was interesting because I raised and sold my own puppies and those of other people.

One fascinating aspect of this business was the dog breeders that I bought dogs from. They were farmers with small operations to large kennels which raised dogs as the sole money making project.

One person who stood out was a modern day product who reminded me of the horse traders of the Old West. She loved nothing better than getting a better deal out of something than the other person. For example, she had sold some breeding stock to individuals on time. They defaulted on their payments.

She went to Iowa and came home with a station wagon and a house trailer to pay for the dogs. She used both items for years. She also wanted some of my breeding dogs. I needed horses for my daughter to ride for the summer. Lady Luck seemed to be on her side in trades. She came out top dog.

Another complex individual I met was a gentleman who owned a pet store in Florida. I shipped him dogs on credit, and apparently, he was close to bankruptcy. It took me one year to get my money for those puppies. He left Florida and was hiding from his creditors in New Jersey.

He called me from there and asked how much he owed. A check came to me that next week with a note saying, "I am only paying you and not the others, because I like you." He took bankruptcy for $500.000.

The dog customers who came to the kennel to buy dogs were a diversified lot. About 5 o'clock one morning, I got a long distance phone call. The voice on the other end was sobbing. "My Fluffy died." As she continued, I found out that Fluffy was a female, black Pekingese I had shipped 20 years before.

She had a funeral for Fluffy and put her ashes into an urn for burial when she herself died. She wanted to buy another female Peke. As providence would have it, I had one to ship. I put the Peke in a shipping crate and put it on a plane. Every year at Christmas time, I get a Christmas card and picture of Fluffy.

Another plus of this occupation was having one hundred dogs and their puppies, because they gave you unconditional love. It didn't matter to them how you looked, what you were wearing. I used to go into my dog house and yell, "Hello, dogs," and 100 enthusiastic voices answered me.

I also traveled to Eastern cities like Norfolk, Va., and Boston, Mass., to meet the people I sold dogs to and see what the pet shop where I was sending them looked like, If I didn't like what I saw, I didn't send them any more dogs.

I still have dogs: one lazy Dalmatian and one small noisy Pomeranian. Dogs have given me much in my lifetime, a good income, memories and lots of love. If a dog comes walking down my road with no place to go he is welcome to stop here and stay.

Interesting Dog Owners

In the 1970's I ran a kennel. Most of my time was spent with dogs, buyers, breeders and agriculture officials. The most enjoyable part of these times was the dogs themselves.

One dog who gave me many silent laughs was Norman the Yorkie. A beautiful dog that had on idiosyncrasy—he did not like having his kennel cleaned. If you touched his feet he would bite you. Everyone who worked at the kennel enjoyed teasing Norman with. a sponge. If you touched his feet he would bite you.

I fell in love with the red miniature daschunds and bought several pair. They demolished their quarters by promptly eating the wood inside. Unsuspecting Poms would lie to close to the wire and Maggie daschund would get a clamp on their tails and hold on with her teeth. Maggie and her destructive friends were sold when I had to take two sore tailed Poms to the vet.

I have had heroic dogs too. Such a dog was Paula Poodle. She was a tiny thing with two small puppies. A Peke climbed out of her quarters on night and was roaming the kennel. She tried to get into Paula's kennel and bit Paula's foot to the bone. Her pups were fine. Paula was several weeks recovering from the bite, but still took care of the baby puppies.

211

One lady donated me a black lab male, George who had been her companion for several years. She changed the picture of her life by getting married. George didn't like his rival and would bite the husband every time he got into bed. Poor ole George came to live with me until I found him an owner with two people already in the family.

People who bought dogs were characters too. One lady called me crying "my black Peke died, I need another one", It just so happened I had one to sell her and I shipped it to New York City. She told me she had all her pet friends cremated and when she died her will specified they would be buried with her.

I had a strange pair of men buyers. They chartered a private plane and flew in from San Francisco to Kansas City. They rented a car and drove to the kennel. One bought a chow puppy and the other bought a westie. The westie owner went on vacation and left dog with the chow owner. The chow killed the westie. The replacement westie was ordered to be shipped before the man got back from his vacation. I don't know if the westie owner ever knew the original westie had been killed or not.

The kennel received Christmas cards from dogs. A race car driver bought a male Pom and named him Kidder. His cards were signed with paw prints. I got a picture of him wearing his racing suit. I still receive cards from Kidder Junior.

One of my male Yorkies, Killer sponsored a product for reducing bicycles. His owner would take him on selling trips to conventions where his product was displayed. The dog has stories written about him in the Kansas City Star and he always rode In the Kansas City Saint Patrick's day parade. That's enough of the dog tales for now. Catch you later.

Keeping puppy warm

When I was in the kennel business, it was all important to me that my newborn puppies lived. One poodle mother decided she didn't want a puppy and pushed it out to the side so it would get cold. I found it and brought it inside my home. The puppy slept on my chest under my night gown nice and warm.

Sunday morning dawned; time to get ready for church. I did not know what to do about the puppy. I got dressed for church and put the puppy inside my bra and off we went a normal looking family.

Everything went well until the priest started reading the gospel. The puppy must have been hungry and started crying and moving around in my sweater in the bra. At the sound of the loud cry everyone looked around to find the source of the cry. I am still trying to keep the puppy from escaping under my sweater. My children were horrified at the attention I got.

For weeks after that everyone checked me out to see what weird thing I would be doing in church. The female poodle lived and I called her "Mary's folly". She became on of my pets. If you do things out of the ordinary you can get labeled as weird. I think that God and St Anthony would approve of someone taking care of his smallest creatures. I really do not regret my unusual act.

Kerosene heaters warm kennels

Whenever I think of snow, ice and old man winter, I go back twenty or thirty years ago. At the time I had just started a kennel and brokering business. I did not have a furnace installed in the new kennel buildings but, just used kerosene heaters. Some were modern and some were antiques that I bought at auctions. I was always afraid that the heaters would run out of kerosene and that some of the dogs might freeze.

I would set my alarms at 11 p.m. and 3 a.m. I put on a heavy sweater over my night clothes, sweat pants, boots and wool socks. My coat always had a hood. I woke up the dogs. I think they thought I was their worst nightmare come true. I stripped down my winter clothing and went from building to building checking the heaters. I was always glad I went because some of the heaters would be low on fuel.

On icy wintry days I walked with a shovel so I wouldn't slip and fall. Some times when the ice crackled on the trees our lights would go out everywhere. The kennel building would be dark and I had to take a kerosene light or flashlight.

My children Marijean and Julie would be home from school on snow days and they helped me with the chores in the doghouses. Unlike most children mine the longed for school.

They were glad when we got full time kennel help and they no longer had to help with the animals. Marijean had sheep for her 4-h projects and Julie had horses and dogs.

Snow days also seemed to fall on dog shipping days. We used to have snow pile up in the driveway and we had to scoop it out to get the car out. How my daughters complained when we hauled them out of bed and handed them a shovel! Eventually we made a deal with our neighbor who would plow out the driveway and the road down to the highway. That sure saved our aching backs.

Ice storms are beautiful but deadly. One ice storm cut off our electricity for two days. The only heat we had in our house was a gas cook stove. If we wanted to get warm, we went to the dog's house to share the kerosene heaters. My husband was snug and warm in St. Louis those two days.

I am writing this story on Jan 5, 2005. It has been a combination of ice, snow, sleet and cold temperatures. The only difference in my life is I no longer have a kennel. I have two spoiled cats and three small dogs.

They peek out the door shake their feet and run for the house. They use newspapers to do their business, so they will not get wet. Such are the pleasures of being retired in the winter.

Storms bring conniptions to canine breeder

The Great Plains is noted for its hurricanes, tornadoes, floods, cyclones and thunderstorms.

The storm that stands out in my memory was a thunderstorm during which water gushed down the windows high winds blew down trees and the electricity went off for 24 hours. Naturally that's a period of time when Eugene, my husband was on the road with this bus and my daughters and I were at home alone.

I had a dog house full of dogs with a whelping room full of expectant mothers and other mothers with puppies. Wouldn't you know? Two Pomeranian females decided that was the night to have puppies.

At 2 a.m. in my nightgown, boots and raincoat, I made my way into the whelping room. I was carrying a kerosene lamp for light. It was pitch black except for the light for the kerosene lamp. All the dogs woke up, their hair standing on end at the sight of this creepy figure invading their doghouse.

I started talking to them and they quieted down. I checked my two dogs that were close to whelping and both dogs were getting down to business. Each dog took its time between puppies. I remember thinking to myself: Why couldn't I have chosen a profession where I worked days? I sat there from 2 to 5a.m. the rain poured down and the florescent lamp flickered.

Bo Bo Pom had four beautiful puppies and her sister, Yogi Bear, had three puppies. An individual from Chicago who bought one of Yogi's puppies named him Kidder for the town he was born in. These two Poms retired from kennel life at five years of age and went to live with my brother in Nebraska.

Another connection I had with storms was with Old Man Winter. Most of the dogs I sold went out on airplanes a KCI airport. Snow would invariably fill up our driveway on nights when dogs had to go out the next morning. Many nights, we would be outside digging our way to the top of the hill so that the dogs could go to the airport.

Finally we made a deal with our neighbor who would come over with his tractor and snow plows and not only plows our way out to the highway from the gravel road we lived on.

On nights we shipped dogs, we got up a 2 a.m. to get them to the airport. We packed each order and checked all our animals to make sure the right puppy were going to the right pet store. Many were the nights that the lights flickered when snow was loading up electrical lines.

Storms now do not seem as fierce as they did when I had dogs to ship. I can sit and watch the snowfall and stay in. If it rains, I don't worry about the lights going out.

T.V. station error surprises unsuspecting family

For 20 years I raised dogs, sold dogs and bought other people's dogs. We had five people working for us to take care of my animals and animals that were kept for a week after we bought them. A veterinarian came to our kennel weekly and the chief inspector from the USDA in Washington D.C., visited our kennels and brokering business as a model kennel and housing for dogs. We had buildings with germ-proof lights, where puppies coming in were housed to keep down the spread of disease.

Around 1970 we had a neighboring kennel where the conditions were not so ideal. She lived a mile from us with her son and dogs. Her CB handle was "Puppy Love." I think she spent more time on her radio and the road than she did taking care of her animals.

Conditions there became worse and worse until finally the humane society and the county sheriff stepped in.

An area televisions station got wind of this problem and sent out a car and a cameraman to take pictures with a long-range camera from the road, one night I was looking at the television standing in front of it. The newscaster went through the story about dead and dying and neglected dogs. The pictures were of my kennel but, the story was about her abuse and neglect of dogs. I called up the television station and told them about their mistake. It seems that the news reporter taking the picture went to the wrong place.

The television channel put a retraction on the news at 11 that night and 6 the next morning. Everyone in my area missed that broadcast. The topic of conversation on the school bus was the story about us. My children had to listen their classmates talk abut our dead and dying dogs. All the children recognized my kennel even though the story was about "Puppy Love."

I wanted to sue the television station for slander and wrongful information, but my husband talked me out of this. Since this experience, I am always careful about what I see and read on television or in the newspapers. The printed word and spoken word as new can damage a lot of lives. Believe me, I know from experience.

Taking a bite out of poachers

My father-in-law Paul Bechtold hunted with a rifle in the early 1900's. He hunted ducks, geese, rabbits and squirrels. He used a rifle and shot them all in the head so all the meat would be edible. He killed many wild ducks and geese that made the large lake on the farm their home. Many of the animals that he hunted wee raised by the family. My husband was fond of the meat on the tame ducks.

My dad hunted wild game. When money was short, the wild meat sure helped out the menu. I liked fried squirrels and rabbits with mashed potatoes and gravy. My dad always enjoyed hunting in later life. When the deer season came around he would get his deer clothes and go off hunting. When he got his deer he had it cut up and stored in the freezer. It made into lots of hamburger and roasts.

Four wheel trouble

After my husband and I moved from the city to an acreage, we had our problems with deer hunters. When the deer hunting season opened here came the four wheel drive vehicles and scads of pickups. Men in orange suits and vests dotted the landscape. I don't see how they kept from shooting each other they were so plentiful.

We were very possessive of our acreage and resented people trespassing and killing the wildlife who lived there. We spent many hours running off the deer hunters. Especially annoying were the individuals in the winter who were so lazy that they would sit on the snow covered road and shoot at the starving rabbits from their car. Some sportsmen they were.

CHAPTER 11

PRISON

My retirement problem and how I solved it

Have your ever been busy seven days a week, twelve hours a day? I have! Twenty years ago when my oldest daughter was in kindergarten, I quit my job as an elementary school counselor so I could be at home to take care of my preschoolers and meet the bus at noon.

On one of the excursions I visited a Pomeranian kennel near me. As I looked in the whelping house, I saw mother dogs with lots of puppies. There must have been at least 100 puppies from newborn to six weeks of age. I bought an adorable golden female puppy. We lived on a farm of 180 acres. We visited many kennels and I found myself buying adult females. Soon I had about twenty female and three males with no place to put them.

Talk about putting the cart before the horse. We built a kennel and whelping house large enough to accommodate 300 dogs. At first I sold only my own puppies and shipped them to pet stores. Within five years I was buying other peoples puppies as well as shipping my own.

While my children were growing I remained in the kennel and brokering business. I had seven employees and shipped 7,000 dogs a year. I had always enjoyed teaching and counseling and had intended to go back into it when my children were going full time to school.

In 1988 I decided to sell my business to the local veterinarian. I could hardly wait to be out of the business. I counted the days until the business transaction was completed at Thanksgiving. How nice it was to be able to take a bath without having to talk to a perspective pet buyer.

I enjoyed Christmas holidays with my family. I could decorate my house with no interruptions from my employees or emergencies with my dogs in the middle of the night.

I had never been sick in all the years of running my own business. In February 1989 I began to awake in the middle of the night with my heart beating rapidly sweating profusely and my blood pressure and pulse were high. I couldn't concentrate on any tasks and at hand or sleep at night. I began to doubt my own abilities to drive or do simple household tasks. All of these anxieties culminated in a three a.m. visit to the hospital emergency room I thought I was having a hear attack. I felt foolish after spending the night in the intensive care unit hooked up to a heart monitor. The next day I was dismissed and told that there was nothing wrong with my heart and that I had had and anxiety attack. My doctor said I needed to go to work and get something to occupy my time.

Soon after my hospital visit, I went to an American Legion meeting. Our speaker for the evening was Carla Franks Director of volunteers for Western Missouri Correctional Center in Cameron, Missouri. She told about the need for volunteers at the prison. Many of our members were appalled at the idea of doing volunteer work at the prison. Working as a volunteer there intrigued me. I signed up and was give 16 hours of training for the prison. Two months after I had taken the training I was cleared by the state as a volunteer. I was assigned to the Education Department as a tutor for a fifty—six year old inmate who could not read. I worked with him on a one-to-one basis four days a week. He progressed from non-reader to the third grade level in seven months. He wanted to learn to read so he could read his grandchildren stories when he got out of prison.

I also worked as the substitute librarian and took her place when she was absent. In this way the library remained open extra days for the prisoners use. I enjoyed my work in the library because I got the opportunity to know and help the inmates find books. Also, I got to know them as people. I saw picture of their children, helped them find books and information they wanted. I listened to their problems and discussed local or national problems with them. These men ceased to be inmates in gray suits behind bars and became people I got to know well. When they were paroled and left I missed the association with them and felt like I had lost a friend.

A teaching vacancy came up in September, 1991 and the head of the Education Department asked me to apply for it. I did and became a part-time evening teacher in adult education in December, 1991. I went to school at Moberly Junior College in early December over a weekend and started my new job December 10, 1991. I have sixteen students ranging in age from 18-56. Three of my students are being taught to read basic Math. The other students are studying so they will be able to take the GED test and receive their high school diploma.

I can't think of any job I've ever had that's more rewarding to me personally. When my students first arrived there was this gap between them and me. They were mistrustful of me as an authority figure. They had low opinions of their ability to achieve in school. Some of them covered up their low esteem by being noisy and cocky. The gap between us is closing as they are learning to trust me because I want to help them learn and they see the really can master school skills. This my first experience in adult education and I am learning right along with them.

The student I tutored as a volunteer is now enrolled in my class at night and is progressing right along. He is writing simple words and sentences as they are dictated to him. Soon after I started volunteering at the prison, I started sleeping better and my anxiety attacks disappeared. I wake up each day looking forward to the challenges that a new day brings.

My problem of not having enough to keep myself occupied solved itself. Looking outside me and helping others was what did it. You can make yourself sick with imaginary ailments when you are bored and only have yourself to think about. I certainly don't intend to spend my retirement years knitting and sitting in my rocking chair. My fellow man has a need for my devices and I grow as a person when I use them for the benefit of others.

Interesting Job Experience

In my lifetime I have been interested in many different areas of employment. After I retired from running a busy kennel I got bored no place to go for give days a week. The Cameron Medium security prison was built and opened. I took Criminology when I got my Master's Degree in Sociology. There was an ad in the paper wanting volunteers to help in the library. Right up my alley I had worked in the library during my high school and college years. I went for an interview and was promptly accepted after a thorough background check. I worked as a volunteer in the library for a month. I then found myself running the library with six inmate helpers and no paid staff for half a day. The first time I entered the prison yard and heard the doors slam shut, I knew that I was on the yard. Two library inmate helpers met me and took me into the library. I spent an uneventful half day checking out books and helping keep people quiet. Many inmates asked for law books. I found out later that they were preparing their own briefs for an appeal.

For three months I was a volunteer. Then I was approached to be a GED teacher. I signed on for three years as a teacher. My classes had at least 30 students in them. One set in the morning and one in the afternoon. Each inmate in the institution had to have a job. My student's jobs were going to school. We had one officer for 200 students in the entire building. These students ranged in age from 18 to 60 and older. I had two inmate assistants who helped with the classroom.

The students were of many different nationalities, races and religions. I had many nerve wracking experiences in the classroom. One individual sat in class and wrote on his paper, "I am going to kill myself" I wrote him up and he was put on suicide watch and isolated. This made him angry and he couldn't understand why I wrote him up. He came back to class and never wrote suicidal message again.

Another time occurred when an inmate came to me telling that a group was going to attack one of my helpers when he went to church. I reported the incident that was going too happen and it was averted.

I enjoyed my three years at the Cameron prison. I met many inmates who got there by peddling drugs, assault, theft, domestic disturbances, etc. I felt good every time one of my students passed the test and received his GED. I got to see them receive their diploma and wear caps and gowns. Christ says "Love one another and help your brothers." The old adage "Do unto others as you would have others do to you,' was my philosophy.

Happy times

I believe the happiest times in my life have been associated with a school or a library. Books are lying all over my house—biographies, love stories, horror, non-fiction, to mention a few. Looking backward makes one nostalgic, the people that one is close to at one period of your life move away, marry or lose contact except by mails or occasional telephone call. My life now is one of the happiest periods that I have experienced. I am retired and enjoyed the first few months of retirement: shopping, visiting neighbors and playing with grandchildren. I soon got bored and wanted something else to occupy my time.

My entry into my present occupation came about a year and a half ago. I heard Carla Franks, the director of Volunteers, at Western Missouri Correctional Center talk about the need for volunteers at the prison. I signed up and was assigned in April of 1991 as a volunteer attached to the Education Department. I thoroughly enjoyed working there. I worked three hours a day four days a week with an inmate who didn't even know his ABC's in the beginning. He progressed to about the third grade level before I was given a different assignment. Another fascinating job I was given was to work with an accident victim who needed some help with his speech.

I enjoyed working as a substitute librarian when the librarian had to be absent. I helped many a prisoner find information and books. What I couldn't find the inmate clerks helped me with. We talked about all of the current topics seen on television and in the newspapers. Many of their insights made me look at things in a different way.

A paid teaching position opened up in the Education Department in December of 1991 and I was asked to apply for it. I am now working nine hour a week with adult who want to receive their GED and better themselves when they leave prison . . . I like working with these individuals because they are motivated to improve their ability and get better jobs when they leave us.

I'm happiest it seems when I am growing by helping someone else and learning new skills. I may be helping others but I certainly am repaid by the satisfaction I see in their faces as they master a forgotten skill they left behind when they quit school I can truly say this is the happiest time of my life.

Reflections of a Prison teacher

Ace, a tall slim Afro American man, ambled up to tell me good-bye. He was being released after twenty years of incarceration from the state prison. He said as much to me as to him "how will I make it? What's it like on the outside? I hope to make it, if I don't I'll just commit another crime and come back home." This attitude may seem strange to you, but when you've lived the same way for twenty years with someone telling you what to do 24 hours a day, you don't feel you can think for yourself.

My farewell to Ace, at the prison library where I work as a volunteer, brought back memories of the two years I'd worked as an adult education teacher in a medium security prison. Many experiences and thoughts of those years crowded in my mind.

One of my first experiences was with inmate X whom I worked with in night school. We were watching videos, and they were taking notes on them. The next night they would be writing me essays on what they saw and practicing for the essay part of the GED. Inmate X hesitated before he finally started writing. He was still writing after all the others were finished. I wondered what he had to say that took so much time. As I read his paper, about 100 words were devoted to the film and abut 1000 words were telling me about the anguish he felt inside. He and his sister had been abused as children and now they both suffered the mental anguish of the damned. I showed this letter to my supervisor and he recommended my referring him to the psychiatrist. I talked to X about it and he filled out a medical service request.

Later, he told me that he was seeing the psychologist and it helped to get all these experiences talked out. He never completed his GED with me because he said whenever he was quiet nightmarish flashbacks flooded his mind.

I have never been able to effectually teach a person I don't understand and have a rapport with. Perhaps this is why I spend about one tenth of my time talking to my students in the hall while I watch the others through the door. I pick up changes in their behavior very quickly because this effects how they perform in the class. Many times a student will want to talk to me privately; you can never escape the fact that the inmate culture and motivations are different from those of us who represent their custodians. We the custodians look at life and morals differently that the inmates do.

Inmate Z enlightened me on the way ghetto men look at selling drugs. They see it as a business opportunity and a way of getting out of the ghetto. He rationalized selling drugs to affluent people because he said they were going to get them anyway somewhere. In retrospect, Z said that he was going to get his GED and go into a legitimate business because selling drugs is like a one-way street back to prison. "You're always looking behind you for cops who are going to bust down your door or another drug dealer who will shoot you because he wants your territory." He sees education as a way to help him earn a living that is legitimate. Perhaps education is getting our message across to the offenders better than we think it is.

Another trait that inmates exhibit in my classes is the willingness to help each other. As they grow in self-confidence, they share their newfound knowledge with classmates. Many of my students pass their GED and go on to become tutors in Vocational Technology School and education in the prison.

One of the most irritating traits I run into is one inmate wanting to torment another about his stupidity. The tormentor is having self doubts and trying to make himself feel better by belittling another. I warn the culprit and if he persists I will write him up on a violation for creating a disturbance. That usually takes care of that.

Prejudice also rears its ugly head at times. Inmate DO called inmate AC a "bean-burner". This was a reference to AC's Mexican origin. I called the guard as witness and warned DO, the offender that he could be written up on a violation. I told the class that name-calling would not be tolerated.

Inmate society is a microscopic picture of our larger society. I noticed that one inmate; MA was shunned by all the others. No one wanted to be around him. Over a period of four months I watched MA deteriorate. I became concerned about him and he told me that he was HIV positive. He was released soon after that and I don't know what happened to him.

As will happen when I was passing down a hall someone in the crowd called me a "bitch". When we got back into class one of my Afro-American students came up and said, "I want to apologize for my race. We all appreciate what you're trying to do." That kindness of my students made me forget the incident. This reinforces my idea that inmates are human beings with consciences and care about others.

Inmate AB came in on 120 day shock-time. He thought he'd be getting out at the end of that period. Instead, he has to complete a one year sentence. He said that working on his GED and completing it was what helped keep him sane. He is now tutor in education and taking college courses. He wants to teach and go to college when he gets out. To me, education it the key to rehabilitation and attitude change for an inmate.

A lot of inmates use going to school as a way to escape being assigned to the kitchen. My job as a teacher is to keep my students working toward getting their GED. I check every day to be sure my students are working on the objectives that they need to pass the GED. I force unwilling workers to keep on course. Very few of my students drop because they can't sit and write letters, sleep or read materials not related to the goal of getting a high school diploma.

Inmate BQ entered my class with precisely "escape food service" on his mind. He started to work reluctantly. As his successes in completing his objectives mounted, he balked when it came time to write his essay. He stalled and talked and couldn't pick a subject. Finally he decided that he'd write about discrimination against American Indians in the United States. The essay he wrote showed me an intelligent man who is capable of deep sensitivity. His paper is the best I've received. To look at him and listen to him you'd think a brainless macho man. He has been in AD Seg. For two weeks. He needs to take a pretest and I'm eagerly awaiting his thoughts on that in the essay.

Inmate Detag stands out in front as a very memorable individual. He was in my night class. He enjoyed saying things that would shock me. One night we were discussing the justice of Hammurabi. He surprised me by saying that since that type of justice was "an eye for an eye and a tooth for a tooth", he'd probably lose all his limbs since he stole things and made his living by going in and out of window's. Another quiet evening when we were discussing people we'd like to be like, he came up with Al Capone. There was never a dull moment with him.

Inmate saying and a vocabulary kept me laughing many evenings as I left school. One of my con artist tactfully admired different things I'd wear. One evening as we were waiting for the guards to dismiss class, Slick, as I nicknamed him to myself, told me he was going to marry a rich widow so he'd never have to work a day in his life. He's been paroled so suppose he's a kept man now. Another inmate asked me to jump-start his battery—translation: give him ideas for the GED essay he had to write.

Despondent inmates occur also in the classroom E inmate came to class very squirrelly one night. There was a complete personality change.

As soon as I got the class started, I took him into the hall. He had been served divorce papers that day. He said life was not worth living. Our correction training tells u to be on the alert f or possible suicides. I wrote up a conduct resolution and gave it to the custody officer. She notified the Captain who talked to E. This story has a happy ending since E's wife changed her mind. E got his GED. He is now paroled and working as a cabinet maker on the outside.

When we give the MOBES test to inmates wanting to get into GED classes, we are screening these individuals for placement within our classes. One man stands out in my mind. He came in and told me he couldn't take the test because he couldn't read. He was later place in a literacy class where he is being taught to read in the Laubach method on a one on one basis.

Inmate F and I discussed recidivism and career criminals. He felt that the difference between inmates who learned their lessons and career criminals was based on their family backgrounds and their experiences when they were children. No one in his family had ever been in prison except him. He had moral values taught to him as a child and a job waiting for him when he got out of prison, teaching adults in a literacy program. He said his crime hurt no one but himself. On the other hand, career criminals had been taught no moral values in their families. They scratched and struggled to survive as small children. With no caring at home, they sought belonging and a sense of identity by becoming members of street gangs.

Once in prison an inmate who has a sense of strong family solidarity accepts his punishment because he feels he deserves it. The career criminal in prison quickly absorbs the prison culture and learns how to be a better criminal from others who share their skills with him. This is where those of us who work with inmates feel the division between them and us "the prisoners". Many of my inmate students have fathers, brothers, uncles and mothers in prison. The only loyalty this career criminal feels is towards his gang and to other criminals. Killing doesn't bother him because he has no sense of right or wrong.

The key work to teaching is caring. Caring about helping the ones you teach to plod up the mountain, which is taking the GED test and passing it. Making a difference in one's individual's life by helping them learn and feel better about themselves when they receive their diploma, may keep them from becoming career criminals. A famous writer once said in passing through, "My time on earth can be measured by my impact on my fellow man." This then is the essence of my teaching philosophy.

An Experience with a Mass Murderer

Working at the prison I had many memorable experiences. I met B, the serial killer who was incarcerated and working in the prison library. He was a balding man with glasses and a face that you wouldn't be afraid of. I had a prison aide as a helper in my room and had a vacancy for another one. Robinson applied for the vacancy. Some of the inmates told me he was trouble. I took their advice and stayed away from hiring him. He continued to work in the library with B the head librarian. She resigned and Robinson had been released.

B had dinner with Karen Ray and me, the night before she left for an interview with a new employer. She would be selling American products in England. Before she left that night, she said that she would write. We never heard from her again. Her son was killed and she never returned for the funeral.

Time went by and articles came out in the local newspaper. It showed pictures of our old inmate Robinson. He lured women into Kansas and they ended up missing. Where were they? Further investigations showed that he had a storage space in a building on one of his properties inside the building were barrels. To my horror in one of the barrels was B.

John lured women and killed them. They gave his address to have their checks sent there while they were away. The Kansas police came to visit me because I had been one of the last people to see B alive.

Who would have ever thought a man who looked like a preacher or professor would be so evil. He was a consummate con artist. He advertised in a local paper to find his victims. I think now about how evil comes in serious disguises. He was probably was the worst individual I ever met in my prison and later life.

No to Sleaze and violence

You are right about society needing a radical change. We have become a "me" society—each person concerned only about himself and what's in it for me. Many individuals feel what they want to do is right regardless of whether they are infringing in the rights of others. I've

Mary Bechtold

heard this view many times from the inmates I taught in prison. "So I killed someone, that's not my fault. I'm this way because of where I lived and what society did to me. "How can inmates respect other people if they don't have respect for human life and for themselves? Families are not teaching the Ten Commandments which are the basic tenants we should live by.

Little children are not loved by many parents but just grow up scratching out their daily existence like little rats. No one is there when they come home from school. No one cares about whether or not they do their homework. Walking to and from school and being in school is like being a wild animal living in a jungle.

Our society is a nation of window peepers. The press tries to pick our nation's leaders apart to see whether or not they are good role models or have any hidden secrets. The Charles Manson and serial killers become love objects for sick women. Sick people buy instruments of their torture used in their killings for many thousands of dollars. Normal people in earlier times would have looked at these killers with revulsion and horror.

Many inmates I taught had no conscience no remorse for murders and crimes they committed. Three times and you're out is not a bad idea for convicted felons. Perhaps this would keep repeat child molesters and rapist from doing the same thing over and over.

One inmate expressed his feeling in poetry. Soon there will be more of us in prison then there are of you on the outside. Prisons need more psychologists. We only had two psychologists' for two thousand inmates-no consulting psychiatrist. I would take a prisoner in to the intake center and psychologically try to determine whether or not he could be helped by being treated by psychologist or classes in group therapy to keep him from coming back to prison. All prisoners have low self esteem, quick tempers and could benefit from classes showing ways to prevent violent out bursts and ways of controlling the temper. Educational classes and trade classes should be offered in prison. Industry could be subsidized to take inmates paroled and trained in their specific areas when they are released.

Juveniles who commit felonies like armed robbery, car jacking or murder should be tried as adults and put in a juvenile prison. Why keep releasing them to commit more crimes until they finally become adults. Appropriate programs should be worked out for these juvenile prisons.

I would reinstate the death penalty for serial killers and mass murders. Why pay for housing someone who should never be released and whose crimes are so heinous.

The use of temporary insanity for murders shouldn't be accepted. Incarceration in maximum security prisons would be appropriate punishment. All of us are temporarily insane at some time or another, but we don't' commit crimes. We need to accept responsibility for our actions instead of blaming someone else or something else. Claiming you killed your parents because they sexually abuse you is wrong. Charge them with the crime, but don't take the law into your own hands.

We need to take the perks away from Congress. How can we teach honesty and obeying the law when our elected officials use government helicopters to go play golf?

We can't correct all the ills wrong with our society but we can help in our own individual way by volunteering in prison, hospital, etc. A smile or kind work and your own actions speak louder than words. The contact you may be the only outside contact they have for the day. If you help one person each day then the world will be a better place.

CHAPTER 12

STORIES OF ANIMALS

Animal Lore begins at home

Living in a rural area of Caldwell County Mo., helps you become acquainted with all kinds of critters—wild as well as domesticated. Both my daughters were in 4-H in high school.

My youngest daughter, Julie fell in love with the neighbor girl's horse, Cowboy when she went to a birthday party. After the party Julie thought she wanted a horse of her own. We went to look at a pony for sale when she was six. It was as wild as a March hare; we didn't buy him. We rented two horses for the summer from a dog breeder. She rode both of them. My other daughter was not interested in horseback riding.

After the summer the horses went home. We went horse looking again. We decided on a nice horse name Arabet. Arabet was gentle, but she didn't like to be caught. We decided Julie needed a new horse.

She joined the Caldwell 4-H horsemanship club and we bought her a new horse name Swing. Swing was easy to catch and Julie went to horse shows. She still goes to horse shows and wins trophies and ribbons.

Her daughter Megan carries on the family tradition and has been riding since she was four.

She also liked dogs and trained a Doberman named Dusty for dog shows. Dusty enjoyed terrorizing the mailman and UPS delivery truck.

Julie worked in a pet shop after graduation from high school. I got a parrot a lame hamster and a Himalayan cat from that job.

Megan her daughter would like to have a lizard or a snake. Thank goodness that was something I didn't have to contend with.

Marijean my other daughter had to have a 4-H project. She chose registered Hampshire sheep. We built a barn and one adult male and two females of the previously mentioned species moved in. She went off to college and I sold the sheep, so much for them.

I still inherit stray dogs and cats that they can't keep in apartments. It is a good thing I like animals. Two small Poms and one Dalmatian still live here. I also have five tanks of tropical fish, so much for the Bechtold menagerie.

Cats in garage

Animals play part in family's life

Critters have been a part of my life for the last 30 years. I had pets as a child. My favorite was a banty hen. She traveled with my family when we moved from Missouri to Kansas to Oklahoma during the Second World War.

When my children were growing up, I ran a kennel and raised small toy dogs. My daughter, Julie inherited my love of animals. She had dogs, horses, parrots, cats and guinea pigs. She even worked in a pet shop in Metro North when she was 16. She rode horses and went to horse shows. We bought her a horse named Swing who was nine when we got her. Swing is still living in Colorado with five other horses.

After I closed the kennel many dogs and cats have made their home with us. Mabel, a Dalmatian will be 14 years old. She puts up with my small poodle and Pom.

Cats entered my life after my mothers' senior housing complex had stray cats. My beauty operator took two of them that I cat napped for her. They made excellent mousers for her. She wanted two more so I caught them and brought them home. I made the mistake of letting them out. They promptly took off. I could see them watching me from the evergreen trees. They kept our mouse population down.

One black and white cat had kittens in the garage. She had five live kittens; three grays and two black and white ones. The mother didn't show up one morning. I found her dead on the road. The kittens were hollering and I became a momma cat. I used kitty milk and a baby bottle. This went on every four hours for three weeks. They finally graduated to eating wet food and milk. To these kitties I was a mommy cat.

Mabel never offered to hurt the kittens. At six weeks I put them outside during the day and brought them in at night.

I have one tom cat and one spayed female cat left. They are so tame that they follow my husband and I like dogs. When we go to the mailbox we have three dogs and two cats trailing behind us.

My cats cannot be left loose in my house because I have five tanks of tropical fish. They love to watch the fish when I am holding them. I know the cats are thinking yum yum.

My animals and finny friends give us a lot of pleasure. Their antics are so funny. It is nice to see our canine and feline friend get along so well. Mabel the old Dalmatian is an exceptional dog.

Boston

One of the most interesting trips I ever took was to Boston, Mass., the home of Paul Revere; I sold puppies to Doctor Pet centers. The corporate headquarters were in Boston. This large chain had pet centers all over the United States. Ross Johnson, one of their buyers and vice presidents, invited me to Boston. I had never met anyone from the doctor pet center in person. I only knew their phone voices.

My trip had all of its expenses paid by doctor's I decided to take Julie, my 15 year old daughter, with me. We flew into the Boston airport. It seemed as thought the plane was going into the water instead of a runway.

Ross and his wife met us in an expensive Rolls Royce. I thought to myself, "They must have been making lots of money from pet stores." They delivered us to the posh hotel where we were staying. When they picked us up in the slick car for dinner, they took us to a restaurant way up in the sky that revolved so you could see all the sides of the Boston landscape. It was beautiful to see Boston at night and we enjoyed a wonderful seafood dinner.

The next day we were picked up by the manager of the Braintree, Mass., store. We visited his store and other stores in Methuen and Danvers. It was fascination to see some of the puppies I had shipped them looking at me from their cages. The stores were all clean and full of people buying pets.

The next day was Saturday and I rented a car and drove through the New England countryside. The fall trees were changing color and it was absolutely beautiful. We drove to the Atlantic Ocean and got on a rowboat. They rowed us out in the Atlantic Ocean. We looked for souvenirs in the various that lined the oceanfront. I bought a necklace and bracelet made out of while bones with elaborate carvings.

All tourists go on tours so we took a tour of Boston on a tour bus. It was fascination to see places that you had read about in history books. Especially fascination was the U.S.S Constitution nick named "Old Ironsides." The Constitution is operated by the Navy sailors in period costumes. They lead groups through this magnificent piece of American history, telling stories of the battles of Old Ironsides and the conditions her crew lived in. We love the New England Aquarium. We enjoyed spying on the exotic sea dwellers.

We had dinner with Ross family in a large house in Boston. His mother had been given the job of getting us to the airport on time. She left half and hour before time for us to get there. We almost missed our plane. We had to run with our bags to catching it.

Ross was out in his boat watching whales.

Mary Bechtold

Dalmatian lying down

Dalmatian demands obedience

The common ancestor of our pampered pet the dog (scientific name—Canis familiars), is depicted in scenes on the walls of caves in France, Arizona and South America. He warned our ancestors 3,000 years ago that danger was near as he continues to do today. The ancient dog gave the same devotion to his owners that we have from our papered modern day pets.

My life has been intertwined with dogs for the past thirty years. I ran a kennel and was privileged to share my life with many different dogs. They didn't live with me but, condescended to let me live with them.

My current pet is a female Dalmatian. She appeared overnight in a pen with one of the adult Dalmatians. It was always a mystery about how she arrived; she has an uncanny way of answering you when you ask her a question. She will howl, and her vice will continue to get louder. She likes warm places in the winter and cold places in summer. No amount of bribery with food can lure her out of our comfortable people home. She has my husband and I well schooled in dog obedience for people.

My husband bought her a shiny new igloo doghouse last winter with a soft pad, to be placed in the garage. Only one thing was wrong with the dog house: Mabel thought it was haunted.

My kennel dogs had many unusual character traits too. One I remember was Max a very shy Pom who would not breed when watched by people. We hit on the idea of putting a blanket around the breeding pen. Bingo!

I had a female Yorkie named Morgan. To make her pregnancy uneventful, we kept her inside with us. My husband traveled and was home on certain nights. One of Morgan's favorite pursuits was hiding under the bed and biting my husband on the heels.

The many Pekinese who lived with us were quarrelsome characters. We had a male Peke named Curtis as stud. Some people gave him to me. I didn't know why they did until I decided to clip him and he bit me. I hadn't had him very long when a biker with tattoos drove up. He wanted to buy the meanest dog I had. I immediately put him and Jaws together. When the dog bit the biker, he said, "Awesome," and I know that he was a satisfied customer. I never knew what role Jaws played in his life.

Ten years ago we sold the kennel. I miss my furry charges and the pet lovers who bought them. Life around them was never dull. When stray dogs come down my road with their suitcases they always stop here because they feel my love of the ever faithful dog.

Killer   Little girl holding first
                                catalog puppy

Even puppies can be bought via catalog

We always had a Sears and Roebuck or Montgomery Ward catalog to look at during Christmas time.

This year I've added the J.C. Penney catalog to my collection. I find it much easier to shop at home that to fight the crowds in shopping centers and malls. Wal-Mart during the holidays is wall-to-wall people.

Would you believe at one time that you could look in a catalog and get pets shipped all over the country? When we first started the kennel a catalog order company contacted us and we filled orders for their customers with Yorkies, Pomeranians, Pekinese and Maltese. We received a lot of letters at Christmas from people all the country with picture of their dogs in them.

Another purchaser of Yorkie pups saw them in the catalog and drove from Michigan to pick them up. Another satisfied customer bought a

Yorkie and called him Killer. I received a Christmas card every year with Killer's picture on it.

We lived in the country on acreage for 40 years. When my daughters were small they wore out the Christmas catalogs looking at the pictures and putting their names beside what the wanted so that Santa would know. It was difficult to keep them from knowing what they got. They were slick and would rewrap their presents so that I'd never know it. I finally would hide their presents in a gunnysack hanging up off the floor.

They have left home and have families of their own and wrap their presents and have beautiful trees. It is lonely until they come home to celebrate Christmas with us.

I still order my gifts from catalogs. This year I bought gifts from Blair, Figi's and Swiss Colony. Even my dogs get present from Upco and Petco. Never a day goes by in late November or December that the mail doesn't bring catalogs.

I looked through my Christmas pictures and found some Christmas trees and presents from years gone by. I always went to Kansas City for Christmas with my mother and family. All my Christmas presents came for the catalog of course. My pictures look like Christmas past, present and future.

Catalogs were used for other purposes that I remember. My brother and I cut out pictures, furniture and made houses and played for hours making up make believe lives for them.

When we finished with the catalogs we read them in the outhouse and make toilet paper of them. During the Depression you made do with what you had.

Wish books were the old fashioned way of selling goods before T.V. with its high powered advertising. Catalogs are her to stay.

Fall Harvest

Whenever I think of autumn and fall days, one of my favorite memories is of seeing hundreds of beautiful butterflies that gathered at the back of our house and barn in the warm autumn sunlight. They were beautifully colored-yellow, red, blue, and almost all the colors of the rainbow. The monarchs would stop on their way to Mexico for their winter home. This was God's harvest of beautiful creatures to feast our eyes on.

As if this wasn't enough we were blessed with apples. Red and golden, the trees that surrounded our house would deck out with beautiful red and green leaves we had more than enough apples to share with our neighbors.

Our pond would fill up with geese winging their way South to warmer climates their visit was short. While they were there, they spent their time honking. The dogs in the kennel would bark and bark and drive us crazy with the noise.

The fall meant that students were beginning a new year and the teachers were getting a new crop of children. I always liked the smell of a freshly polished classroom and new. Books, School buses were running up and down the gravel roads carrying their precious cargo of children twice a day. The roads would become dusty when they passed and it was hard to see.

Hayrides were popular at this time of the year. You needed a jacket because nights were cool. As the children would troop in after the ride they devoured hot dogs and marshmallows cooked at the bonfire. Our church sponsored the hayrides and my husband and I got to ride along with them.

Only one thing spoiled my remembrances of fall. You would hear bang in our woods and know that hunters had sneaked onto our property to hunt the game in the woods. They ignored no trespassing signs. I would get so mad that I would go down in the woods hunting them to run them off. They always told me they had permission to hunt. No way. A call to the sheriff would help them to find another place to hunt.

I think fall was my favorite time of the year because it was the end of the growing season and crops were harvested. I went to school for eighteen years of my life. I taught school for almost twenty years. I still feel the urge to find a classroom and go to teach. My mind would like to do it but the old body protests it is too old.

Fall then is the end of the growing season and it is time for the Earth to rest itself until spring. Old man winter raises his white head and covers the ground with white.

From a dog named Daisy to a fish named Dempsey

Animals have been my companions ever since I can remember. They could crow, fly, hop and run on two or four legs. Some of my pets lived in fish tanks.

One of my first chores was getting eggs out of the hen house. I always like banty chickens. One of my favorite pets was a banty chicken who moved across Kansas, Missouri and Oklahoma with us. My family moved with Koss Construction Co at the time.

When we moved to Kansas City in the late 1940's my brother Tim acquired a dog named Daisy. The fact that Daisy was a he made little difference. Daisy ran away from people who mistreated him and moved in with us. Daisy loved Timothy and even went on trips with my parents. Daisy wasn't exactly my favorite. He would try to bite my friends and he especially liked to nip my husband Eugene. Daisy lost his life in a dog fight over a female. He was buried with pomp and circumstance.

At the time Daisy lived with us I had adopted a tomcat. He moved in slept with me and fished in Mother's guppy bowl.

When I worked for Katz Drug Company after I was married, I discovered exotic pets. I'll bet the fish I've lost would cover a path from here to the moon. My favorite fish was Ol' Jack Dempsey. I bought three of them for companions and he promptly ate the other two. He was aptly named after a prize fighter. He grew to 8 inches and lived in a tank by himself for four years. We move to Kidder one cold January and poor old Jack didn't survive the trip. While he lived, he was and exotic eater. He ate flies, raw hamburger other fish and earth worms.

With this kind of a background it wasn't surprising that I developed a kennel. We had a white Pekinese who loved chasing my daughter Julie to the house trying to bite her. He would sit on the steps washing his paws and grinning.

A male Pomeranian liked his privacy and wouldn't breed a dog unless you covered him up. One of my female Yorkies lived with us and would stay under the bed and rush out and bite my husband's bare feet.

My Doberman watch dog hated UPS trucks. Animals give unconditional love and devotion. I still raise tropical fish and have three dogs.

Al Krietler and Killer

Killer an Unforgettable Companion

Angels leading the recently deceased persons to heaven have appeared on true life accounts from "Unsolved mysteries" and "Eye to Eye". I couldn't help but think while watching them of the story in Ann Lander's column about people's pets when they die, waiting on the Rainbow Bridge for their masters to come across and go to heavenly land with their beloved owners.

On May 20, 1994 the owner of one of my most famous dogs from Bechtolds kennels called me to say the killer, his dog had passed on. I hadn't heard from Al Krietler in many years. Killer was 14 years old and had died from the last throes of cancer in his owner's arms. Killer's picture appeared on stickers, stamps, shopping bags and Christmas cards to advertise Al's inventions: rollers that make all bicycles stationary,

Killer headwinds resistance fans to keep you cool and Convertible fork stands.

Killer was a Yorkie with a baby doll face and less than five pounds dripping wet. Al got Killer when he wwas six weeks old. Killer's favorite spot was riding in the front of Al's bib overalls. Killer was Al's constant companion for overfourteen years. Al said "I cried at much at Killer's death as I did when my mother and son died."

Al and Killer visited my kennel to buy Killer a girlfriend. They found the right female, and Killer left two daughters as a legacy for Al.

Killer went to work every day with Al and to trade shows in the 48 states. Most people in the bicycle industry knew Killer better than they knew Al.

Many articles have appeared in the newspapers and magazines about Killer. Killer had been in the Kansas City St. Patrick's Day Parade starting in the 1989 and continuing until March 14. Killers costume a green coat and green ribbons saluted the Irish. He ran beside Al's bicycle for the three mile journey. The crowds would roar, clap and whistle as he went by.

Killer did an Rgbrai commercial twice and is in one of their videos and barked most of the way. He went to an event called Gear 90 and had a Gear 90 t-shirt cut up so Killer would have a shirt like everyone else.

I like to remember Killer running along beside Al as he exercised on his bicycle, and when he got tired Al put him in his overalls. Killer is the picture of a man's best friend always loving, never criticizing and constant friend and companion. All a human being has to do is exist for his four footed friend and give him food, water and loving care.

Al is looking for a new Yorkie male companion, not to replace Killer but to fill the lonely hours until he crosses over and Killer joins him on the Rainbow trail as a young vigorous happy dog.

Memories are made of . . .

The pleasant memories that I had going back to my childhood are related to animals. My very first pet was a Banty hen. She followed me everywhere. I would stroke her eyes and she would fall asleep. She was perfectly content to sit on my lap.

Dogs and cats came next on my list of pets with special memories. Dogs are tuned in to your feelings. They comfort you if you are feeling sad. Dogs are content to sit on your lap, lie in a pet bed or just be in the same room with you. They are non judgmental and adapt to any living conditions. My cats and dogs like each other. I may sit and hold a cat or dog on my lap.

Dogs have been domesticated for thousands of years. They cave man and his dog shared his quarters with him in the cave or beside his fire. Dogs have diversified jobs today. They can be trained to guard sheep and goats, drive cattle and other herd animals. Blind people have specially trained dogs to lead them when they need to go and help with doing simple tasks.

The residents of nursing homes will respond to an animal that is brought to visit the nursing home. Residents who do not respond to people will break out in a smile when a dog comes up licks their hand and wags their tail.

Prisoners in a maximum security prison will train their dogs to become seeing eyes for the blind and handicapped. This interaction between the dog and the prisoner helps even the most hardened prisoners become more emphatic and more responsive to their fellow human beings.

Mentally ill children in hospitals respond to animals before they respond to people. Horses and ranches are used with delinquents that have committed serous crimes. Caring for and working with horses brings about their rehabilitation.

As a former kennel owner, I have had people call me and want another dog exactly like the one who has died. One lady was embalming her dog and wanting a dog exactly like him. I just happened to have a puppy that looked exactly like her lost friend. I shipped it to her and she thought that it was her older dog reincarnated. She treated her animals like children.

If you have animals long enough they communicate with you in barks and body movements. A Pom I had used different bark tones to tell me what she wanted. Many dogs that crossed my path, past and present leave me with lasting memories.

Mary holding dogs

My animal companions

The most interesting of my animals is Stormy my tomcat. His mother was killed on the road by a car when his litter was nine days old. There were five kittens in the litter. I raised them on a bottle with kitty formula. They were able to eat canned cat food and moistened kitty pellets at three weeks. Before that I fed them every four hours on the bottle.

He still thinks of me as his mother. Stormy is a very large gray and white cat with white feet and a white face. When he was about six months old a small starving kitten came up and I took her in. She became Stormy's project. He slept with her and he cleaned and protected her.

On my wedding anniversary I received a three pound Yorkie that I named Cricket. Stormy adopted her and she still eats with him at night. They both sit on my lap as I watch television.

Stormy has a very playful side. He will jump out and attack my feet and shoes. He hides and jumps out to scare my small poodle that shrieks as he pounces. When he wants attention he jumps up and lies right in the middle of whatever I am doing. Today I was repotting a flower and he knocked off the pots and dirt. All he wanted was a little attention.

243

He also thinks he is a watch dog. Certain cars that travel our road alarm him and he growls. If a strange dog or cat comes up he looks like a Halloween cat hair on end, tail straight up. Other strange cats that come up are run off.

Our garage doors open automatically. If the cat gets in the doorway up they go. He likes to run to the door when it is give inches from closing. He likes to live on the wild side and use up his nine lives. Life with him is never dull. I feel like we might have been soul mates in another life.

Saved by howling dogs

It was about 2 o'clock in the morning, I heard my kennel dogs banging the doors as they came outside and where running around barking. As usual, my husband was gone driving his Greyhound bus to St. Louis. Dusty Doberman and I peered out the windows toward the kennel. It was the dark of the moon that night. All I could see was lights in the pasture behind the dog house. As I looked toward the pond on the south of the house I could see someone flashing a light on a creature behind the pond trying to climb a tree to safety. I hear a big bang and the critter dropped to the ground. I opened the door and went out on the deck and let Dusty Doberman out. I could hear cursing and running as the individuals were trying to get over the barbed wire fence to the road in front of our house. A car was coming down the road to pick up our invaders. Dusty was following the car up the road until I called her back. The next morning I looked at the barbed wire fence by the pond. It had the rear of some overalls covered with blood on them. I guess Dusty hit her mark with the teeth.

Another time that I was scared occurred about thirty years ago. An individual who lived about a half mile from us was trespassing, carrying a gun and hunting on our property. I call the conservation department and an agent promptly came out and caught him with game in a not-hunting season. He was arrested and had to appear in court. The agent told me I had to go to court so he could be prosecuted. On the day of court, I saw the hunter sitting on the front steps of the courthouse. He didn't think I would be there. He was fined and warned about hunting out of season. Later in the year, I saw his name in the paper and he was sentenced for an assault.

I came out in good shape on both incidents, no more night raids and spotlighting coons happened. The neighbor who was trespassing went to jail and moved on. I thank my Doberman and noisy dogs for alerting us.

Ornery rooster attacked everything

In the 1930's we lived on a farm in Grandview Missouri. We kept chickens for the eggs and food. These chickens were Plymouth Rock pure white with red combs and waddles.

Chanticleer the rooster was a magnificent specimen. He weighed fifteen pounds and stood about two feet tall. He woke us up each morning at daybreak with his sun worshipping "Cock-a-doodle-doo." He had spurs on his feet that were razor sharp. He was lord and master of the hen house and the hens dwelled therein.

All he did all day was chasing hens and preen himself for his next conquest of the adoring hen population.

He attacked anything and everything that came close to his courtyard. Unfortunately for us children we did not have indoor plumbing facilities. If you had to use the bathroom you went to the outhouse, which sat right beside the chicken yard. The only time you were safe from being attacked by Chanticleer was after he had gone to roost.

None of us made too many unnecessary trips to the privy. You put off going to the bathroom as long as possible because of that old rooster. As surely as the sun came up The old rooster would slip up and start flogging you with his spurs. I had a 2 year old brother at the time and I had to take him as well as myself.

When you were finished in the outhouse you peeked out the door if no rooster was in sight you cautiously let yourself out. That rooster had extra sensory hearing which allowed him to hear the outhouse door opening.

I put up with that obnoxious rooster and his flogging for six months. One day after being spurred and coming in with bleeding legs I decided to do something about Chanticleer. It was him or me preferably me. I took a board on my next trip to the outhouse and he charged me. I cold cocked him with the board. I never intended to kill him only stun him.

There on the ground the fine feathered rooster lay bleeding. I had broken his neck with my blow. I cried and cried because I had never killed anything before.

My mother consoled me by saying that at least the old rooster had fertilized all the eggs and we would have more roosters and hens coming on.

Chanticleer was our Sunday dinner. He cooked up and looked magnificent with dressing and noodles. I couldn't eat any dinner because I was the culprit who "done" in old Chanticleer.

Reminiscing

The common ancestor of our pampered pet the dog is depicted in scenes on the walls of caves in France, Arizona and South America. He warned our ancestor 3, 000 years ago that danger was near as he continues to do today. The ancient dog gave the same devotion to his owners that we have from our pampered pets today.

My life has been intertwined with dogs for the past 30 years. I ran a kennel and was privileged to share my life with many different dogs. They didn't live with me but, condescended to let me live with them.

My current pet is a female Dalmatian. She appeared in a pen with my adult Dalmatian overnight. It was always a mystery about how she arrived. She has an uncanny way of answering you when you ask her a question. She will howl and her voice will continue to get louder. She likes warm places in winter and cold places in the summer. No amount of bribery or food can lure her out of our comfortable people house. She has my husband and I well schooled in dog obedience for people.

My husband bought her a shiny new igloo doghouse last winter with a soft pad to be placed in the garage. She thought it was haunted. I put the pad out and she would lay on it. I inched it back into the dog house. Finally one morning after about 3 months she started lying in the dog house on the pad, miracle of miracles. Her favorite place is on a rug in front of my TV in the family room.

I had a female Yorkie named Morgan. One of Morgan's favorite pursuits was hiding under the bed and biting my husband on the feet when he took off his shoes.

Ten years ago we sold the kennel. I miss my furry charges and the pet lovers who bought them life with them was never dull. When stray dogs come down my road with their suitcase they always stop here because they feel my love of the ever faithful dog.

CHAPTER 13

INTERESTING LIFE STORIES

Diagnostic lab helps insure safer herds

A farmer goes outside to feed his cattle. The unthinkable happens. He finds two dead cows. He calls his veterinarian for advice.

A dog breeder checks his pregnant dog-much to his horror, he finds that his pregnant poodle has aborted her puppies. He calls his veterinarian to come out and inspect the premises.

What do these two incidents have in common? Both have cost our livestock producer's significant income and short-circuited the chain of livestock sales to the consumer.

The veterinarian will advise the producers to take the deceased animals in for a necropsy at the diagnostic lab in Cameron. The mission of Cameron Diagnostic lab is to diagnose the course of the producer's problem and to get his livestock production bock on track

The Cameron lab opened in 1979 with Dr Rob Tharp as the veterinarian in charge. At the time of its opening it had five people on the staff. Today there are seven people working there.

They are director, Dr. Rob Tharp, Chretta Mastin, Master Bacteriologist; three Laboratory Technicians, Adrienne Scott, Glynis Dotson Nancy Robinson; Secretary Receptionist, Karolyn Brashears and Robert Edwards, laboratory Custodian and Necropsy assistant. The Missouri Department of Agriculture Director is John Sanders.

The state Veterinarian and Director of Animal Health is Dr. John Hunt. Dr Hunt supervises three state labs which cooperate with veterinarians, diagnostic labs and the University of Missouri. Missouri has three labs:

Jefferson City, Cameron and Springfield. The lab in Springfield has ten employees and is the one used for diagnosing diseases and problems for Missouri's poultry producers.

The Diagnostic lab in Jefferson City has nineteen employees. The lab does mainly brucellosis testing. Brucellosis is a disease that causes animals to abort their fetuses early and can infect humans as well as rendering producing hers useless.

Some of the procedures performed at the Diagnostic Lab in Cameron are necropsies, preparation of rabies suspect heads for examination by the Division of Public Health, bacteriology—isolation and identification and antibiotic sensitivity testing, serology on blood samples such a equine infectious anemia in horses, phraseology, the identification of internal and external parasites.

The Diagnostic Lab in Cameron has an educational function. Some of the veterinarians' in Northwest Missouri come to the lab to get their brucellosis training. Many veterinarian practitioners also train in the lab with the bacteriologists, so they may be qualified to do bacteriology at their practice locations. 4-H groups come to observe the functions of the diagnostic lab. At one time, the laboratory hosted feminine farrowing schools.

Dr Jerry Rainey, one of the veterinarians in the area, uses the diagnostic lab as a management tool to help his agricultural clients, whether it is a swine producer or exotic animal raiser. Dr. Rainey says, "When a dead animal turns up on your farm, you should take it to the Diagnostic lab for a necropsy. You should be concerned for the well being of the other animals in your herd." After the animal is autopsied the results are sent to the consulting vet. After talking to the vet and following his suggestions, the producer can safeguard his herd and therefore his livelihood.

The role of the Diagnostic Lab is problem solving and the finding there are only a management tool to be used by the processor and veterinarians for a healthier and hopefully a profitable livestock operation. Another function of laboratories in Missouri is to run tests that are required by law for intrastate, intestate nod international movement of livestock. Diagnostic labs are tools that will help your "Heartland producers "the breadbasket of America, compete in world commerce. This brings the midland agricultures in to the twenty first Century.

Sadly the Diagnostic Laboratory was closed in Cameron and all of the farmers miss the skills that were available to them there,

Mary Bechtold

Gutenberg press leaves lasting imprint

The greatest invention of the last century, I think, was the Gutenberg press. It allowed the common man to learn to read and write, and helped open doors in the United States to put a free public education before all our citizens.

Because of the press, we can mass print books that are available to all our citizens at prices they can afford.

For my fellow senior citizens, I hail the advent of the computer as the second-greatest invention. It helps the seniors by alleviation their loneliness, boredom, helplessness and the decline of mental skills due to lack of stimulation.

I retired in 1998 as an elementary school counselor. I use my computer to keep me connected with fellow senior citizens all over the globe and in my own country. For example, through e-mail I have met people in Australia, New Zealand, England and my own country with interests similar to mine. My friend in New Zealand sent me pictures of her beautiful flower garden. John Webster, who lives in Australia, sent me (information on) Web sites where I could get acquainted with the area where he and his wife live. I talk via-email to a lady who lives in Lebanon, Mo.

I think, for homebound, isolated senior citizens and nursing home residents, that computers are a godsend. Computers in nursing homes could give residents a way to combat loneliness, learn new skills, get and interest in living and stimulate mental skills.

I, myself, enjoy a challenge. I have never been mechanically inclined. My Internet provider has helped me with many of my computer mistakes. It was some time before I learned computer technology. The statement "You can't teach an old dogs new trick" is simply not true. My e-mail friends are as old as I am and more advanced. One lady sends m e-mail with music and pictures that she has put together from free stationery sites.

There are many senior citizens sites on the Internet. Forty percent of Internet users are seniors, according to one statistic I saw.

The computer and therefore, the Internet have their drawbacks. One day as I was investigating senior citizens resources with a search engine, I clicked onto a site that advertised pornographic pictures of senior men and women. There are charlatans and crooks that are ready to help you and your money part company if you're stupid enough to fall for their tricks.

Every search engine—Yahoo, Hot Bot or Exite has personals where you can click and meet a future friend. I put my name on a senior site e-mail list and much to my surprise, got e-mail from men in foreign countries who made romantic overtures in forest e-mail messages. I never replied.

I know of two people who met their mates online and are happily married.

One should exhibit the same caution in meeting cyber friend that you would in getting acquainted elsewhere. You could meet Jack the Ripper types who are waiting to find the next victim on the Internet.

Computers are here to stay. The Internet represents the whole world just waiting to be explored. All of us should take advantage of the good things it has to offer.

Cyber police are being enlisted in larder numbers to help police the darker side of cyberspace: the pedophiles that hide behind e-mail to pry on children, and the sexual perverts who pry on men and women both.

History traces rights efforts

The struggle to achieve equal rights for women began in the English speaking world with the publication of Mary Wollstonecraft's "Vindication of the Rights of Woman" (1792).

The demands for the right of the American woman to vote began and were formulated at the Seneca Falls Convention in 1848. Some of the famous United States suffragists were Lucy Stone, Julia Ward Howe, Susan B. Anthony and Elizabeth Cady Stanton. Lucy Stone organized the American Woman Suffrage Association. In 1890 Wyoming entered the Union, becoming the first state with general women's suffrage that was adopted as a territory in 1869.

Woman take office

In 1915, Carrie Chapman Colt was named the president of the National American Woman's suffrage Association. Another prominent suffragist was Alice Paul, who resigned from AWSA because she used militant tactic. She organized the Nation Woman's Party. This party, led by Paul marched in Wahsington, D.C. When its members were thrown into jail, they were mistreated and sent on hunger strikes. The party's perseverance led to victory. On Aug, 26, 1920 women were granted the right to vote by the 19th amendment.

In sleepy rural areas like Gower and Paradise, Mo, where I was born, the farmers and small town people were isolated. They had radios but could not afford the newspapers. Many houses did not have electricity. The women worked from dawn to dusk taking care of their families. The breadwinner of the family worked long hours in the field trying to keep his family fed. My mother knew she had the right to vote but was not concerned about it because daily living took too much of her time.

It has been within my lifetime that women have moved to having equal rights with men. Women can no longer be beaten and mistreated like they were second-class citizens by their husbands.

Roles remain rigid

When I was going to high school in 1945-49, women only had had the right to vote for 25 years. The men worked and the women stayed home caring for their children. The Second World War was over, and jobs were plentiful. Women's roles were as cook, child-care giver and homemaker. The married woman who worked outside the home was unusual.

During World War II women were encouraged to help in war plants; this marked the beginning of women getting outside the home. Accepted jobs for women were teacher, nurse or secretary in offices.

Men were still the final authority figures in the home and the bread winners. Education beyond high school was considered nonessential for women. My dad's hair stood on end when I wanted to go to college and won scholarships. He didn't think women needed to learn to drive either.

From 1920 to 1960 militancy on behalf of a single issue diffused into a number of women's political groups, such as the League of Women Voters and the Nation Council for Negro Women. Such group's supported various types of liberal reforms related to the rights of both men and women. And Equal Rights Amendment drafted in 1923 by the National Woman's Party remained dormant for another 50 years.

The preamble to the United Nations Charter referred to equal rights for women. In 1948, the U.N. Commission on the Status of Women was established. As an outcome of the international feminist exchange, the number of countries granting voting rights to women rose for 25 in 1945 to 106 in 1971.

Now pushes issue

The force of the entire women's movement, spearheaded by NOW (National Organization for Women) was brought to bear single issue: ratification of the Equal Rights Amendment to the Constitution. As of 1981, 35 states had approved the amendment. Women are just now coming into their own; they are no longer dominated by their husband. They can hold property, be educated and climb as high as their dreams and intelligence will let them in the work world and the political arena.

To me, nothing is sadder than the picture of a late 19th century woman who has no rights of her own and is dependent on her husband for property and existence. Give me the outspoken females of today who make their contributions in our modern world.

Humor highlights drives by means of Burma-shave sign

When I think of "Jingles and Rhymes." I think of Berma-Shave songs. I learned to read and increase my vocabulary on these signs. From the back seat of a car, you can take the time to read signs as you pass. We didn't have books and puzzles to use when we were traveling. We spent our time looking at the scenery, reading signs, or making faces at the cars that we passed. We didn't fight or tease each other because retribution was fast-coming from my father. There was a mean look or the car stopped and you got disciplined.

Burma-Shave signs reflected the history of the years they were written in. I have copied some of the ones that were the most memorable, with the years they were written.

1930

Does your husband Misbehave
Grunt or groan and grumble
Rant and rave?
Shoot the brute some
Burma=Shave

Early to bed
Early to rise
Was meant for those
Old fashioned guys
Who didn't use
Burma-shave

Uncle Rube
Buys tube
One week
Looks sleek
Like sheik
Burma-Shave

1932

You'll love your wife
You'll love her paw
You'll even love
Your mother-in-law
If you use
Burma-Shave

1940

Soldier
Sailor
And Marine
Now get a shave
That's quick and clean
Burma-shave

If man bites doggie
That is news
If face
Scares doggie
Better use
Burma-Shave

Let's make Hitler
And Hirohito
Look as sick as
Old Benito
Buy defense bonds

1960
Henry the Eighth
Sure had trouble
Short term wives
Long term stubble
Use Burma-shave

I miss those old signs as I cruise the freeways. Life was sweeter and slower when you drove a two—way highway and were not hurrying your life away.

Jingles were popular when I was growing up. People advertised their products on radio and television. One of the ones that I really like today is the Oscar Meyer bologna song. I like the cute kids they us on television.

The bologna song goes; "My bologna has a first name it's Oscar. My bologna has a second name it's Meyer. Oh I love to eat it every day and if you ask me why I say, "cause Oscar Meyer has a way with bologna!"

Another of my favorites is the Armour hotdog song. Sometimes, it's better than the program it is sponsoring. "Hotdogs, Armour hotdogs. What kinds of kids love Armour hotdogs? Fat kid, skinny kids, kids who climb on rocks, tough kids, sissy kids, even kids with chicken pox love hotdogs, Armour hotdogs, the dogs kids love to bite"

Another catchy jingle was the ad that showed Charlie Tuna trying to get caught and he never did. They always withdrew the hook and said, "Sorry Charlie." That was for Starkist Tuna.

255

Everyone is intrigued by mermaids, those legendary creatures of the sea. Their jingle was: "Ask any mermaid you see, 'What is the best tuna?' 'Chicken of the Sea."

I think food jingles are my favorites, and who could for get the catchy Oscar Meyer wiener song. "Oh I wish I were an Oscar Meyer wiener that is what I'd truly like to be. "Cause if I were and Oscar Meyer wiener, everyone would be in love with me."

Probably the reason why we have so many obese American adults and children is because we watch television and head for the refrigerator after hearing and seeing all the delicious food pitched at us in primetime before bedtime.

"Iron horse" facilitates shipping of livestock

As the railroads grew, they began to stretch from coast to coast, thus connecting the East Coast to the West. This mechanical monster and its cars that could transport people and goods all over the country superseded covered wagons, steamboats and other modes of transportation.

St. Joseph was already established at the headwaters of main rivers for steamboats bringing immigrants in to begin the journey west. After gold was discovered in 1848, thousands of immigrants purchased covered wagons, oxen and supplies to go west. This established the economic foundations of the city. In 1859, when the railroad came to St. Joseph, it became a supply and distribution center for the entire western half of the country. St. Joseph grew rapidly in the 19th Century.

In 1886, the Chicago Times reported that St. Joseph was a modern wonder city of 60,000 with 11 railroads with seventy passenger trains each. It had 170 factories, 13 miles of the best-paved streets, the largest stockyards west of Chicago and whole sale trade as large as that of Kansas City and Omaha combined. One count of the U.S. census had the city's population in 1900 at 100,000. With the opening of the St. Joseph Stockyards in 1887 and the opening of several new packing houses from then through 1923, St. Joseph became an important meatpacking center, one of the leading resources of revenue for the city and surrounding agriculture areas.

At the outbreak of the Civil War, Chicago's meatpacking industry was primed to furnish much of the meat to soldiers. Many people began to call for a consolidation of stockyards so all sellers and buyers could meet in open competition. In 1864 the Chicago Pork Packers Association led the way to build a Union Stockyard. The General Assembly chartered the Union Stockyard and Transit Company in 1865 and opened for business Dec 25, 1865. It grew and reamed its peak year in 1924; it went out of business in 1971.

In small towns and cities where the railroads stopped, holding pens for livestock were built. Farmers from neighboring farms would bring their animals. Farmer's animals were branded. My father-in-law Paul Bechtold accompanied animals to Chicago. At the stockyards, he received the checks and brought them back to the farmers. This took place in the 1920's and 1930's.

Gradually, Henry Ford's truck started hauling the animals to market and the railroad holding pens were no longer needed. The iron horse still runs, but in no longer hauls animals to market. Trucks do the job now. They are faster, keep the animals' weight on better, and thus the farmer makes more money.

Orphan trains carry children to country

From 1800 on the Unites States beckoned to thousands of families in the countries of Europe. Times were hard in many countries; so many immigrants packed their bags and headed to the land of limitless opportunity.

When they arrived in the New York harbor and saw the Statue of Liberty, they thought they could do whatever they set out to do. After a stop at Ellis Island, they were ready to begin their new adventure in their adopted country.

The history of the orphan trains, an ambitious and controversial effort to rescue poor and homeless children, begins in the 1850's when thousands of children roamed the streets of New York searching for money, food and shelter. They feel pry, like homeless children of today, to crime and disease and worse. Many children to survive had to sell matches, rags or newspapers and even their bodies. Survival is a very powerful instinct. Because they are so vulnerable, they banded together for protection in street gangs. Police were arresting children as young as 5 and locking them up with violent criminals who preyed on them and used them as sexual objects or worse.

Charles Loring Brace, in 1853 was appalled at the plight of these "street Arabs," so called because of the wanderings. Brace was completing his seminary training in New York City. He thought there was only one way to help these children and get them off the streets and into kind, Christian homes. Move them from the city to the country.

In 1853 Brace founded the Children's Legal Aid Society to arrange trips, raise the money and obtain the legal permissions needed for relocation. Between 1854 and 1929, more than 100,000 children were sent, via orphan trains to new homes in rural America. Recognizing the need for labor in the expanding farm country, Brace believed the farmers would welcome homeless children, take them into their homes and treat them as their own. His program would turn out to be a fore runner of modern foster care.

One child tells the story, at eight of being on the train. His mother had died when he was two. His father had been alcoholic. The children's aid society took him away from the father. Placement into new families was casual, at best. Hand bills heralded the distribution of cargoes of needy children. As the trains pulled into town the children were cleaned up and paraded on make shift stages before crowds of prospective parents. The eight year old child found a warm and loving home.

The children's aid society likes to point with pride to other success stories, like those street boys Andrew Burke and John Brady, who grew up to become governors of North Dakota and Alaska respectively. But the record of placements was mixed. Some of the farmers saw the children as nothing more than a source of cheap labor.

I, myself, believe that this was a practical solution to a problem where children's lives and futures were at stake. No program is perfect. The children's aid society did it's be to help the children.

You can find the stories of the survivors of the orphan trained on the Internet. Most of their stories have happy ending.

Priest dedicates himself to helping others throughout his life

When individual think of people who respond to a different drummer, they think of someone who has the courage to be themselves regardless of what people say or think. These people think for themselves and follow the dictates of their hearts. I met such a man in1969. His name was

Father Thomas Gier. He was our parish priest at Sacred heart Church in Hamilton, Mo. I had two small children at the time and my hormones went haywire. I was suffering from depression and was on Thorazine. This made me sleepy and slow moving. Father Gier came to visit and he noted my condition. He said, "What are you taking?" I told him and he advised me to stop taking it immediately. He had been a psychiatric social worker before he became a priest. I stopped taking the drug and began to get out and go on home visits for the church. I owe him a debt of gratitude since I recovered over a period of several months. Very soon thereafter I became interested in raising dogs.

Father Gier had this effect on everyone he came in contact with. He never met a stranger and picked up hitchhikers and helped those in need in any was he could. He was a dynamo of energy and visited everyone in his parish.

My nephew, Paul Hartley, wanted to become a priest but did not have any way to go to college. Father Gier went with my husband and Paul and helped him get a four year scholarship to Rockhurst.

He then moved to Borneo, the land of headhunters, to set up churches and carry the gospel to those isolated natives. These tribes fought each other and collected scalps and heads. He was successful in setting up churches.

Before he left for Borneo, he was sent to the Philippines and set up churches on the different islands. This was a man whom God was very proud of. He devoted his life to others and to the church.

State's living history book" remains etched in memory

The most interesting vacation that I ever had was in October 1987, and it lasted five days. It was sponsored by the National Trust for Historic Preservation. The tour started in Washington, D.C., and was entitled the" Great Homes of Virginia." It ended in Richmond Va.

One of the first stops was at Montpelier, a great estate in Orange County and the home of James Madison, our fourth president. It was a center of renowned hospitality and was visited by the great statesmen of our country's history.

All of the tour participants enjoyed our stop at the Barbourville Winery, the oldest winery in the United States. It originally was owned by the statesman James Barbour, the Virginia governor from 1812 to 1814. The tourist got to enjoy tasting wine and eating cheese, the ruins of Governor Barbour's mansion—designed by Thomas Jefferson and gutted by fire on Christmas Day 1984 were very impressive.

At Charlottesville, we visited Monticello, residence and estate of Thomas Jefferson, the third U.S. president. The estate is located in Albemarle county Va. Begun in 1770 and completely designed by Jefferson, the building was completed in 1809 in a complex architectural style. The 35-room house was made of red brick, trimmed with wood. It has a Greek portico and is capped by a Roman style dome. An illusion of compactness is created by a terrace on either side of the structure that conceals stables, laundries and servants quarters. The president is buried in the family plot on the grounds. This unique home on 1,000 acres was given in a grant to his father.

From Monticello, Jefferson could see the University of Virginia, which he founded, designed and wrote the curriculum for. He served as rector for the university. This university was founded in 1819 and opened for instruction in 1825.

The University of Virginian had red brick buildings with white trim and ancient trees. We got to see the alderman Library, including the archives and rare book room. We touched the original charter signed by Thomas Jefferson and saw many rare books copied by hand by monks in the Dark Ages to keep learning alive. These books were stored under glass in climate controlled rooms.

Thomas Jefferson, like Leonardo da Vinci, had many interests. He was a great inventor, scholar, architect and agricultural innovator. As you gazed around the plantation, you could almost see this genius at work if you closed your eyes.

In Richmond, we saw the state capitol, where America's oldest continuous legislative bodies still meet, where Aaron Burr was tried for treason and where Robert E. Lee accepted command of the Virginia forces. We also saw the governor's mansion, which still is in use by the current Virginia governor. It was built in 1813 after the capital was moved from Williamsburg.

I saw many homes of our country's first leaders and president. You could picture in your mind's eye stately ladies in their fancy dresses and gentle men in their powdered wigs living in theses palatial homes with their slave attending to their every need. Virginia is a beautiful state and a living history book of the past. This is one vacation that will be remembered by me forever.

Superstitions still playing role in our moderns-day lives

Have you ever wondered how much of a role superstitious sayings play in your life and those of other people? You say to yourself, "I'm not superstitious; it's only ancient peoples like the Druids and the Irish with their little people called leprechauns who live their lives around sayings and stay away from black cats."

I, myself am a college graduate and a product of modern science. So you think. You get out of bed when the alarm clock rings and look at the calendar-Friday the 13th. "Oh," you say to yourself, "bad day" I should stay home."

You go to work-climb in the car and back out. Halfway to work a black cat crosses your path. You tremble and remember that a black a cat crossing your path is bad luck, and on Friday the 13th!

Finally, at work you rush in, hair on end, and get out your pocked mirror. You drop it, and it splinters into a million pieces. The words go through my mind: "Seven years of bad luck coming."

I start off to lunch with the girls. The handyman left out his ladder, and I walk under it. More bad luck, if I believe in certain sayings. At lunch, I couldn't avoid the devil. I spilled my water and salt and dropped my meat. All of these things let the devil lean over my shoulder. If I throw salt in his eyes, I can escape by blinding him long enough to avoid ill fortune. Salt is saving grace, for it is the purest substance on earth and stronger that holy water.

I take the afternoon off to go to a wedding. The bride wears a garter for good luck. If a brides man pulls the garter off before the bride enters the bedroom, he gets good luck.

At the reception, I see a woman with one brown and one blue eye. She could be said to have the evil eye. Just looking at a certain person can bring misfortune or illness to people if this person looks at them.

I drive home and get out of my car, and I sneeze. I didn't have time to put my hand in front of my mouth, and my soul has escaped from my body, according to old sayings.

I hurry inside and make my husband and myself a cup of tea. I stir his cup and the old superstition says that this will cause strife between us. My son has brought a live frog in to the house. One of his friends told him that warts could be cured by rubbing a frog across the warts. If he would kill the frog and put it in a bag, he told me he would avoid epileptic seizures and other fits. He would have to wear the dead frog in a silk bag around his neck.

I cross my fingers for good luck at dinner because the day has brought me so much bad luck. I cross my toes and fingers before I go to sleep.

There are literally hundreds of such common daily activities like I've mentioned above which we still think of with some trepidation. We may have lost the original meaning of these sayings, but most of us prefer to observe ancient lore just in case.

Symbols and Magic of Christmas

Whenever I think of the magic of Christmas, I automatically think of Christmas lights and sounds that put me in the holiday spirit. When the radio plays Silent Night I begin to feel soft and mellow. In my mind's eye I see a quiet landscape with snow softly falling and the whole world is quiet as if waiting for something to happen. The sound of sleigh bells on Santa's sleigh or the approach of the wise men bringing gifts to the Christ child. A picture I still cherish is my children stretched out on the floor marking the Christmas catalogs so that Santa will know what they want. We still get many Christmas catalogs including the Sears and J.C. Penny catalogs that I used to order most of my presents from for them.

One of my favorite Christmas symbols is the Poinsettia in its many variegated colors. I have good luck with them and I have one now that will be blooming at Christmas. My favorite flower came from Mexico and was named after the United States first ambassador to Mexico in 1828. This was Joel Poinsett who introduced it to our country. The Christmas tree is widely used to decorate the homes at Christmas. I like the true live pines best with their smell. We always went out and cut our own trees as did my husband's family. The Christmas tree originated in Germany in the 16th century. Trees inside and out were decorated with roses, apples and colored paper. Trees now are sprayed with artificial snow, covered with candy canes and ornaments. The Christmas tree came to America in the 1820's with the Pennsylvania Dutch.

At Christmas parties the mistletoe is used to give party goers and opportunity for a kiss. It was believed by pagans in the centuries before Christ that is has special healing power. It also meant peace and harmony.

The greatest magic for me is at Christmas mass celebration the birth of Christ. The people and the church itself are dressed in their finest at the Lord's birth. The church has a beautiful Christmas tree with lights and the children's faces beam with anticipation on that evening because the next day Santa Claus will have come and there will be presents to open and a bounteous feast with lots of good food and relatives.

The most famous individual

The most famous individual, who lived in my town Kansas City, was Girard Bryant. I remember him because to me he was synonymous with Integration. At that time I was a beginning teacher who was getting ready to help integrate schools in the 1950's in Kansas City. Girard Bryant was the vice-principal of the school Central High School where I taught. He spent many hours helping the beginning teachers plan their lessons, listening to their woes and working to help them correct a classroom situation with rebellious students. Like many white people I had never been exposed to the black sub culture. Girard Bryant helped all of us in a new teaching situation understand how difficult it was for a black child from a different culture to try to fit into an alien culture. Girard was a member of the NAACP and he wrote articles for the Kansas City Star. I taught at Central for eight years.

I have been privileged to have Girard Bryant as a friend and mentor during my lifetime. He helped me grow as a person by helping me look beyond my white skin color and accept all individuals regardless of their color, religion or nationality. Before he retired he became the head of the Maplewood Junior College where he inspired many young students to become teachers. He also helped many aspiring young black students receive scholarships and thus help other individuals of their race reach for goals that he bee unattainable without his help.

The odyssey of a tugboat captain
As told by Ormand Douglas
Written by Mary Bechtold

I was born in Bend, Oregon in 1925. I had four brothers and one sister. I grew up during the Great Depression. My father was a Canadian. My mother's folks lived in Northwest Missouri. We moved to Northwest Missouri to take care of mothers folks.

I left home when I was seventeen. I headed out to make my fortune. I ended up in Port Arthur, Texas. I recall liking out over the eater and watching the tugboats towing the barges. It occurred to me that I might like that life.

I went out to talk to the Captain of the boat; I was hired as a deck hand. It didn't take me long to decide I wanted to be captain of a tugboat.

At eighteen, I was the captain of the boat, pushing barges from Port Arthur to Florida, on inner-coastal canal and bays.

During the days in Texas, I pursued a life long love. I loved horses from the time I was old enough to know what a horse was and this love has lasted a lifetime. I had a Shetland pony. Shetlands are known for their stubbornness.

I lived in East Texas close to Dalton in Liberty County. I was close to a racetrack, which made it easy for me to be on the horses. I bought some race horses and they turned out to be Champions. My wife at the time took care of the horses while I was gone.

As a captain of a tugboat, I had many experiences. My tugboat handled as many as three to four barges. I studied the coast and the rivers so I knew the most treacherous areas to the barges, where the snags could be found.

Empty barges were dangerous. They could run right over the top of the tugboats.

The tugboat companies wanted their captain to make the miles; they did not want them to be stuck on sandbars. This cost the company money. Too many barges stuck and you were and unemployed tugboat captain.

The cheapest way to transport goods is by barge. The most common products transported on barges are petroleum products, lots of grain, lumber and wood products sand, gravel, pulp and paper.

When industries that depend on the river systems for transportations take into account over 400, 00 jobs and 700 million in tax receipts can be attributed to inland waterways according to National Waterways Conference.

The most important employee on the tugboat was the cook. The food was good. Many of the cooks were females. Make employees who hassled, the cook were put to shore at the nearest town.

Many of the tugboat employees were of questionable character and unknown pasts. Many like their alcohol.

The tugboats took on supplies at various river ports. Boats would pull right up to the tugboat with their supplies.

After working the coastal areas of the Gulf of Mexico, I found a better job, paying more money being a tugboat captain for the inland rivers. The most treacherous river is the Missouri. I worked many rivers the Mississippi Tennessee, Colorado, and the Cumberland to name a few.

My military career consisted of being a 4-F in the Second World War. I had to serve a year at Ski troop training in Colorado.

The towboat captain worked 30 days on and 30 days off. This made it very hard to maintain a relationship and marriage. I was married four times. No children resulted from these unions.

When I lived in the Houston area, I invented and patented a stroke exercise machine. There was an article in the Houston Newspaper about my invention. I never sold the machine but I had some made for the poor people in the area.

As the 20th century progressed, improvements on the tugboats and barges were made. Barges were pushed not pulled. The tugboats were called push boats and were equipped with radar sonar equipment that can tell the captain of dangers in the waters.

I have been everywhere in the United States that tug boats and barges can go. I retired eight years ago. I moved to Kansas City, Missouri to be closer to my brothers. I chose the Cameron Veteran Home because I feel at home here.

Veterans remember some Christmases past

Many of my stored Christmas memories have been told to relatives and have been printed. This article will be mostly about the memories of other individuals that I have talked to.

It is fitting that I begin with the memories of Julius Ellerman form Conception Junction, and now the oldest resident of the Cameron Vets home. He is ninety one years young and was born in South Dakota where his father homesteaded 100 acres near Cole Springs. His first recollections of Christmas begin in a sod hut.

Winters were severe there and his Christmas Eves were spent waiting for Santa to land on his roof and come down the chimney.

When Julius entered the service in 1941, he was sent to the Hawaiian Islands where he worked as a mechanic on airplanes. His Christmases there were sunny and warm compared to his Christmases in South Dakota.

In the little sod house, his dad played the guitar, mandolin and violin. One of Julius brothers and one sister were musically inclined. The little sod house rang with Christmas music and songs.

At 60 Julius wanted to learn to play the violin. He didn't like the violins that he could buy so he made and played his own until recent years.

Cleo Simmons says that his most memorable Christmas is not the away most people would like to celebrate. He was in the army in Italy. One Christmas the United States Army provided the soldiers with wine, turkey, dressing and coffee. What he remembers most about that Christmas was two real boiled potatoes with the meal, the first ones that he'd had in three months. Cleo also resides at the Cameron vets home.

Mrs. Hines wife of another resident remembers Christmas as a bleak time during the Depression. Her Christmas tree was a small oak tree that was cut and branches of pine were attached to the tree. The children put popcorn strings and homemade decoration on the tree. Each child in her family got one present. Bob Hines, her husband remembers as his most memorable present a movie projector that you cranked, it showed a World War I filmed in red.

My daughter Julie's first Christmas was a time of wonderment for her. She could walk with help and was fascinated by the bright lights and ornaments on the tree. She kept reaching for the ornaments and presents. We saw Christmas in a new light by watching our daughter's firs Christmas. We felt especially fortunate to share Christmas with her.

Writer recalls Edison's bright impact on family

Over 200 years have passed since Benjamin Franklin ventured out into the storm with his kite and his hypotheses. Tremendous progress in the study of electricity has been made since them. There is still more to understand; even today, scientist still experiment to learn more about electricity.

Thomas Edison, called the wizard of Menlo Park, N.J., had been working to invent electric lights for many years. Back then, people used candles and gaslights to light their homes. But gaslights were smelly and smoky. After two years in his new laboratory, Edison boasted he would invent a safe, mild and inexpensive electric light.

Edison searched for the proper filament or wire that would give good light when electricity flowed through it. He sent people to the jungles of the Amazon and the forest of Japan in his search for a perfect filament material. He tested over 6000 vegetable growths as filament material. In 1879, after spending $40,000 and performing 1,200 experiments, he succeeded. He made a light bulb using carbonized filaments from cotton thread, the light bulb burned for two days. The electric lights took the greatest amount of time and require the most complicated experiment of all his inventions.

At the laboratory in Menlo Park, scientists could turn different lights off and on. This was something very rare for the world. His bulbs were first installed on the steamship "Columbia" and later in a New York factory.

Edison invented a system where many lamps could get electricity all at the same time. He set up the world's first electric light power station in lower Manhattan. New York City was the first city in the worked to have electric lights. The Edison Electric Light Co. sent electricity to houses and homes.

We take our comfortable lives using electricity for granted. When the electricity for our homes is down or shut off, life stops. I have had this happen to my family several times in my life. One of the memorable times was when I ran a kennel and the ice storm lasted for two days. Our furnaces shut off because of an electric switch that controlled the thermostat that started the furnace; I used kerosene heaters in my doghouses. They stayed warm the temperature was 40 degrees in the residence where we lived with no heat. We camped out in the kitchen in front of the gas stove and wore many layers of clothes. We slept on a mattress In front of this cooking stove.

I used kerosene lamps to see at night during the storm and whelped two litters of Pom puppies. One of the lamps belonged to my mother's parents. This lamp could tell many colorful tales of the past. I still have this lamp and two others that use kerosene. I have had to use them when we have storms that caused the electricity to go out. I can remember my children playing Barbie by kerosene lamps during this storm.

One of Edison's engineers, William J. hammer, made a discovery that later led to electronics. Electronics is the branch of science that is related to electricity. Without electronics, we might not have radio, TV, CD's computers, X-ray machines or space travel. The discovery of electronics was patented as "Edison Effect," which is the basis of all electronics.

Ben Franklin sure started a trend with his kite that thrust us into the modern world. Thomas Edison went on to give us the electric light bulb and electronic. The "ole" days without electricity sound romantic, but give me the modern conveniences.